# AL QAEDA'S
# GREAT ESCAPE

# AL QAEDA'S GREAT ESCAPE

## The Military and the Media on Terror's Trail

PHILIP SMUCKER

POTOMAC BOOKS, INC.
WASHINGTON, D.C.

**Library of Congress Cataloging-in-Publication Data**

Smucker, Philip.
  Al Qaeda's great escape : the military and the media on terror's trail / Philip Smucker.—1st ed.
    p.  cm.
  Includes index.
  ISBN 1-57488-628-2 (cloth : alk. paper)
    1. War on Terrorism, 2001—Press coverage—Afghanistan.  2. War on Terrorism, 2001—Journalists.  3. Bin Laden, Osama, 1957–  4. Qaida (Organization)  5. United States—Armed Forces—Afghanistan.  6. Smucker, Philip.  7. War correspondents—United States—Biography.  8.  War correspondents—Afghanistan—Biography.  I. Title.

  HV6431.S642  2004
  958.104′6—dc22                                                2003016233

ISBN 1-57488-629-0 (paper)

Printed in the United States of America on acid-free paper that meets the American National Standards Institute Z39-48 Standard.

Potomac Books, Inc.
22841 Quicksilver Drive
Dulles, Virginia 20166

First Edition

10  9  8  7  6  5  4  3  2  1

*For my father, Rev. John R. Smucker III, who taught me to question authority. For my mother, Louisa Fontaine Washington Dawson Smucker, who tried to teach me to be a gentleman. For my wife, Ivana Veselinovic-Smucker, who tolerated my obsessions and encouraged me to keep writing. Last but not least, for my intrepid colleagues, some living, some dead, and the daring fighting men and women of the U.S. military.*

# Contents

# List of Maps

# Acknowledgments

It would be hard to thank everyone who helped me along the terror trail. I would like to start, however, by acknowledging the loyal and brilliant services of my Afghan guide, Lutfullah Mashal. Mashal, as he prefers to be called, risked his life for the sake of the news as none other has. He did it out of loyalty to a friend, but also out of a personal drive to come to grips with the radical Islam implanted in his homeland in the wake of the Soviet invasion. Mashal traveled clandestinely into al Qaeda camps and strolled nonchalantly through Tora Bora as the bombs were falling, always with a sense of humor to guide him. He made it an unusual pleasure to work in a war-torn land. My hopes are with him in his new job as the interpreter for the U.S. ambassador in Kabul.

Next, a big thank you to my foreign editors, whose patience with my ramblings and faith in my nose for news was, as always, extraordinary. Thanks to Alec Russell and Francis Harris at the *Telegraph,* along with their brilliant team of "youngsters," including Paul Hill and Patsy Dryden, for arming me with hard cash and constant inspiration for the hunt. A special thanks to Faye Bowers and Dave Scott at the *Christian Science Monitor* for handing me the ball and allowing me to run with it. Faye, a fellow Michigander and an incorrigible sleuth on the terror trail, kept me on my toes and always in the thick of the hunt.

I would also like to thank my colleagues who have kept my spirits up in times of gloom and doom. Tom Walker of the *Sunday Times,* my partner in crime at "Tricky Dick's," always encouraged me to pursue the twisted truth. Also from the *Sunday Times,* I was blessed with the good company of Jon Swain, survivor of *The Killing Fields* and man forever rowing his own boat down the river of romance. Jon provided our entire team with constant good cheer and comradeship at the battle for Tora Bora. From the BBC, I have two great friends who have encouraged me to write: the intrepid Paul Wood and the indefatigable Jacky Rowland.

To complete *Al Qaeda's Great Escape* I needed access to persons in the know. Some of these individuals, who will go unnamed here, were greedy warlords, others innocent-eyed warriors, some "anonymous" government officials.

Then there were the American soldiers, men who despite my occasional critique of their choice of tactics I still consider the best and brightest in the business. When I asked the Pentagon for help with this manuscript, I got the usual runaround from the gatekeepers, those charged with keeping the drooling dogs of gloom at bay. But when I came up against brick walls in Arlington, there were U.S. officers (you know who you are) who suggested creative ways to work around the bureaucracy. For the officer who told me that Secretary of Defense Donald Rumsfeld was opposed to airing anything that "could be considered dirty laundry," I thank you profusely for pointing me in the right direction. I owe you a beer for helping me run down the likes of Green Beret colonel John Mulholland, one of America's finest and a man not averse to providing the unvarnished truth to a lowly hack. The colonel's frank and straightforward discussion of the battles of Tora Bora and Operation Anaconda stood in contrast to other senior officers who ran for cover when the "Sec Def" sent down "the word." In addition, I would like to acknowledge the help and hospitality of Col. Bryan Hilferty at Fort Drum, Maj. Gary Kolb with the Green Berets, and Maj. Hugh Cate at Fort Campbell. I will forever cherish your help and assistance in the chilly winter of 2003.

The most essential work on the manuscript of *Al Qaeda's Great Escape*, however, was provided by my editor, Christina Davidson, with Brassey's in Dulles, Virginia. Christina, young in years but wise in advice, provided sharp and focused editing throughout. Her sense of "the story" helped me stick to the essentials of the hunt. One manuscript reader was crucial to the final product. National Public

Radio's Mike Shuster, who read early drafts, offered priceless insight and encouragement.

Finally, *Al Qaeda's Great Escape* would never have seen the light of day had it not been for the diligent efforts of my literary agent and friend, Elizabeth Frost-Knappman at New England Publishing Associates. When I resisted, she persisted. Elizabeth's insightful suggestions helped make this a story worth telling, particularly the sections concerning members of the Western press.

# Introduction

## MAD MULLAHS RUN AMOK

> That a Mad Fakir had arrived is known. His power was still a secret. It did not long remain so. Whispers of war, a holy war, were breathed to a race intensely passionate and fanatical. Vast and mysterious agencies, the force of which is incomprehensible to rational minds, were employed.
>
> —Winston Churchill,
> *The Story of the Malakand Field Force*

When I tried to walk ahead, balancing on the narrow mud dyke that held the water inside the rice field, a little man with a big gun and a bigger scowl stopped me. He held a long, shiny carbine of World War II vintage, curled his forefinger around the trigger, and pointed it down at my shredded Nike tennis shoes. I stopped, looking up again in the direction I had intended to walk. Set in stone high on a cliff above us, a sign reading "WINSTON CHURCHILL'S PICKET" overlooked the surrounding expanse of terraced rice fields. A small British fortress where Churchill had apparently spent time nestled at the base of the hill along a road snaking toward Afghanistan. The sturdy outpost—obviously a former colonial redoubt with thick, impenetrable walls designed in a simple, puritanical way—appeared humbled beneath the awe-inspiring presence of Mother Nature.

The man dropped his gun to his side and looked up with me— seeming to suddenly embrace my own curiosity—before clearing his throat.

"Winston Churchill looked down on this valley from those heights," said the skinny, bearded cop whose bulky uniform made his body beneath appear no thicker than a scarecrow's. "Well, some people say he was a good man, but as far as I'm concerned he was just another infidel."

Hmm. Just another infidel? What had he done to deserve such opprobrium? I felt an uncanny need to know. But when we asked more about the famous man whose specter still commanded the heights, the guard just sneered at me, pointed his gun back toward the road with one hand, and itched his chin with the other. He said that to approach the picket was forbidden, since "someone might attack you," adding, "We have *jihadis* hunting down journalists just like you even as we speak."

Determined to pursue answers elsewhere, I turned back with my trusty guide, Mashal, and stepped up into the front seat of our Pajero jeep. It was a bright autumn day, early in November 2001, in the remote tribal areas of Pakistan hard up against the Afghan border. From the valley where we stood, surrounded by cliffs and crags, I could not see U.S. jets but knew from the incessant roar and occasional thunderous burst across the mountaintops that the B-52 and F-16s were prowling the skies in Afghanistan nearby.

Mashal and I passed through scrub and pine forests and began to swing through a series of rising, twisting foothills. The landscape had a sharp, disturbing edge. These were not the untamed peaks of the Rockies or the sharp, pointed rocks of the Alps but rather more slopping, regal rocks rising majestically toward the confluence of two mighty ranges—the Himalayas in the north and east, and the Hindu Kush in the west. As our driver, Jamal, jammed the gearbox stick into four-wheel drive, we rose to the top of a rocky ledge, from where we could see mountains surge like a rough, dirty ocean in the direction of Ladakh and Tibet, heavenward to the roof of the world for miles and miles in undulating white snowcaps, rolling ahead as far as the eye could see.

Our jeep slowed to a crawl as a young boy tried but failed to beat back a herd of black sheep scampering across our path. As we descended into a gorge, we looked down on the rice paddies. A barefoot peasant covered in dried mud clung to an iron plow and plodded knee deep behind a water buffalo. The force of man and beast gently pushed the waters in small waves out over the rice plots down over the terraces, sending ripples of water that turned to cascades, falling into the cool valley below. On this fertile soil one of the richest Buddhist cultures in the world had once flourished, populated by a placid nation of begging monks aspiring toward Nirvana—until Alexander the Great came charging across Persia and down from the Hindu Kush with his minions. Since then, half a dozen empires had come and gone, and the valley had alternated from savagery to tranquility and back again.

Pakistan's Northwestern Frontier Province is, with its bearded tribesmen, private gun factories, and absence of female faces, not the most hospitable place on earth, and so our unexpected discovery of a monument to Winston Churchill—a personal hero—had been reassuring. It provided me with another fleeting mission in life—to find out what his exploits had been. He wasn't set in bronze or chomping on a cigar, but his name was written in great white letters, beaming in the sunlight against the forbidding cliffs. This curiosity couldn't be just let rest—it had the scent of a good feature story—so Mashal and I started snooping around in Malakand, the district headquarters.

Soon enough we found ourselves in a wooden government outpost stacked with pile upon pile of moldy court documents. As we passed into the courtyard, we were confronted with a disheveled prisoner, secured to the musty floor by a ball and chain wrapped around his bare ankles. Malakand's chief prosecutor, a moderately chubby, mustachioed man, offered to sit with us for afternoon tea amid the pines and sycamores behind his district jailhouse. As we reclined in large wicker chairs and began our inquiry, it quickly became clear that the prosecutor, who also conveniently served as the district judge, was convinced that Churchill had served as some sort of junior colonial official. He praised him for bringing law and order to a wild frontier. "He was a fine man," he told us. "The system that Churchill administered worked well—it delivered to the people," the prosecutor offered, plunking two cubes of sugar in his tea, one in my own, and another in the cup of Mashal, my trusty interpreter and right-hand man. As he spoke, a flock of birds chirped in the surrounding trees, nearly drowning out the distant buzz of U.S. raids coming from the direction of the Khyber Pass.

The prosecutor displayed exceptional cordiality, in that familiar way common to South Asians schooled by the British. He could not, however, give us any specifics on the exploits of young Winston, who he calculated would have been twenty-three years old at the time of "his gallivanting around these parts."

We left the magistrate's office in a renewed state of confusion. A quick call to the foreign desk of the *Telegraph* in London offered the only solution, so we set up the satellite phone on the hood of our Pajero and dialed through. My foreign editors, Alec and Francis, said something about Churchill's travels as an "aspiring writer" and passed me over to a sage librarian for confirmation and clarification. As it turned out, young Winston had been no colonial administrator at all. After he graduated from Britain's famed Sandhurst Academy, he served some time in a wretched colonial outpost but soon resigned from the service of Her Majesty Queen Victoria. Afterward, he signed up for the "Malakand Expedition" of 1897, one of the British Empire's classic "punitive campaigns." Churchill traded in his commission as a warrior. Instead, he planned to rush around Pakistan's Northwestern Frontier mostly on horseback as a freelance journalist chasing down the news. As a correspondent for the *Daily Telegraph,* one of the two newspapers I worked for, Churchill did his best to keep a wary eye on the empire's efforts to subdue the rebellious spirit of the locals.

Despite his apparent lust for a good story, young Winston hadn't gone easily into a profession that lacked decent pay and any semblance of respectability. Something of a dilettante still looking for his true calling in life, he had begged his American mother, Lady Randolph Churchill, to find a newspaper that would publish his erudite ramblings. She failed miserably with the *Times* but landed the *Telegraph,* the editor of which messaged back the standard advice for the prose style he preferred from a war zone: "Tell him to post picturesque forcible letters." When the young author received back the edited results of his work in the *Telegraph,* he was outraged to discover that he had not been provided with a byline in his own name, writing back to Lady Randolph that "I had hoped that some political advantage might have accrued." He also informed his "Mum," who managed his personal finances, that he would "not accept less than ten pounds [an extraordinary sum for the day] a letter and I shall return any cheque for a less sum." Churchill justified the extra payment by adding, "I think of the circumstances under which those letters were written, on the ground in a tent temperature 115 degrees or after a long day's action or by a light which it was dangerous to use unless it drew fire." It was a well-worn sob story of which I could recall using versions to bolster my own paltry earnings.

Churchill, the novice scribe, had a special mission, or at least he viewed it that way. When I finally got my hands on a copy of his first book, *The Story of the Malakand Field Force: An Episode of Frontier War,* published in London by Longmans, Green and Company in 1898 and based on his work as a reporter in a Pashtun tribal region along the Afghan border, I recognized a certain idealism and ambition reminiscent of my own first days in journalism at the age of twenty-six, some fourteen years earlier. His lucid ramblings reminded me that the attraction of war reporting had not changed much in the preceding century. Churchill noted that an observer of war has a unique window into the human spirit: a war reporter "may remark occasions of devotion and self-sacrifice, of cool cynicism and stern resolve. He may participate in moments of wild enthusiasm, or of savage anger and dismay—the skill of the general, the quality of the troops, the eternal principles of the art of war."

The sporting spirit of the fight and the educational value it held provided another attraction of the trade for Churchill. "To some the game of war brings prizes, honor, advancement, or experience; to some the consciousness of duty well discharged, and to others—spectators, perhaps—the pleasure of the play and the knowledge of men and things." While Churchill would highlight the rogue characters—the mad dogs and the Englishmen of his day—he clearly believed that the rigors of the work, despite his occasional complaint, were worth the price of admission, mildly joking that war made "his chances of learning about the next world . . . infinitely greater." The exhilaration and abandon of the front line had, however, to be taken in reasonable doses. Conjuring up the image of the famous imbiber he became in later life, he wrote that "a single glass of champagne imparts a feeling of exhilaration. The nerves are braced, the imagination is agreeably stirred, the wits become more nimble. A bottle produces a contrary effect. Excess causes a comatose sensibility. So it is with war and the quality of both is best discovered by sipping."

I couldn't have agreed more. Beyond the addiction, I suppose, war reporting also offers a strong element of voyeurism—your very own view of the kill. Through the years, I had kept the faith that exposing a little of the world's evil might do some genuine good. In Burma, I jumped over the entry rail at the airport and ran past soldiers to report on the slaughter of student protesters in August and September 1988. I had scaled a cactus-infested mountain in the middle of the night to get into Haiti to write about the evil deeds of the island's new Tontons Macoute. In Kosovo, I trekked through a blinding blizzard and down into an Albanian village controlled by Serbian paramilitaries as U.S. bombers pounded the valley and an old lady lay dying in her husband's arms. It had been in the Balkans that I imbibed too much; I started slipping into a deep abyss populated by bloody babies and headless rebels.

I inherited a stoic approach to life's ups and downs, possibly attributable to my father's grimmer-than-thou Pennsylvania Dutch descent and my mother's old Virginia stock, her grandfather having been the last of her founding father's family to inhabit the estate at Mount Vernon. I have plenty of warriors and politicians in my family tree but not many journalists. Sometimes I feel that if I had chosen a profession that permitted a modicum of revenge, I might have managed better, but in war reporting, objectivity always stands as your last line of defense. You condense a slaughter of unarmed civilians into a thousand-word dispatch and do your best to keep your outrage and disgust from showing through—an excellent recipe for emotional distress.

After fourteen years of horror shows, the endorphin blasts have long since worn off. At forty, the killing haunts me; I experience recurring nightmares. Sometimes, bloodied faces, deep purple with death, distorted with hate and fear, turn up in the twilight to welcome me back to the war zone. In my most fitful hours of sleep, my well-cultivated war correspondent's emotional detachment can't protect me from visions of Burmese soldiers with maggots in their eyes scattered along the Salween River, the dying Cambodian we dragged through paddy fields, or the skinny little Haitian father spurting blood from his neck into monsoon-swept streets of Port-au-Prince. In the worst nightmare of all, I'm standing in a pool of blood and muddy water in a village in western Kosovo. I have a hole in the sole of one of my two duck boots, and I can feel the cold, sticky liquid seeping through, soaking my toes. Two dozen Albanians lie at my feet oozing organs and blood as Serbian cops rifle through their pockets. About half the corpses have gaping holes in the head or neck, and some of the dead are actually missing their faces. In the center of the courtyard, splattered flesh and brains mark the interior of a red Isuzu minivan, sticking like globs of jelly on the bullet-riddled metal walls. As I peer inside, a square inch of gray brain tissue drops from the van into the pool of blood at my feet, splashing against my leg. I slog through the mud. Many of the dead are in bizarre postures, curled up with a finger on the trigger of an imaginary gun or doubled over in a vain attempt to hold in their intestines. I feel nothing. Not even the slightest nausea. I can't explain how unemotional I feel about it all. Then I look up at a frosted window overlooking the courtyard. There, the eyes of ten small children peer out. They are blue, brown, and filled with terror. My heart sinks as my eyes meet theirs. The vision begins with me on the outside looking in, then shifts to me on the inside, as one of the petrified children looking out. This would be something to shake off, just another bad nightmare—that is, if I had never been there on that frosty afternoon.

By the time I left the Balkans at the end of the Kosovo conflict, I had become convinced that there really wasn't much glory to be had in journalism—at least in my lifetime. I tried, but failed, to convince myself of the "noble cause," the idealism of getting the untold story, "the scoop." This motivation had driven me when I had started out in the middle '80s, my early days of reporting on what is sometimes opaquely called "man's inhumanity toward his fellow man." As far as I could see, the only "respectable" exit out of this highly addictive profession, already discovered by many close friends, was to end up on the losing end of a bullet and six feet under. Even those rivals who raced alongside and cut you off into ditches full of antitank mines, would, of course, pay their respects once you bit the dust. That made our profession, I reflected sadly, something akin to the Cosa Nostra. After the Balkans, the idea of having to cover yet another war was worse than a bad dream. Only so many times could I look on a scene of scattered limbs and cracked skulls and say to myself, "Poor bastards—I'm glad it wasn't me." It didn't occur to me that any of my own reporting had served much of a moral imperative, and so when my London editors told me that they needed to base someone in Cairo, Egypt, I jumped at the chance. I had visions of writing about the unveiling of vast new Pharaonic tombs and uncovering—or, at least, adding to—the mystery of the Pyramids.

Instead, one year later I found myself watching the collapse of the World Trade Center towers on CNN as if in another obscene dream and wondering what the world had come to. It didn't take long for the phone to ring. Gordon Witkin, the chief of correspondents at *US News & World Report,* wanted to know if I could make my way to Pakistan. Reluctantly, I bid a wistful farewell to my lovely Yugoslav wife, Ivana, and two hours later found myself squeezed into economy class of a Pakistani Airlines carrier bound for Peshawar, heading toward yet another conflagration—one that none of us had seen coming or asked for. My employers, the *Telegraph, US News,* and the *Christian Science Monitor,* briefed me simply enough. I was on a mission to break through the front lines and hunt down—by all necessary means with the exception of firearms—one well-known villain: Osama bin Laden.

I numbered just one of the hundreds of journalists who descended on steamy Peshawar, Pakistan, in late September 2001. The Pakistan–Afghan border provided all the palpable doom that a war correspondent could have hoped for, and the media lacked no shortage of interest in the story, in contrast to so many other conflicts I had covered. After 9/11, many in the United States itched for retribution, and the new "war on terror" offered the vehicle, emotional and practical, to set things right. The war promised high drama, excitement, and justice for all. I was glad that some of my competition believed that the "mission" was to free Afghanistan. I didn't. Liberating Afghanistan, to me at least, looked like a cakewalk. It wasn't what I signed on for, either. The world's most powerful military—

with air power that could, after all, put missiles through a three-story window as needed—was far better equipped, I assumed, than any of the invading armies that had failed in Afghanistan before us. I had no doubt that America and her allies would "win" in a conventional way by liberating the oppressed masses, but I also took as the real objective my own commander in chief's vow, albeit possibly stated in a fit of Western bravado, that the U.S. military would take down Osama bin Laden "dead or alive."

Early on, my interpreter, Mashal, and I had made a pact of sorts that kept us on the edge of our seats in the thick of the hunt. We pledged to split the twenty-five-million-dollar reward on bin Laden's head two ways and to give five million to our driver Jamal. We didn't exactly expect to see "The Sheikh," as he was known in these parts, suddenly prancing toward us through a mountain pass on horseback, but in preparation for all contingencies we always carried an empty whiskey bottle and an eight-by-eight Persian carpet in the back seat. Given the chance, we planned to whack the bastard over the head, roll him up, throw him in the back of the Pajero, and speed to Delhi with our precious cargo.

Speculation was already rife on bin Laden's possible where-abouts, not to mention his vile nature. A journalist looking for a "great story" could hardly have asked for a more sinister culprit. Details about bin Laden's austere, monkish existence circulated, but one had to imagine that as an extremely wealthy man with four wives, he had a few creature comforts—maybe a complete harem—hidden away in the dark recesses of some cave. He had long since taken on the image of a real-life Bond villain plotting to destroy the civilized world in his dark, underground enclave flush with confer-ence halls, vast office spaces, and sundry torture devices. With its eerily calm, steady-handed message of total destruction, Osama's face had invaded living rooms around the world—my own Cairo digs included. Bin Laden appeared to be goading all of us, George W. Bush included, with the taunt, "Catch me if you can!"

The Saudi mastermind, however, was not the first nasty character in the region to taunt a Western army. In fact, brave "holy warriors" had roamed the barren wastelands of Central Asia long before even young Winston traipsed the Malakand, following the British cavalry in their efforts to clear the frontier of unwanted tribal elements. That expedition had ended in relative success, with the troublemakers run out of the valleys, but by no means hunted down or eliminated. Churchill had wisely reminded his readers that the Pashtun locals on the Afghan border, of the same ethnicity as the Afghans beyond the mountain passes, still lived in hope of reviving a lost empire, the same glorious dreams that inhabit the minds of twenty-first-century Muslims from Tangiers to Mecca. He wrote, "The Mullah will raise his voice and remind them of other days when the sons of the prophets drove the infidel from the plains of India and ruled Delhi as wide an Empire as the Kafir [infidel] holds today: When the true religion strode proudly through the earth and scorned to lie hidden and neglected among the hills: when mighty princes ruled in Baghdad, and all men knew that there was one God, and Mohamed was his prophet."

Indeed, Churchill documented how in 1897 the British troops and their South Asian proxies faced down their own "mad mullah," or "fakir," a holy man who had inspired the tribals to brazen, self-sacrificing attacks on the very fortress Mashal and I had come across that bright November day in 2001. Churchill attributed the rising storm, the challenge to British hegemony in Asia, to this "madman." Though written in another century, his description of the holy man's influence echoes a standard view of bin Laden's own appeal: "Though he was known to be a physical coward, his sanctity and the fact that he was their own particular holy man, not less than his eloquence, powerfully moved this savage tribe. A 'Jehad' was proclaimed. He urged them to rise and join in the destruction of the white invaders. Those who fell would become saints; those who lived would be rich." Young Winston, who would go on to become the greatest menace that a twentieth-century tyrant ever faced, understood the enigmatic magnetism that his foe held for his followers, writing that the Afghan masses he came upon "were powerless to resist. Like one who feels a fit coming on, they waited. Nor did they care very much. When the Mad Fakir arrived, they would fight and kill the infidels."

Written over a hundred years before my own rude stumbling through the former homeland of the mad mullah, these words rang in my ears as I stood on the precipice of a much greater war—my own nation's offensive against a modern extremist religious leader. I suspect that among Churchill's many virtues that would show up in spades later in life, a few were already evident to his colleagues who accompanied him on that sweltering summer campaign in the remote mountains where the Hindu Kush converges with the mighty Himalayas. His last defense, which would also be my own, was that he had done his best to convey the objective truth of the matter, however challenging that might be—while, at the same time, remaining aloof from the temptations to assume the defense of his own empire. He wrote, in words that I assumed to contain both an age-old belief and a hint of his own idealism, that "the impartial critic will at least admit that I have not insulted the British public by writing a party pamphlet on a great Imperial question." He added, "An honest and unprejudiced attempt to discern the truth is my sole defense."

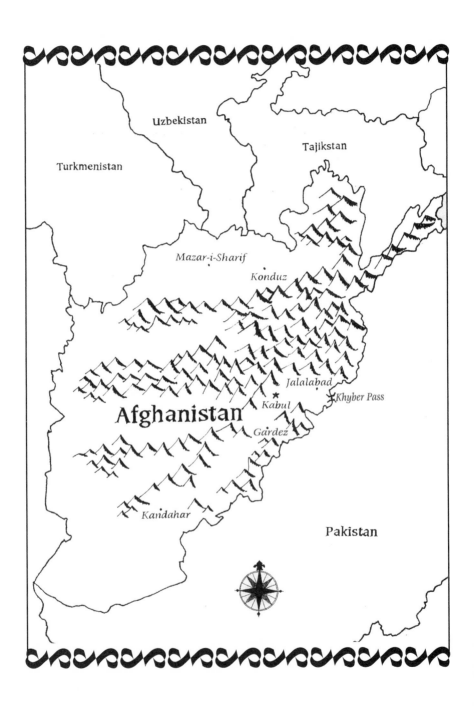

# 1

## BEEN LOADIN' FOR BIN LADEN

> Then it was that Alexander's difficulties began. Nor need we wonder, when the historian gravely asserts that "so stupendous is the rock in this land that it was found impregnable even by Heracles, the son of Zeus."
>
> —Winston Churchill,
> *The Story of the Malakand Field Force*

### Two-Thousand-Gun Salute

The hope of good fortune and the hunt for a good story had every brand and variety of reporter descending on the Afghan war zone in the autumn of 2001. Established stars, freelancers, and foreign agents just posing began arriving in droves soon after the September 11 attacks. The Pakistan–Afghan border provided all the palpable doom any of us needed for a sense of adventure. As much as any confused CIA agent in Langley, the foreign press had been stunned by the events of September 11. Ever since, we had been writing about the "intelligence lapse"—without, of course, having to examine the same shortfall in our own ranks. Just as bin Laden and company had blindsided the Pentagon, so the world's press, particularly the American press, had been found napping.

After five- and twelve-hour flights from the homeland, with the hangover and jet lag that followed, we all plunged into a chaotic wilderness of intrigue and spite. If Osama bin Laden had attacked the

Pentagon and the World Trade Center to draw the great infidel armies of the world onto his home court, he was about to get just what he was looking for, plus about four thousand entirely unwanted reporters, who didn't play by the rules of any military. It was enough to make even a hardened reporter despair over the future of civilization as we had known it behind our white picket fences, weaned on Superman and Batman comic books. What would happen if the U.S. military came in guns blazing was an entirely unpredictable business, which provided the ingredient that gave this story the greatest buildup of attention I could recall in my decade and a half as a foreign reporter.

No one could predict what kind of reception the Western press corps would get once its members made it into Afghanistan, either. With the approach of "D-day," the expected wild rush through the Khyber Pass to Jalalabad in eastern Afghanistan, and ultimately on to Kabul, I was reminded that I would have at least to attempt to alter my appearance. Blending in and looking as Afghan as possible became the goal of all correspondents. For female journalists it usually meant dying their hair dark and swathing it in a veil. For men, achieving "the look" meant dressing in the pajama-like *shalwar kamis* and cultivating unwanted, prickly facial hair. I hadn't yet acquired the patience the average Pashtun male took with preening— trimming his beard with metal scissors while holding up tiny Chinese mirrors in teahouses and at bus stops. With my driver's encouragement, I had made several false starts and finally arrived at something resembling a Brillo pad, set awkwardly on my lower jaw. As I passed a final assessment in the bathroom mirror, I judged that I was beginning to look—if not feel—about 30 percent Afghan.

Early on in the conflict, the prospect of getting a scoop inside the closed borders of Afghanistan had compelled some of the less risk-averse correspondents to test their fates in their pursuit of the story. Almost all of them, male and female, had disguised themselves in head-to-toe light blue *burqas*. No one could see in the crags and cliffs from a face mask that resembled a Catholic priest's confessional grill. A burqa fit so loosely that even the BBC's most senior international correspondent John Simpson, a huge man by any standards, could fit comfortably underneath one for a day. What still poked out at the ground level caused the most problems. Reporters invariably forgot to remove their telltale sweaty sneakers and replace them with an old pair of leather sandals. Captured hacks, in any case, had, thus far, only ended up in a Jalalabad prison, fitfully trying to recite the Koran.

After Simpson's successful day trip, in which he admittedly only put two feet in Taliban territory very briefly, reporters in Peshawar started getting calls from anxious editors. "Why aren't you in there, disguised as a tent?" asked one. "If all six feet two inches and two hundred pounds of John Simpson can get in, surely a woman can." Within days, the Taliban had captured Yvonne Ridley, a British reporter and a single mom who wrote for the tabloid, the *Sunday Express*. The Taliban information minister quickly accused her of "ill intentions"; her editors, who had approved her trip in advance, shot back that their star reporter was actually a Taliban sympathizer whose nine-year-old daughter, Daisy, really needed her "mummy" home. (Ridley's subsequent conversion to Islam would prove half of their point.) After she was released unharmed after ten days in captivity, Ridley astounded her colleagues at the Khyber border crossing by praising the Taliban for treating her with "respect and courtesy"—this even after they had severely beaten her Afghan student guides.

The Taliban had responded to the border hoppings by putting out a "red alert" along the Pakistani border; their guards kept their heads up for blue-burqa invaders. For the rest of us, it was obligatory to write kind things about these captured journalists, pointing out in our reports that these folks were not, after all, government spies. That was of course true, and besides, there was no need to caste any suspicions on our colleagues once they were in the hands of the Taliban, whose fondness for public executions was infamous. Video footage of executioners shooting a burqa-clad woman in the back of the head in Kabul's football stadium, filmed for the documentary *Beneath the Veil*, reminded all of us how quickly things could go belly-up in Afghanistan. The stories of the few journalists who had slipped over the border clandestinely had sufficiently deterred future sneak attacks, while the rest of the media patiently waited in Peshawar for a more secure opportunity to travel into Afghanistan.

For five weeks, I lived in "Auntie's" stately guesthouse in University Town on the edge of Peshawar, a city of two million official residents but now teaming with Afghan refugees, just down the road from the Khyber Pass. A warm, diminutive soul, Auntie viewed most of her Western guests as naïve children lost in a strange land. She quickly assumed the role of my guardian angel. I found it reassuring to have someone who cared so much if I lived or died, and it meant that much more since I knew Auntie had been hard-pressed of late, making frequent trips to the city jail, where her husband, a political dissident, languished as a "guest" of Gen. Pervez Musharraf, the president of Pakistan. Everything Auntie did seemed all the more selfless and gentle. Her lunches on the lawn and lamb curries beat staying at the posh Pearl Continental Hotel in Peshawar, the preferred two-hundred-dollar-a-night lodging of the network reporters. Jamal, Auntie's lone driver, had already agreed to take me when the moment arrived up to the Khyber Pass, at which point, he insisted, he would be begging off. He told me that to continue my journey across the border I would have to hitch a ride with one or another of the bands of armed men. He could not have been more terrified of the idea of riding into Afghanistan. Jamal was an orphan whom Auntie had trained from an early age to watch out for himself in an unkind world. Now a burly father of three children, he had none of my own fascination with the idea of plunging into a war zone. "Crazy people, crazy people," he would start, shaking his head from side to side when you mentioned Afghanistan. "The Afghans know only, 'kill da infidel, kill da infidel.' That mean, you, Mr. Philip. No. Not me. I no go there."

As the day of my journey into Afghanistan seemed imminent, not only did I feel at a disadvantage for having to hitch a ride from the border, but I felt shorthanded. My usual partner in crime, the brilliant Lutfullah Mashal, was locked in a woodshed somewhere on the outskirts of Kabul, waiting for an invading army to liberate him. Mashal could best be described as the "dream fixer," the best man any foreign reporter could hope to find in a war zone through serendipity or any other means. Fluent in five languages—Farsi, English, Pashto, Urdu, and Arabic—Mashal had provided me with endless grist for my newspaper mill since the day I met him in his home village hard up against the Afghan border. He was both courageous and scholarly. A jocular, chubby thirty-three-year-old with a constant grin, an endearing chuckle, with a voracious appetite for lamb kebabs and news, he had until a year ago run an Internet café in the Pakistani tribal areas; it had been shut down by religious zealots. When I met him, he gave me a tour of his home village, explaining that his father had been an Afghan Supreme Court judge under the rule of the exiled King Zahir Shah, years before the Soviet invasion. After a time in jail in the hands of the Communists, his father had fled with the family to Pakistan, where in the absence of formal schools he had personally taught Mashal to write and speak fluent Arabic. The language had been his son's password into the al Qaeda haunts.

For over a month, Mashal had been at my side when he was not making regular "undercover" reporting trips inside Afghanistan, beginning early each week and returning by Thursday in time for my end-of-the-week magazine deadlines. On his own initiative and daring, he had visited three functioning al Qaeda camps, at grave risk to his life. On one occasion, he had watched a three-ring combat training circus of al Qaeda fighters on motorbikes, strapped with TNT, and aiming rockets at imaginary U.S. helicopters. Another time he had landed in a Kabul hotel with a Filipino scientist who had a signed letter from al Qaeda's number two, Dr. Ayman al Zawahiri, authorizing him to help the network develop biological weapons. The man had described his own efforts to develop an "anthrax bomb," a nice "scoop" in itself. In our last meeting three days before my own foray into Afghanistan, I had asked Mashal to cover the fall of Kabul from start to finish and report back to me in Peshawar as soon as he could. As the days passed, I became concerned that he had been taken captive, or worse, strung up for spying. I had already begun to kick myself for sending him off; I had no idea where Mashal was, but I knew I had to find him if I wanted to stay ahead of the competition. The *New York Times* alone had several dozen reporters on the story. I was working on a lower budget, but I knew that Mashal's talents could put me on equal ground with anyone.

My replacement guide, Karim Abdul, was the best second choice I could have had. The tall, strapping peasant could frighten off most people with a quick glance. I had found him begging for work, any work, outside the UN's refugee center in Peshawar. The lanky, full-bearded Pashtun had fled Jalalabad just two months prior, after the Taliban had raided the British Christian charity he worked for. For him, our race into the fray would be a grand homecoming of sorts. The anticipation in his jet-black eyes was palpable.

Finally, on November 12 and 13, after two months of waiting at the gates of the inferno, the Taliban regime imploded. A government that had ruled Afghanistan with ruthless ineptness for a half-decade had only fringe extremists still on its side. First, the warlords, backed by Green Beret fighters and bomb spotters, had ridden in on horseback and in jeeps to Mazar-I-Sharif in the north. Next, their tanks had rolled into the capital, Kabul. Finally, the manhunt of a lifetime had begun, or so I thought. Al Qaeda and Taliban, who had long vowed to turn their struggle into a guerrilla war, were on the run, retreating into their old Soviet-era mountain redoubts. Somewhere in that mix was bin Laden, and it was anyone's guess if he would stand and fight or flee for his life.

As I prepared to rush into Afghanistan, however, I worried that the real story might rush right past me going the other direction. Panicked Afghans along the border spread stories that al Qaeda was filtering out into Pakistan, just as we were heading into Afghanistan. If Osama and his boys gave all of us the slip just as we were finally getting in, we would all look a little foolish, ending up—as was often par for the course in our profession—in the wrong place at the wrong time.

The fall of Kabul, in itself, gave a strong hint that the floodgates were about to open from eastern Afghanistan on the great highway running into Jalalabad. Among the warlords the attitude had changed, and they were making last-minute preparations for a possible plunge into Afghanistan. We followed suit to the best of our ability. As Jamal, Karim Abdul, and I rushed to pull together a few supplies and ready ourselves for the journey to Afghanistan, Auntie was talking a mile a minute. "Now, remember to drive slowly on those icy roads, and if they start shooting, don't be silly, now," she said, waving her tiny hands in the air and speaking in that South-Asian English that sometimes sounds more like a hen cackling than a human talking. "Just turn back, and I'll have your room waiting for

you. Now, here are your ten chicken salad sandwiches with hot peppers—hot peppers just as Jamal likes them. They should last forty-
eight hours, but I wouldn't risk anything beyond that—you might
poison yourself in this heat." All the coddling, as we prepared to
plunge into the unknown, was more than welcome.

We hopped into Jamal's Pajero and set out into Peshawar, racing
past rickshaws and horse-drawn carts as we hurried to make the final
arrangements. Karim Abdul was snapping his fingers and singing a
little ditty, unable to restrain his joy at being on his way to see his
mother and four brothers again. His cool, collected demeanor acted
to assuage my own fear and uneasiness. Jamal swerved for a man on
a bicycle, and as we entered Peshawar's ancient marketplace, we
passed by a bookstand selling numerous biographies of Osama bin
Laden as well as creeds against the latest "greatest infidel" of all,
George W. Bush. Aptly named, Qissa Khwani—the Bazaar of the Sto-
rytellers—the market stank of diesel fuel and camel dung. The bustle
of travelers and the loose-lipped gossip of what might or might not
be going on down the road reminded me that a thousand years earlier
caravans had gathered in Qissa Khwani to listen to bards and gos-
sips. All those "authorities of the day" loved to embellish and expand
on the truth, creating the very legends that still lived on in the name
of the latest and greatest warrior for Islam. The vendors appeared
nervous, waiting for news—possibly word of the lone wolf himself—as they hawked their spices, silks, and tapestries. Lamb and
goat kebabs sizzled on spits; a legless man holding a basket asked for
donations for the Taliban.

We dropped into Peshawar's Western Union office, a cramped
booth in the back of the bazaar. A neatly dressed man in a shalwar
kamis sat cross-legged like a Buddha statue on an elevated floor
behind a glass window counting thousand-rupee notes. He tossed me
a form to fill out and asked for my passport before handing me seven
thousand dollars in Pakistani rupees, an advance on my expenses.
The transaction, we figured, wasn't much more sophisticated—nor
need it have been—than the crude methods of money transfer preferred by Osama bin Laden's al Qaeda. We walked briskly, nearly
running, back to the Pajero, swinging a suitcase full of "funny
money" through the maddening crowds.

In the marketplace, Jamal had bought a cassette tape with an insignia of two crossed guns on the plastic casing; he shoved it into the tape deck and began playing it at high volume. The lyrics, which Karim Abdul dutifully translated, were devoted to the cause of Osama bin Laden. One of the cuts—the one with the best melody— had a mother and her warrior son serenading each other in a hearty duet as the young man prepared to go off to war. The soldier sang, "Mother dear, let me go there where my brothers are being bombed. Let me go and make a place for you in Paradise!" She sang in response, "Go, go, my son, but don't come back alive unless you've defeated the infidels!" Jamal found the rhyme amusing enough to sing along at the top of his lungs. As we raced through the streets of Peshawar on our way to warlord Haji Zaman's compound, Jamal slapped me on the back and tried to get me to join in the chorus. However, the lyrics only turned my mind back to worrying about what kind of reception we would receive at the gates of the Afghan inferno.

No one—especially those of us who had spent the last five weeks in Peshawar waiting for just such a break—was quite prepared for Haji Zaman's offer that afternoon of November 15, 2001. We had been lulled to sleep watching warlords work their satellite phones and hand out blank checks to followers.

When we arrived, Zaman, a grizzled and unsmiling man, was holding court outside his small brick house just across the street from the UN refugee center, where the starving masses had gathered day in and day out for the last two months. Several dozen disheveled reporters hung on the warlord's every word. The handsome old Afghan could well have been a cowboy western star in another life—he wore a Zapata-like brown blanket across his shoulders, sat cross-legged on the floor, and motioned with his hand, more often than not waving forward timid petitioners, listening to them diligently, chuckling a bit and then dispatching them with vague promises of rewards once he had regained his seat of power in Jalalabad, the largest Afghan city east of Kabul.

Lining Zaman up for our journey had required some real "shoe-leather" reporting. It had meant drinking countless cups of tea with the right warlord. The trick was in determining which ones wanted their homeland the most and which ones were just posing for dollars—or, if you will, which ones were getting the largest retainer from the CIA. Our man Zaman was loathe to admit that he was a sucker for promises of hard cash and a chance to reclaim his orange grove, but as far as I could see, he understood the stakes and what it would mean to his fellow Pashtun tribesmen, as a sign of courage, to be the first back. It hadn't always been that way. When the Taliban claimed Jalalabad a few years earlier and his assets appeared to be drying up, Zaman had fled Afghanistan for a leisurely life in Dijon, France. Just a few years at the top of the heroin trade in Jalalabad had given "Mr. Ten Percent" a ticket to just about any destination he could have chosen. In late September 2001, British and American officials, keen to build up an opposition core to take back the country from the Taliban, met with and persuaded Zaman to return to Afghanistan.

The fresh hordes of "holy warriors" lining up on his doorstep looking for work indicated that Zaman had the "mojo" working. The lax recruitment standards of Afghan warlords allowed for very little exclusivity indeed. Almost any old friend or unknown rogue who showed up at his house was taken on board, as would be the journalists dragged along for his next adventure. Zaman's fresh recruits were a mix of the Pashtun warriors who had defeated the Russians and a new generation of down-on-their-luck refugees who just needed the work. I guess Zaman knew that if he didn't sign them up—be they criminal, murderer, or con artist—his rivals certainly would.

After several hours early that morning of making his own final arrangements, Zaman had emptied his quarters and paraded with his entourage out onto the front lawn, which in addition to being flooded with his current pool of new recruits, also served as a distribution point for blankets and food packets for refugees. As he waded into the crowd, it became clear that Zaman's best bodyguards had no experience beating back a Western press corps. Within seconds, reporters, stumbling over electrical cords and whacking each other in the head with microphones, swamped the warlord, who, perhaps as a means of self-defense, wrapped himself in a putrid sheepskin. He started by saying all the right things—that he was determined to teach Osama bin Laden's al Qaeda network a lesson in modern warfare and would, come hell or high water, return that very afternoon to his hometown, Jalalabad, where he had fought the Russians in the early '90s. Zaman extended an invitation to anyone in the media who wished to accompany him on his journey. Several mouths in the audience dropped precipitously.

"Is it safe?" a Frenchman asked. Well, no—*"pas exactement"* was the warlord's quaint reply.

After Zaman's announcement, about half the journalists in the pack outside his home remained impatiently waiting for the adventure to begin. It was hard to tell how well our "escorts" would perform. Except for the gray and brown *pakols*, woolen berets that had replaced the black Taliban turbans, most of Zaman's men had beards cut nearly as long as those of their ruling compatriots. With knives hidden beneath their wool blankets, they could well have passed themselves off as a band of eighteenth-century cutthroats. Noticeably missing were guns. I assumed, rather hoped, that some contingency plans were now being made closer to the Khyber Pass to arm our party properly. Then came word over the radio that Zaman's advanced party still hadn't brokered a deal for a "peaceful return" for his men. One of Afghanistan's most-feared warlords, as it turned out, would have to go for the gusto—prove he hadn't gone soft dining on filet mignon in Dijon.

At 2 P.M. on November 15, 2001, Zaman decided that if we didn't leave immediately, we would never make our destination by sundown. Our convoy had grown to some seven four-wheel-drive jeeps, one or two Toyota Corollas, and several small trucks with enclosed wagons, inside each of which from a dozen to two dozen would-be fighters had been crammed, squatting against the tin walls. By my own count, twenty to thirty journalists were riding along, several television network correspondents having dropped out at the last moment over the concerns of their company lawyers about the prospect of rising insurance premiums. In our own Pajero, which was about ten years old and one of the best looking in the lot, we had just the three of us—Jamal, Karim Abdul, and myself.

Our convoy inched forward through the diesel smoke and a herd of braying sheep on the edge of Peshawar. As we rounded a corner, I caught a final glimpse of Auntie waving her red scarf and running after us, but failing to catch up, with yet more chicken sandwiches to send along for the trip. We sped through the marketplace toward the Pakistani tribal areas. On the Peshawar City side, heroin, hashish and machine guns were illegal. In the marketplace across the muddy alleyways on the tribal side, though, dealers sold kilo upon kilo of white and brown heroin. You could even drop in for a free sample. A train of pack camels, chewing cud and flashing their long yellow teeth at us, lumbered across the road in front of us. Jamal's left rear-view slapped the tail of the last beast in the train as we raced to keep up with the rest of the convoy. In the distance, I could just make out the first of the dusty, red, rocky hills that marked the precipitous rise into Afghanistan. Out my window, I saw the huge marker set in stone for Pakistan's "Khyber Rifle" brigades, the elite guardians of the frontier on our side of the border.

Jamal was managing to hold second place in the long, snaking convoy when suddenly the lead vehicle, in which Zaman was riding, came to an abrupt halt. Zaman and two of his armed sons jumped out of their car, and one son waved us over to explain quickly his new plan. From the look on Jamal's face, the change had come as a complete surprise. The son asked Karim Abdul to move to the front, and while one son jumped in after Karim Abdul, Zaman and his other son squeezed into the back seat with me. It didn't take long to figure out that Zaman didn't want to ride with us simply to chew the fat about his prospects for a dramatic homecoming. Zaman, the clever fox, was trying to avoid an ambush against his own well-known vehicle and had chosen to hide his person in our jeep instead. His car, if I judged correctly, was now the decoy, and we were the real targets. He hadn't even asked, nor would it have been useful for us to object; a journalist sometimes just has to accept the story as it develops. I wasn't going to let the opportunity slide, and I began a soft interrogation of the crusty fighter, who smelled (it seemed inappropriately) of Old Spice aftershave.

Was he surprised by the sudden collapse of the Taliban? He chuckled, "Wars are won mostly on morale," adding in French, "Esprit de corps, my boy. They just collapsed, and now it is our turn again. Jalalabad has always been a city for peacemakers." The fib, of course, being that he counted himself among the peacemakers. He obviously took himself very seriously, but it sounded as though he had been drinking too much Perrier water during his sojourn in Dijon.

I dared to ask the honored warrior why he had only now returned to the fray. "Events have conspired to create an opportunity. The Americans, the British, and the Afghans all want me back, so how can I refuse?"

He had given us a ticket into Afghanistan, so I didn't press him too much on that point. "Blessed be the peacemakers," I mumbled to myself. Our convoy came to a sudden halt on a nearby ridge so everyone could take a moment to face Mecca and offer prayers. I noticed that Jamal, who had still not fully realized that our Pajero had been hijacked, was wisely going in for the full genuflections. It was a touching moment. South Asia's brilliant autumn sun was just beginning to make its way down toward the blood-red earth of the Afghan frontier. No one was sure what the mountains of Afghanistan had in store for us—certainly, nothing nice. They had served as near-perfect cover for Afghan snipers who had wiped out British colonial armies on two occasions in the last two centuries. In the distance were the sharp crags and peaks that I had looked out on only two days earlier, wondering if Mashal had made it safely into Taliban-controlled Kabul. On that day, I had been in the border-crossing village, Torkham, where I had watched Taliban guards with thick rubber truncheons beat back Afghans who did not have proper authorization to return to their country. But as our convoy approached the village on the way to make our own border crossing, we saw nothing, only an empty, abandoned valley full of dust. Bleak rumors began to circulate.

We stopped again, and for about ten minutes it was unclear what was causing the delay. From my window, I could see we had arrived at another of the ubiquitous roadside arms bazaars that line the thoroughfares in the Pakistani tribal areas. I began to feel somewhat relieved as I realized our convoy would not be continuing on completely defenseless. The bazaar sold everything from rocket launchers to homemade machine guns. A gunsmith in Pakistan could make a Russian Kalashnikov almost from scratch, but the guns that Zaman's two sons started tossing to our own ragtag fighters were the real

McCoy, Kalashnikovs from the era of the Soviet invasion. In addition, some of the young men now appeared with jerry-made, hand-held rocket launchers. I saw one kid, maybe fourteen, jam a rocket into the barrel of one of these things and point it toward Torkham. If we had been in the market, we could have bought an American-made Stinger missile, also left over from the fight against Soviet aggression. The going price was from fifty to a hundred thousand dollars, depending on the condition of the timer.

Zaman's brother, who headed up a delegation that had reached Jalalabad a day earlier, caught up to us in the bazaar as our men bought up guns like candy bars. He brought what was decidedly bad news, warning that Arab al Qaeda stalwarts held at least one village along the road to Jalalabad. The warlord's brother was short and fat, clearly not a man who could jump out the back of a truck and run up a hill. He said things that made all kinds of sense to me, and my hunch, though I held my tongue, was to agree that we might consider postponing our dash into Afghanistan.

"Don't go today, al Qaeda fighters are still in the mountains," the trembling brother told us, trying to reason with his elder sibling. He reminded Zaman that less than two weeks earlier, Abdul Haq, one of several Afghan warlords believed to have had Washington's strong backing, had proved to have had very little indeed. Haq, a jovial, heavyset man and a Western-leaning "holy warrior," had told me in an interview sometime earlier about his plans to take back his own province, though he had remained standoffish about the timing. It had been genuine patriotism that kept him in an Afghan fray dominated by power-hungry extremists. Indeed, the Taliban had run him out of Afghanistan and then Pakistan. Haq had been, it seemed, an excellent ally, one that Washington should have signed up early in its battle to oust the Taliban and their special "guest" Osama bin Laden. But as Haq rounded up his own posse and set out on horseback for his old haunts, Pentagon officials had been helpless to prevent his death. Taliban fighters had surrounded him in a valley with nowhere to ride. The CIA managed to unleash a single "Hellfire" missile from an unmanned Predator drone. It had been to no avail and, in fact, demonstrated one of the first signs that Washington's war cabinet viewed the Afghan conflict as something they could win with a newfangled Nintendo game created in the Florida's Central Command headquarters. Haq never stood a chance of riding out alive. In the end, the Afghan, who did not have enough friends in high places, swung from a tree in a hangman's noose. His rigged, bloated body waved in the autumn wind in the desolate town square of Jalalabad, our own destination. It was a tough way to go, and it sounded like an awful end to a good western.

As Zaman's brother's warnings grew more strident, I waited impatiently for the translation of Zaman's answer. He ultimately said just what you would expect an older and more brazen Afghan warlord brother to say: "Don't be silly!" The comment struck me as almost humorous, given the circumstances.

Whom was he kidding? I wondered. After all, he had just jumped into my Pajero to avoid an ambush. If al Qaeda fighters crossed our path, I didn't expect Zaman and his brothers to give a friendly wave out of the window. As we prepared to run what we all now expected would be a gauntlet into Jalalabad, I looked over at Jamal, whose large forehead had gathered beads of perspiration. He had begun to understand that he was now on his way to where only the "crazy people" went. I advised him against trying to oust Zaman from the back seat and offered him double the salary for making the run across the border. He shook his head resignedly: "Mr. Philip, you crazy too! What about my family?"

As we passed a sign noting the Islamic Republic of Afghanistan, I felt as though we were riding in slow motion, creeping ahead in some hostile moonscape, a treeless land of rock and dust. The red rocks shimmered in the dimming light. It was almost as dramatic as I had hoped, and I might even have enjoyed crossing the border if I hadn't been frightened of what lay ahead. It was so silent, like driving into a strange twilight zone where humans, like rodents, might only come out at night. An eerie silence—apart from the sound of rubber on asphalt—descended on our convoy. A bedraggled old man encrusted with the dust of ages stood beside the road alongside several hungry-looking children. He looked a little bitter to me, as though we owed him something that someone had promised years ago, but his gaze provided no clues of what lay ahead. A twosome from the *Times* of London leapt out of a jeep three vehicles behind us to take pictures. The pair, which had been in an advance party, had planned an exclusive "How I became a holy warrior for a day to slip clandestinely into Afghanistan"—the only problem being that they had no facial hair, which made them look like blonde Swedes trying to slip into Uganda in blackface. One of Zaman's sons started shouting and hustled the two reporters at gunpoint back into the car as we carried on into the approaching twilight. I had the feeling that all of us had become hostage to the warlords and their ally, the approaching darkness.

Still nearly an hour outside of Jalalabad, the first sound of trouble had begun. A stray rocket fired from a distant mountaintop rocked the silence. "Where did that come from?" I asked Karim Abdul, snapping my head back to look at a receding ridge. No signs of any gun smoke, but it appeared to me that someone, maybe al Qaeda, had fired down on us from one of the surrounding hills. As Jamal increased our speed, I could see a large, green antiaircraft gun about five hundred meters in the distance. The setting sun highlighted the gun's contrast to several mud-brick homes in the background, and as we moved closer, I could see the gun had been freshly oiled by someone who apparently intended to use it. Only at the last minute did I make out two men manning the machine gun at the back. My heart sank. The gun ripped the twilight with a chorus of rage that unleashed all my fear at once. My stomach seized up, and I dove under the seat as the wild, incessant staccato unfolded. I expected to hear the side of our Pajero ripped to shreds by incoming shells. Suddenly, I wished for the life of me that I had joined the blue-burqa brigade instead. Anything but this!

Then I heard something more disturbing, which sounded like someone mumbling in fear. I looked over at Zaman. He appeared unmoved by the ruckus. Soon, one of the warlord's bodyguards' nervous chuckle broke out into a hearty laugh. He looked over at me, smiled a very patronizing grin, and told Karim Abdul, who quickly translated: "It is only a two-thousand-gun salute, you fool!" Jamal, who had begun to swerve from his own fright, now straightened the wheel and breathed deeply. I sat up in my seat and forced a timid grin.

As we approached the village center, bands of smiling villagers appeared beside a tank with its turret pointed away from us into the distance where the mountain valley opened up, unveiling the spectacular beauty of the turbulent Kabul River. To the north of the river we could see mountain peaks, like a camel train fading into the darkness. The natives shouted that they had seen Arab fighters and some stray Taliban flee over the same mountains. They went "thataway," a kid pointed with a bony finger. I scribbled his remark in my notebook. Some of the Arabs—apparently wary of their lives as holy warriors— had, another young boy raising a Kalashnikov shouted, handed in their guns to the villagers as they boarded boats. The Arabs, their children in tow, had headed north to cross into Pakistan on foot, he said. No one was there to stop them, and I immediately worried again that the greatest prey of all, Osama bin Laden, might have already fled to safety.

Our convoy set out again, speeding ahead to catch the last light until Zaman ordered a halt to pray a second time on the outskirts of Jalalabad. Jamal couldn't have agreed more with the idea, and this time he used a large red rock to rest his forehead on as he bent down like a large bear examining the soil. The sun slipped out of sight over the parched, flat valley leading into Jalalabad. Naked, shoeless children raced out of mud huts to greet the warlord's convoy, and a woman beat a mule to keep it walking in a straight line. After our crew said their prayers, several of the young men holding the largest rockets pinched a cigarette laced with hashish, stealthily passed it back and forth and smiled at the hometown they hadn't seen in five years. We moved out again. At a military fort that had served five years earlier as Zaman's base, a band of young men stood at attention in the darkness beside an aging artillery piece. The image stuck in my head for hours. It looked like one of those old black-and-white shots of the ragged Confederate Army saluting General Lee toward the end of the Civil War. Most of the soldiers, their loyalties unknown until this very moment, acknowledged us with poker faces as we passed into the city. A twelve-year-old boy waved to us with one hand and clutched a shotgun in the other. The warlord had arrived home. To his misfortune, several dozen shell-shocked Western journalists had arrived with him, with all their lives still intact.

## "Hotel Tora Bora"

Zaman had, judging by what he had explained on our journey, expected to waltz—along with the jittery press corps—into Jalalabad's only two-star hotel. But as it soon became apparent, the Spin Ghar (White Mountain) Hotel had already fallen into the hands of his rival warlord, Hazret Ali, and his fellow Pashay tribesmen—local hillbillies with no blood ties to Zaman's Pashtun. Ali and his men had slipped down out of the mountains a day earlier, as soon as the Taliban and their Arab guests had cleared out. Their advance arrival at the hotel—in Afghanistan, at least—amounted to a long-term rental agreement.

The Spin Ghar, a low, sprawling hotel set in a tropical garden of sorts, offered all of eastern Afghanistan's strange, alluring mix of foliage—pines, palms, apples, and oranges. It must have looked to the young Pashay fighters like a luxurious base for their marauding about town. By strict comparison with other war-zone hotels I had stayed in, the Spin Ghar was definitely upscale. It even had electricity, water, and a working kitchen.

The Pashay leader, Ali, was standing in the lobby and met Zaman with a tenuous handshake. He cut a short, slim, and handsome figure. His curly hair and blue-gray eyes glistened with a sense of adventure that would soon win him the affections of several female reporters in our lot, who, for lack of any other "heroes," saw him as something of a sexy outlaw. His posse, however, lacked any modicum of sex appeal. Ali led a gang of skinny mountain boys in rags. For Ali's boys, the Spin Ghar Hotel offered more of the same booty that was to be found across the city. As we soon discovered, visions of the modern world had unveiled the vilest urges in these wretched peasants. The security vacuum that had descended after the retreat of the Taliban had allowed them to plunder and destroy everything they came across in Jalalabad. Ali's boys had managed, in twenty-four hours, to steal every running vehicle on four wheels and break into most of the aid agencies to loot televisions, copy machines, and other newfangled devices with keyboards and display screens. They rampaged like kids with the run of an abandoned toy store. Some of them looked to be about fourteen, but the average age was about seventeen. Several truckloads of Pashay greeted us at the gates of the Spin Ghar, each grimy-faced fighter clutching a rocket launcher on his shoulder and smiling from ear to ear. They were a cheery lot, as surprised to see us as we were to see them. They looked at Zaman's press pool with dollar signs in their eyes, and we, in turn, looked through their personas for the stories they knew or might offer us in the future. Many looked like the proverbial descendants of Alexander the Great, rumored still to haunt this corner of Afghanistan. They had dark red, curly hair, which they enjoyed cultivating like gardens on their heads and faces. This was clearly a band of dandies. Many of them stuck flowers behind their ears or in the barrels of their Kalashnikovs—making them look a little like peaceniks turned into beatnik revolutionaries. As their leader shook Zaman's hand, the Afghan beatniks appeared to acknowledge Zaman with their raised rocket launchers—all at once pointed down the road toward the governor's mansion, seemingly indicating that Zaman held no sway here and must continue on his journey. We, the press corps, could remain, but the tone of our stay had already been set.

Ali's boys, the bravest of whom had rocketed the Taliban from the hills around the city for the last six years, had held genuine and relatively profound claims to authority in Jalalabad long before Zaman's men had arrived in town. The warlord from Dijon, which the Pashay couldn't even place on a map, was an immediate social outcast in their view. Zaman's force of three to four hundred, maybe half the size of Ali's six hundred men, would prove no match for their rivals. This wouldn't smooth things over in downtown Jalalabad, though. Ali's band was itself a hated minority group that had managed to seize power, loot, and ravage, with the help of the guns they had only just stolen from the fleeing Taliban. A truck and five fighters with rocket launchers in the back, they had discovered, defined the new Afghan warlord—just as it had for the vanquished religious zealots now fleeing into the snow-capped mountains to the south. Zaman looked peeved, but he copped a diplomatic pose. He recognized that it was wise, for now, to share the spoils. He told Ali that his men had taken over the grounds of the governor's mansion and would prepare for a *Jirga*, council of elders meeting, that would divvy up the turf for both men in a fair and honest way. As Zaman jumped back into his own truck, I felt a sense of relief that he was going his own way. We still agreed to meet in the morning in his orange grove to drink tea and discuss what he had described coming in as "the hunt for the bad guys."

At the front desk of the Spin Ghar, a short fat man in a pakol with a bushy, rounded, brown beard was soon listening to the pleas from journalists for rooms "facing the Indian Ocean, please." Of course, no room overlooked the Indian Ocean; however, the typical Inmarsat satellite phone needed a clear southern view to register a transmission signal. The receptionist couldn't figure out, to save him, why the journalists thought landlocked Afghanistan might have rooms with an ocean view. His assistant quickly chirped in that there was "no water and no swimming! Only showers." In the end, the manager threw up his hands and started handing out keys with a view of the Kabul River, which seemed far more logical, but that was the entirely wrong direction. The few television networks snapped up handfuls of keys. As usual, they demanded not rooms but blocks of rooms, sometimes an entire wing—"facing the Indian Ocean, please."

Once ensconced, we had forty-five minutes to call our desks and file a story. It would be up to "Rewrite" in London, Washington, and Tokyo to make sense of this all. Already on the patio of the Spin Ghar journalists were spinning a web of cables as they opened up a myriad of fold-out and screw-in satellite dishes. I felt a little sorry for a wire-thin correspondent from the Canadian Broadcasting Corporation. I shouldn't have. Having failed to lure his producer into Afghanistan, he was launching his own one-man show—literally. If you've ever seen a musician play the drums with his feet, the harmonica with his mouth, strum a guitar, and sing at the same time, you'll understand what this reporter was about to do. A fold-out dish and a camera on a stand with an automatic switch to roll film allowed him to—lo and behold—complete his own feeds from the patio of the Spin Ghar Hotel. He was describing the two-thousand-gun salute live from Afghanistan before I put my fingers to the keyboard of my tattered Toshiba.

Having abandoned my own broken sat phone in Peshawar, I had to rely on the good graces of my colleagues to procure a few precious minutes on a satellite. I shouldn't have worried about it so much. Several lenders were happy to help. In the end, the *Times* of London, my stiffest competitor, lent me a line. I throttled out dictation—mostly off the top of my head—to some pleasant British secretary in Manchester. After slugging out the best version of the mayhem and confusion I had just witnessed, we filed into the dining hall. It was the first day of Ramadan, which would mean an evening feast every night at sunset, but almost nothing in between then and dawn.

Someone uncorked a bottle of wine, and the entire press corps and a small army of Afghan assistants sat down to eat a precious meal of soft, yellow rice, and glistening Tandoori-style chicken. If this was as bad as it would get, I thought, I'd survive. Karim Abdul had managed to secure us two rooms, and soon after dinner we all collapsed in our beds for our first real dreams inside Afghanistan.

The story in the first few days upon arrival was a "no-brainer." Editors wanted anything and everything on al Qaeda, as well as any indication that the terror network had gone to ground in the nearby White Mountains. There was more than enough fodder for stories to go around, and so the two dozen journalists split up, following their noses and best instincts. Rising early on our first morning in Afghanistan, Karim Abdul, Jamal, and I laid plans to sleuth around the city and its outskirts. The hunt was on, and we would comb the debris for even the smallest hints of where al Qaeda had gone and what its operatives had been up to. Each chemical formula, each charred identity card would be part of the bigger picture, something to spin into a feature story. We raced from one tattered, burned-out terrorist residence to the next. Sometimes we arrived first, other times we had to chew over what others had already picked through.

All in all, catching a whiff of Osama turned out to be easier than anyone had expected. Jalalabad and its environs to the south had had some of the most extensive terrorist training camps in all of Afghanistan. Bin Laden's "people" had literally littered their exit route with enough detritus of terror to fill every journalist's suitcase and then some. On the edge of town, tour guides were touting a local residence as Osama's favorite summer home. The press quickly plundered it, beating all but maybe one or two intrepid CIA agents to the punch. Spy headquarters in Langley would no doubt have to answer for the delay in their own gumshoe work. That a journalist got his hands on a manual or clue didn't mean that it would become public knowledge. It might just end up as a souvenir hanging in some hack's bedroom.

Richard Lloyd-Parry, a tall, raffish-looking Tokyo correspondent for the *Independent,* was more enterprising than many. While Karim Abdul and I were trying to decipher the Arabic of terror manuals, Richard was going straight for dirty underwear—and writing about it. He snagged what he suspected were a pair of bin Laden's briefs off a clothesline in a region south of the city, known as "Farma Hada." At least they were clean. He wrote: "They were striped gray and black cotton boxers, with a label reading Angelo Petrico, a size XXL large for such a lean-looking man. . . . I lifted them from the clothesline anyway, a souvenir from a place full of more sinister and deadly objects. Many before me have seen his guns, his plans and his weaponry, but how many can claim to own the underwear of the world's most wanted man?" That a respected journalist like Richard could get a lead story in a paper about Osama's underwear indicated a good measure about Mr. bin Laden's notoriety. He had taken on the XXL proportions of Elvis himself. Over a typical lunch of crackers and apples, several journalists remarked that the briefs should be immediately turned over to FBI forensics to do a DNA sample. It was our duty, one argued. "Stains of some sort are likely to show up—no doubt," remarked Harry, a Dutchman I had known from Sarajevo. "In the end, these briefs could be more valuable than Monica's dress!"

After lunch, we determined to scavenge the outskirts of town in hopes of yet more booty. American bombers still streaked across the blue skies overhead, but we had received a lead on a possible bomb factory. As we drove from one crime scene to the next, Karim Abdul kept his head out the window, looking up into the clear blue skies. He kept an eye out for American B-52 raids, which came sporadically in the first two days of our stay in Jalalabad; their payloads rocked the earth so profoundly that they brought down most of the mud walls around the alleged explosives factory. The earth near the Taliban's own hidden military installations had already been peppered with fresh, U.S.-made craters, but the ordnance hadn't managed to destroy tanks hidden beneath palm trees or artillery tucked into bunkers. Ali's boys had seized the undamaged goods for themselves.

To approach the factory, Jamal headed west in the direction of an old dam and another of bin Laden's real estate investments, this one a "summer home." We negotiated a mined dirt road, passed by several disabled Russian armored personnel carriers, and finally mounted a ridge littered with rusty mortars. The actual laboratory was set in a tiny mud home, in a village compound ringed by very tall adobe walls. A guard, one of Ali's haggard youngsters, still stood outside the thick mud walls of the factory. A few dusty children running circles around his feet, he greeted us as would a tour guide meeting his new charges and as though he had somehow been expecting us. I shook his bony hand, which gave me the immediate impression that he was malnourished. Little did we know, he was about to earn his dinner—since he had a gun and we didn't, there was a price to pay. He started by offering a package deal including Osama's summer home for two hundred dollars. When Karim Abdul finally had him down to something within reason, about 25 percent of the starting price, he agreed to take us along, and I marked him down for a "security expense." I didn't kid myself that we were taking along any kind of explosives expert.

I put one foot in Karim's hands as he shoved me over the mud wall, where I immediately tumbled onto my backside next to a few bags of unused fertilizer. So much for preserving the integrity of a crime scene, I thought. A couple of boys who had been playing guns outside the compound had already slinked in through a hole in the wall. They immediately began telling us about how the "evil" al Qaeda chemists had experimented on their village dogs. One of them kicked a glass vial, which shattered against a concrete wall. "They killed my puppy!" said a dirty-faced, angry boy of about ten years. It wasn't a surprise. We soon uncovered enough explosives and bomb-making equipment to blow up most of Jalalabad and probably Kabul. Texts and manuals dedicated to al Qaeda leader Osama bin Laden were scattered around the "factory." In one of the rooms, a chemist's reference book's dedication read: "In respect for our dear brother, Osama bin Laden, who has been a great contributor of wealth and ability to our jihad." Though nothing was specifically labeled "al Qaeda," the preponderance of written materials made it clear who had been the boss. Inside one of the bunkers, a bored fighter had tried his hand at poetry. Next to several sketches of flowers in the notebook, he wrote: "Oh, Osama, we will defend you until death comes upon us. Even in our death, our loyalty will be known by the red flowers that will spring up on our graves." An incomplete sketch of a tombstone with flowers growing at the base accompanied the verse. The display illustrated the poetic, though not very touching, side of martyrdom.

Lest anyone think that al Qaeda wasn't prepared for a little of its own medicine, we also found color manuals for the M-10 Alarm System. Made by a company in Seoul, the device provided "an early warning device by detecting very low concentrations of chemical agent vapors or inhalable aerosols." It added that the system was designed for infantry troops. Given the mess of explosives and chemicals surrounding us, it seemed like a smart accessory for journalists as well.

Keeping pace on the paper trail wasn't easy. Ali had apparently deployed his fighters in most of the old al Qaeda neighborhoods. Often well ahead of us, Ali's hillbilly fighters were ransacking homes throughout the village compound, ripping out computer terminals and emptying drawers. They hunted for gold and paper money, while we looked for hints that Osama had slept here. His men laid claim to the spoils even if they were worth something only to the FBI and the CIA. Locals were arriving home from the battlefield as well—including former Taliban. A former schoolmate of Karim Abdul was guarding one of the homes and trying to weasel a dollar or two out of journalists passing through. He didn't look quite right, and I soon learned that he was suffering from a far more severe case of shell shock than any in our crew had suffered on the ride in. The young man had only just arrived from Mazar-I-Sharif, where he had been fighting on the Taliban front lines until a U.S. aerial assault decimated them. When I tried to strike up a conversation with him, he snapped that he would always be the enemy of America. "Twenty of the twenty-five men in my trench were killed by those bombs," he said. "I'll never help *you* hunt down al Qaeda." No one had yet asked him to, and so far, with an unofficial "amnesty" already in force around eastern Afghanistan, he appeared to be melting back into the already shattered Afghan society in his new incarnation. (It wouldn't be long, however, before we ran into him back up on the "front lines" hunting down none other than Osama bin Laden. Talk was cheap in Afghanistan, a theme we would learn more about in the coming days.)

Chasing the trail of terror was, despite some amusing moments, serious work. Our editors back home couldn't get enough, which left us in a frantic rush throughout the daylight hours, all seeking to trump the competition's latest scoop. Back in the Farma Hada area, a pair of intrepid European journalists, the soft-spoken Italian Maria Grazias Cutuli of *Coriere della Sera* and Julio Fuentes, a flamboyant star for Spain's *El Mundo,* discovered capsules of what they believed to be deadly sarin nerve gas packaged in Russian containers and abandoned by al Qaeda fighters. Russia's leftover chemical weapons had clearly fallen into the hands of the wrong guys. It was an important story. In her dispatch, only days before her untimely and brutal death, Ms. Cutuli, thirty-nine, wrote: "We cannot work out what is inside. Julio Fuentes cuts into one side and one by one removes the white glass phials, which are delicate, like doses of insulin, pinched at the top, and isolated from each other in cardboard compartments. We count 20 of them. The label reveals the contents, sarin gas, written in Russian, and beneath is the indication of the antidote needed: atropine, the only substance able to neutralize the lethal effects."

After a few days of combing through the local al Qaeda files, journalists in Jalalabad felt anxious to move on in our quest for a bigger story. Most of us were getting great showings from our respective news outlets, even without yet having figured out—for certain—that Osama bin Laden was camped out down the road and fixing for a fight. I told my editors that I was thinking of heading up the road to Kabul, and they immediately approved of the idea.

Based on scattered clues that some al Qaeda fighters might be still hanging out in our neighborhood, I decided, along with many colleagues, to wait a couple of days to see what way the winds were blowing. I still had no sense that I might have become among "the hunted." The roads in Afghanistan, which had been extremely dangerous for most of the last two decades, had, ironically, become much safer during the six years that the Taliban held power in Afghanistan.

An authoritarian, extremely devout leadership did wonders for cleaning up the bandits and hijackers who had previously lurked around every mountain pass. This security, albeit at the expense of basic human rights, had won the Taliban many supporters, particularly in the Pashtun belt running from the east to the south, the region through which we hoped to travel safely.

## In the Eye of the Beholder

On the afternoon of November 19, most of us who had remained behind in Jalalabad felt lazy, even relieved, to have most of the day off. The "story," which had been focused on Jalalabad for the past four days, appeared to be slipping down to Kandahar, where the Taliban was making a last stand, and over to Kabul, where the Northern Alliance was extending its old iron-fisted rule. Afghan interpreters, given an afternoon siesta by their employers, spread out in the tall grass under the palm trees in front of the Spin Ghar to sun themselves and bide their time until the evening meal at sundown. Many of the assistants had drifted off to sleep when panicked Western journalists awoke them with shouts.

A group that had left early that morning for Kabul had returned in a panic to Jalalabad. An ABC correspondent appeared profoundly shaken. He trembled as he filled us in on the details. He said he had been in the convoy when it left early that morning. All had been calm as the convoy had begun swinging through a steep valley of barren hills leading up into the highlands that surround Kabul. Then gunmen had ambushed two lead cars, both of them white-and-yellow local taxis.

Four journalists were in the two lead cars. Julio Fuentes was with his close working friend Maria Grazia Cutuli, who had broken the important story on sarin gas only two days earlier; Harry Burton, a slender Australian television cameraman who had offered to let me use his satellite phone only a night earlier, was with Azizullah Haidari, an Afghan-born photographer who had worked his way into international news business from his rough existence as a refugee in Pakistan. Burton and Haidari both worked for the British-based

Reuters news agency; its best war correspondent, Kurt Schork, a friend of mine, had been killed in a similarly shocking ambush in Sierra Leone only a year earlier.

Initially, we had only sketchy reports from those who had been following the taxis from some distance, but as journalists helped one another cross-check the facts, a picture of profound terror began slowly to take shape. It became clear that the drivers of the two Toyota Corolla taxis from which the journalists had been forced out at gunpoint and another driver in a taxi behind him possessed firsthand versions of what happened. As the two explained the incident to a circle of journalists on the lawn of the Spin Ghar, the cars had just begun their ascent through a mountain pass near the town of Puli Estikam in a place where the road runs parallel to the Kabul River. Driver Ashaq Ullah, a terrified twenty-five-year-old, shook as he told the story. Five men in black turbans with their faces swathed in cloth had stopped the cars at gunpoint. When they told the journalists to step out of the car, the reporters had refused, but not for long. The gunmen forced the journalists out of the car and jammed the points of their rifles into their backs to shoo them down the steep embankment. "They were begging for mercy, but the armed men pushed them down and I saw them fire about three rounds into the backs of each person," said Ullah, who spoke through trembling lips. "They fell face first onto the ground."

"Who were they?" I implored.

"Men in black turbans." The second Afghan driver, a slight man wrapped in a blanket, added to the description of the killing: "They forced my passengers out of the car and down toward the river. The journalists were pleading, even grabbing at their beards." This driver added that one of the two men forcing them down the hill picked up a large stone and hit Harry Burton, the Australian, in the head. "After that, they were shot in the back. I saw all of my passengers fall down on the river bank." The motive looked to me to be far closer to pure terrorism than to any kind of a combined highway robbery/ homicide. The men in turbans stole satellite phones, cameras, and the journalist's belongings. But there were also indications that the killers had more profound and political reasons for choosing Westerners. One of the armed men, who had not participated in the actual killing, but remained standing with his gun above the ravine, asked the driver of the first taxi after the shots were fired: "Do you know your Islam?"

"Yes," said the driver, Mr. Ullah, replying in proper Arabic to the turbaned killers. The turbaned killer had added, "There is no God but Allah, Mohammad is the prophet of Allah." One of the four men standing at the driver's window then made a short pronouncement laced with political overtones: "You people say that the Taliban have been removed from power. No. We are here until we take our revenge!" Another one of the killers waved to the driver to turn back in the direction of Jalalabad. All of the men had their turbans pulled over their faces, making it impossible to know their identity.

Curiously, the killers had allowed other reporters to pass them by before moving in for the kill. Several journalists who had left even earlier that morning from Jalalabad had slipped through and noticed nothing unusual. Others had been spooked. Chris Tomlinson, a reporter with the Associated Press based in Africa, said he had passed by the armed men only minutes earlier from the other direction. He sat down with several reporters, myself included, inside the musty lobby of the Spin Ghar to describe his journey from Kabul. He reeled through the scene several times as we tried to pin down the exact location of the attack. "We saw six guys dressed like Taliban and holding Kalashnikovs. My driver slowed down and they shouted at us to stop. They screamed at us, 'Why have you cut your beards?' I shouted at my driver to keep going."

A story like that on a slow day acts like a hypodermic needle of adrenaline jabbed in your arm. Though it is sometimes possible in journalism to immunize yourself from the idea of your own death, when you are least expecting it one of "your own" gets hit, and it reminds you that no one is safe. The news of the attack on the 19th of November shocked me out of my own selfish lust for good news stories, of which there had been plenty of late. It reminded me that sinister powers were in play all around me, far more terrifying than anything a loose-leaf terror manual or abandoned chemical weapons factory could convey. Someone, or some evil, was out to get us, all of us. Of course, I thought to myself, more frightened than before, that was why I had been sent here in the first place.

The killing at noon on November 19 was the second major attack on foreign correspondents in Afghanistan. Thus far, the media had lost more of its own killed in action in Afghanistan than the U.S. military. Eight days earlier, a Taliban ambush had killed three journalists riding on an armored car near Taloqan in the north. Death had come equally quickly. Volker Handloik, forty, from the German magazine *Stern*, and two French radio reporters, Johanne Sutton, thirty-four, and Pierre Billaud, thirty-one, were hanging onto the sides of a personnel carrier that was moving through a battlefield that their armed escorts boasted had been cleared of "the enemy." As the armored car approached a trench, Taliban fighters armed with Kalashnikovs and antitank rockets popped up and opened fire. One of the three journalists immediately jumped down to take better cover behind the vehicle, quickly exposing himself to fire. Two more fell off as the vehicle spun in its tracks. Other journalists survived the attack, clinging for their lives to the armored car as its driver sped back in the other direction.

But whereas the killings near Taloqan looked like a matter of getting caught in the crossfire, those on the road to Kabul looked more akin to a terrorist operation involving members or affiliates of Osama bin Laden's al Qaeda network. By early afternoon, Hazret Ali had sent his fighters—twenty of them, armed with rocket launchers and Kalashnikovs—down the road. The force proved inadequate for the task, and his fighters quickly took fire from the surrounding hills. One of Ali's lieutenants said he had been able to make out what looked like four corpses in the road. He said that he had seen about twenty men on the other side running up farther into the hills, all the while firing back down into the ravine.

Ali's men retrieved the bodies of the dead the next day from the side of the road and at midday brought them back to Jalalabad in an ambulance. The killers had riddled their victims with bullets. Pam Constable of the *Washington Post* was one of two journalists who went in to identify the dead. "The bodies looked bruised with some abrasions and we were told by the coroners that the bullet holes were in the backs and the neck," she said after reemerging, shaking her head as she choked up and turned her eyes away. After brief autopsies that confirmed the violent nature of the deaths, four flimsy coffins made of thin plywood appeared on a balcony where we stood with cameras and notebooks in a half-trance. I stared down on the coffins for several minutes, transfixed by the finality of it all. A sprig of curly brown hair was just visible beneath the top of Harry Burton's coffin. I recalled him laughing and smiling a day earlier as he told me to hang onto his sat phone for as long as I liked. "Someone else is payin', mate!" he had said.

I recalled the day a young Serb, standing ten feet from me on an asphalt road in Sarajevo, had pointed a gun at me and skimmed a bullet within inches of my head. I had been in the wrong place at the wrong time and opened my mouth once too often, but I had lived to report another day. Afghanistan was different. The press corps weren't just in harm's way, minor irritants for extremists and warlords, as we had been in the Balkans, and we weren't peacemongers trying to expose the "war crimes" of the warmongers either—not this time around, anyway. We were part and parcel of "the target" in Afghanistan for several reasons, not least of which because we were helping "the powers that be" piece together bin Laden's own "terror trail" as we went through the motions of our own profession.

Those on our side of the fence often saw our research and findings as the gospel truth of the "free world," at least when they found it suited their political ends. On the other hand, al Qaeda and the Taliban invariably regarded our work as nothing short of vicious lies. The fact that the U.S. military sometimes used the evidence we gathered to plot and justify their attacks bespoke the quality and credibility of information we could turn up. Simultaneously, however, this fact led al Qaeda and the Taliban to brand us as infidels working to advance the goals of our invading regimes. The deaths of the four journalists on the road to Kabul, I believe, shocked all of us out of our own sense of immunity and complacency. It made some of us all the more careful not to promote our role as accessories to our own governments and their efforts to rid the world of evil. Ironically, I believe the attack may have turned other journalists into frontline combatants. More reporters began showing a conviction that they had a duty to take on al Qaeda face-to-face. Some even went so far as to pack guns, a sure sign that we had become the hunters and the hunted. After the killings on the road to Kabul, no one in the press corps could deny that Afghanistan had become "our war" too.

That evening, as we hastened to meet deadlines, we had little chance to reflect on the deaths of our colleagues. There would be neither proper memorial services nor any funeral to remember them by. The four flimsy coffins were loaded onto a flatbed truck the next day by Afghan hospital workers and driven down the road to Pakistan.

A few weeks after the attack, I met a local Afghan, a cave cutter, who had helped bin Laden fortify his mountain redoubts just down the road. He claimed to have spoken to some of the al Qaeda fighters involved in the killings of my four colleagues. "The Arabs tell me that it was right for them to kill those four journalists two weeks ago on the road to Kabul. They even spoke to me about the beauty of the Italian photographer and writer, but they told me that her killing was justified because the American cluster bombs have killed so many of their own people." But the idea that they were even trying to rationalize the killing of these innocents made me sure they were haunted by what they had done. I recalled looking into the eyes of dead women and children in Kosovo and wondering if their butchers had felt just a pang of conscience as they had taken their knives to their throats. Maybe there had been one among the killers who had objected, but who had held his tongue just long enough for the crime to proceed. Murder was a wretched thing, and the conversation with the cave cutter ran all those ugly battle scenes I tried to forget through my head again like a ghastly newsreel. It was tough to say good-bye to a few more ambitious witnesses, and it made me think that just as the victims in 9/11 hadn't lifted a finger to deserve what they got, so too the reporters had been caught in the cross fire of a crazy and unpredictable new terror war. I was also sure that the road ahead, as the Fourth Estate delved deeper into the horror, would be fraught with more peril.

# 2

## THE STAKEOUT

In all this tumult, this wholesale slaughter, the individual and his feelings are utterly lost. Only the army has a tale to tell. With events on such a scale, the hopes and fears, the strength and weakness of man are alike indistinguishable.

—Winston Churchill,
*The Story of the Malakand Field Force*

### Task Force Dagger

Col. John Mulholland, commander of the Fifth Special Forces Group based out of Fort Campbell, Kentucky, could not claim, upon setting foot in Afghanistan in October 2001, to be highly decorated in the line of fire. But he was a dedicated warrior, a man who spent late nights at work, even in the absence of war. He was by now one of the U.S. military's top "in theater" experts on unconventional warfare. His colleagues knew him as a burly, slightly overweight soldier, direct and sometimes gruff but also honest and thoughtful. On September 11, 2001, at the Fifth Special Forces Group headquarters, Mulholland had known almost as soon as the World Trade Center collapsed that he would be tapped for action. As he would explain to me in January 2003 in his wood-paneled office, set in a dingy old barracks building and lined with daggers, guns, and photos of loved ones, Afghanistan was in his "patch"—an area of operations that also included Iraq and much of the Middle East.

31

"Once it became clear that Afghanistan was part of the equation—and you didn't need to be Sherlock Holmes to figure that out—we began our planning," he told me, moving over from his desk to a large conference table and plopping down a detailed map of Afghanistan. "But if you threw a dart at a spinning globe, this is the last place you would have wanted it to land," he added.

On September 13, 2001, Colonel Mulholland's "Task Force Dagger" swung into action. The colonel's forces would be both the eyes on the ground and the key fighting element in the Pentagon's unconventional approach to overthrowing a government and hunting down its enemies. Supporting and directing indigenous fighters anywhere in his patch was what the Green Beret commander did best. Colonel Mulholland would be, himself, the highest-ranking Beret on the ground in Afghanistan for the next five months, America's "go-to guy" for almost all key operations. In the end, the colonel and his elite commandos would garner the lion's share of the battlefield successes in Afghanistan, but they would also take the hit on some of the war's crucial failures.

"We looked on the evolving situation as one that had great potential for what we do best—unconventional warfare," he told me. "There were already resistance groups, even though we knew almost nothing about them. It would be a crash course to learn what we could, but that is what we were trained for."

If Commander in Chief George W. Bush wanted this Afghan war won in short order, as he insisted, there really weren't many other alternatives to Mulholland's unconventional route. Moving large numbers of U.S. troops into the theater required easy access, and at the outset, Pakistan, Afghanistan's most important neighbor and Washington's top ally in the region, had not agreed to allow its bases to be used as jumping-off spots for a massive U.S.-led invasion. The war planners believed that an entirely different approach was required, a new blend of savvy intelligence and sharp targeting. With speed considered to be of the essence, one branch of the U.S. government already had the upper hand. The CIA's loose bureaucratic knit allowed the spy agency to think fast on its feet in the field. Compared to the elephantine, bureaucratic pace of military decision making—by no means an exclusively American disease—the CIA worked at lightning speed. If Mulholland commanded the finesse, Langley promised to provide the brains.

Enter George Tenet, the high-strung intelligence whiz who had also served in the last administration as America's top spy chief. For Clinton, Tenet had done his best to track the elusive bin Laden. In his daily briefings at the White House, he continually stressed the threat that the al Qaeda chief posed. He even came up with a plan, following the U.S. African embassy bombings in 1998, to go after bin Laden in one of his remote training camps in eastern Afghanistan by using Pakistani and local guides. However, the plan fell apart where it required cooperation from a duplicitous ISI, Pakistan's spy agency, which paid lip service to the United States while simultaneously using bin Laden's training camps to ready its own Kashmiri rebels. At that time, the Pakistanis weren't yet our allies. Cynics in the intelligence community were already convinced that if we didn't do it ourselves, no one in South Asia would take out bin Laden for us.

Tenet, like the president, felt pressed to get results—and for good reason. In the wake of 9/11, pundits and common citizens had blamed the spy chief for having no real strategy to combat global terror. He wasn't going to let that happen again, as witnessed by his new "plan of action" for Afghanistan. The chief had a strategy on the table to win the war in Afghanistan a full month before the country's top generals came up with their own.

On September 15, Tenet showed up at the war cabinet with firm recommendations. The number-one goal was, of course, to destroy al Qaeda. This would be accomplished, he argued, through the auspices of the CIA working with the Northern Alliance and its allies, who would sweep across the country under the wings of U.S. bombers. The means were indirect, but, Tenet argued, they would devastate bin Laden and his ilk. Short of a large U.S. ground force, which the plan excluded, just what was needed to make this plan work? Money. Money could move mountains inside one of the world's most impoverished nations, he argued.

Bush was convinced. In late September, he was prepared to move ahead with Tenet's idea, which did not completely exclude U.S.

soldiers rushing into the fray, but worked, in theory, with only a couple hundred Green Berets in theater. On September 23, Tenet argued at a National Security Council meeting that "we need to push the tribals into combat. We need to give them reconnaissance, we need to help them target the al Qaeda leadership, we need to have Afghans fighting Arabs." This would, in turn, he argued, get al Qaeda "moving into enclaves, which may allow us to target them and exploit them." Two days later, Tenet said that his plan could also work to "seal the borders and make sure the Arabs don't flee." That is about the time that Col. John Mulholland's phone started ringing off the hook. His Green Berets had been slated to work hand in glove with the CIA to win this war, and his men were champing at the bit to accept the challenge.

In October 2001, Mulholland's worst obstacles to success seemed to be the harsh terrain and the nasty weather. "The first days in October produced very bad weather, and there was lots of frustration," said Mulholland, recalling the sense of pressure he felt from his superiors to begin work. "There was anxiety and pressure to move fast, but at first we could not get in. If you've seen the Hindu Kush Mountains, that is a massive range, and you know what I am talking about." After a month of planning, on October 16, 2001, "Task Force Dagger" put its first units on the ground inside Afghanistan. The Fifth Group's first two hundred elite fighters did not enter the fray, however, without someone watching their back. In early October, some eight hundred light-infantry fighters from the Tenth Mountain Division, based in Fort Drum, New York, were inserted into Uzbekistan, a nation that had signed up almost immediately as a new ally in the U.S.-led war on terror. After a month on the ground, Mulholland converted the Tenth Mountain Division's mission of security and rescue in Uzbekistan to one of "quick reaction." The Tenth's troops would remain stationed in Uzbekistan, at his disposal, for use if and when he needed conventional forces on the ground.

## Blood Rivals and Bad Guys

Soon after landing in Afghanistan, the first unit of Mulholland's Fifth Group Green Berets linked up with Tajik general Mohammed Fahim in the Panjshir Valley, and the second with Uzbek general Rashid Dostum south of the northern Afghan city of Mazar-I-Sharif.

The colonel maintained no illusions about the warlords with whom he would be dealing throughout the conflict in Afghanistan. "Our guys, who didn't know squat about Afghanistan, could step off a helicopter and meet a warlord for the first time, and all we knew about him was that he was a bloodthirsty bastard—and four hours later, we were conducting operations with him," he told me. "That is just the kind of guys I have got. They knew they were not dealing with Boy Scouts, and these warlords, of course, had in their own minds their own legitimate interests to protect." As the colonel explained to me, as though talking of a New York City street gang, these interests included drug trafficking and rackets in smuggled items. As far as the Green Beret commander was concerned, these unfortunate vices could be left aside for some time, as long as the Afghans agreed to play by U.S. military rules in the hunt for al Qaeda.

The idea of having the Afghans win this war for us had always been a risky proposition, and this would not be the first time in history that a Western army had faced a choice of how to marshal the warlike nature of the local tribesmen. Winston Churchill, in *The Malakand Field Force,* gave long, hard consideration to the pros and cons of the British military's using Pashtun fighters to liberate the Afghan frontier from the dangerous mullahs. He wrote, "As long as they fight, these Afghans do not mind much on which side they fight"—adding, however, "There are worse men and worse allies." As a colonial power responsible for all of South Asia, the British had little choice but to employ the Afghan warriors. Their problem was balancing loyalties to tribe with the legitimate needs of the empire.

Young Churchill also noted the problems presented by the value system of the Pashtuns, who did not necessarily share the Western vision of virtue under fire: "Their system of ethics, which regards treachery and violence as virtues rather than vices, has produced a code of honor so strange and inconsistent, that it is incomprehensible to a logical mind." Churchill even defended the Afghans. He appears to have understood perfectly their unwillingness always to heed calls to arms from their British masters. "It should not be forgotten by those who make wholesale assertions of treachery and untrustworthiness against the Afridi and Pathan soldiers that these men are placed in a very strange and false position. They are asked to fight against their own countrymen and coreligionists. On the one side are accumulated the forces of fanaticism, patriotism and natural ties. On the other, military associations stand alone." In other words, the British military was pressing the Afghans, for the sake of military alliance, to abandon the ties of god and country that bound them to the extremist mullahs. Understandably, loyalties could tilt slightly away from the British toward the mullahs or back again in the other direction, depending on the fight at hand. As the U.S. military learned early on, little had changed since Churchill traversed the hinterlands of Central Asia.

Through the first month, the American invasion "lite" strategy, despite hiccups and false starts, worked like clockwork, disproving the nay-saying of pundits who had called for a massive invasion of Afghanistan that would have targeted al Qaeda camps with conventional U.S. forces. "Almost immediately upon arriving in theater we began calling in close air strikes," said Mulholland. "General Dostum turned out to be the most aggressive of the Afghan warlords. There were vicious fights as he made his way up toward Mazar." Mulholland made a decision to go with the strongest horse. "We had two teams with Dostum, but we weren't getting much out of General Fahim's people. They had been hoping for World War II type of carpet bombing, but we made it clear that we would not do that, particularly because of the overriding concern for collateral damage. Our requirements for positive target identification were very high. We had to see it with our own eyes and confirm it as a target before dropping ordnance."

Just north of Kabul, the Taliban, a feisty band of religious zealots and poor, unthinking peasants, dug into long trench positions fortified against mortars and tank fire. Even with bin Laden's own elite fighters holding the toughest posts and encouraging the rest, however, the Afghan lines quickly began to collapse under the intensive bombing. At a meeting that Colonel Mulholland attended in Uzbekistan, General Tommy Franks, head of Central Command, urged General Fahim to "get moving." Fahim began to whine. He complained that the Americans were now working far too closely with his rival, Dostum, a grizzly and determined warlord who had a dubious reputation with many Afghans because he had fought on the side of the Russians for nearly a decade before switching sides.

"Dostum was, of course, a blood rival of these guys," Mulholland said, by way of explaining his method of playing one warlord off against the other. "There was no love lost between the Tajik and Uzbek-dominated factions, but our answer to Fahim was that we will work with whomever will help us meet our objectives. You must play by our rules and work with us against our common enemy."

In the end, General Fahim's proxy ground force of Northern Alliance fighters didn't have to storm into Kabul under the wings of U.S. fighter jets. It drove in almost casually, so slowly that in some cases Western journalists arrived first, to discover a city abandoned by its former rulers. The desired "regime change"—the overthrow of the Taliban—arrived early, almost unexpectedly. As Kabul fell, Mulholland sent one of his own twenty-two-man "A teams" to Bagram, the old Soviet-built airfield an hour's drive north of the capital.

The Green Beret's forces still spearheaded the U.S. military's operations, but after the fall of Kabul they had an added mission—the long-anticipated manhunt for senior al Qaeda leaders. Both the CIA and the Green Berets were trying desperately to track the mastermind's movements. "In mid-November we had reports of him going to numerous locations, one being to Tora Bora, south of Jalalabad," Mulholland told me, running his thick finger along the still disputed "Durand Line," the Afghan–Pakistan border drawn by the British. "That was an old Soviet-era stronghold where the Afghan holy warriors had fought."

On November 15, about the time my own ragged convoy arrived in Jalalabad, Mulholland had about two hundred fighters spread out in A teams across Afghanistan. Still, Mulholland was complaining to his superiors that he wasn't getting the kind of information he needed to begin attacks on the suspected al Qaeda enclaves in eastern Afghanistan. "We were working closely with the CIA, but, in truth—and I will say this not to steal any thunder from them—they didn't have any more insight on the situation than my Special Forces did. They had a relationship with the Panjshir Valley Tajiks, and that relationship went all the way back to the Soviet era, but they could not provide any great insight on the Pashtun side of the equation."

President Bush, confident that proxy war was the way to go in Afghanistan, had already told his war cabinet that he was no longer sure if conventional military forces would be necessary. The suggestion came as a surprise to many Pentagon planners, who wanted a complete integration of overwhelming U.S. firepower with the assets of the CIA and the Green Berets. The president's choice was fraught with risk, both strategically in the global arena, and politically within his own close security circle. He had stressed continually, as did Secretary of Defense Donald Rumsfeld on several occasions, that the Clinton administration's preference for high-tech aerial assaults without a commensurate commitment of U.S. forces had already left the world with a lower opinion of U.S. strength. Bush said so—months later—in an interview at his Texas ranch with the *Washington Post*'s Bob Woodward. "I mean, people viewed that as the impotent America . . . a flaccid, you know, kind of tech competent, but not very tough country that was willing to launch cruise missiles out of a submarine and that'd be it." Bush's top security advisers had stressed over and over that they didn't want to slam million-dollar ordnance into the sides of mountains only to watch the "cockroaches" scatter to fight another day.

On November 13 a crucial debate about throwing U.S. forces into the fray was still under way in a top-secret NSC meeting. It was the tip of the iceberg of a two-month-long debate about what would be best, a "light" or a "heavy" troop deployment in Afghanistan. Vice President Dick Cheney, who, more than any other "hawk" in the administration, was gunning for bin Laden, asked the obvious question of the day: "Should U.S. forces go in?" Rumsfeld answered that it was still under consideration. Cheney knew that there were a thousand of the U.S. military's best mountain fighters on call already just north of Afghanistan in neighboring Uzbekistan. He asked another question to be sure that the top brass were thinking along the same lines he was: "Tenth Mountain is in Uzbekistan, right?"

## My Man in Afghanistan

After being exposed to years of senseless killing, a war correspondent comes to understand that the grim reaper chooses his victims with the flip of a coin. Missing a ride, bending over to pick up a dropped pencil, oversleeping—so many seemingly minor and random occurrences can unalterably steer one down the path toward untimely death or accidental survival. The joke of fate is that the subjects do not recognize their chosen path until it arrives at a final destination. On November 19, the day the dangerous road to Kabul turned deadly for the Western press corps, I had decided to stay put in Jalalabad, because I thought I had already picked up the scent of bin Laden's presence in the city's environs. A few days prior to my colleagues' tragic deaths, my breathless, red-eyed assistant, Mashal, had come dashing up the stairs to the balcony of the Spin Ghar. We embraced with a Pashtun bear hug, and he began to explain his most recent adventure. He had tried to slip into the Taliban-controlled city just as it was on the verge of political collapse, but the young, paranoid *talib*s (religious students) hadn't trusted his story that he was a trader. They had asked him, incredulously, "What fool, if he wasn't a spy, would be traveling to Kabul as it was about to be conquered?" As the Northern Alliance advanced toward Kabul, the panicked talibs had locked him up in a woodshed on the outskirts of the city and fled with the key. Someone in the invading Northern Alliance heard his pleas and kicked open the door to find him choking for air and water. I told Mashal how pleased I was to see him and promised him, as always, "no more death-defying missions."

"But how did you find me?" I asked, amazed as always at Mashal's sixth sense, particularly since we had said good-bye to him in Peshawar.

"I have my ways," he said with a wry smile. In fact, he had stopped by Karim Abdul's language school on the outskirts of Jalalabad on his way back from Kabul and discovered that a hoard of journalists had taken up residence at the Spin Ghar.

With my "secret weapon" in the war on terror back by my side, we agreed that the most lucrative story to pursue would be found down the road at Tora Bora, a mysterious redoubt that Mashal already suspected had become a hiding place for the al Qaeda fighters who had previously lived in Jalalabad.

The first solid indication that we had of the importance of Tora Bora came on November 17, 2001, two days after our arrival in Jalalabad, when our newly united foursome headed out in the direction of the Spin Ghar, or White, Mountains. We began the day by driving back in the direction of the Khyber Pass, toward the border of Pakistan. Karim Abdul had a friend with a four-wheel-drive Corolla taxi, which ran like a boat on water across the sandy dirt roads. We intended to confirm a recurring rumor we had picked up from fleeing refugees even before we had arrived in Afghanistan. Many accounts claimed that al Qaeda, fleeing from Jalalabad, had sought and found passage across the Kabul River in a tiny fishing village named L'alpur. From there, they could cross into Afghanistan's Kunar Province and head east for a short drive into the safety of Pakistan.

We turned left off the main road and headed into the village. Four twenty-foot, red-and-yellow wooden boats rested on our side of the river. Already in the river, halfway across the shallow waters, was a metal barge strung by a chain to a wire that ran from one bank to the other. A large dump truck filled with sand was on board. Local fishermen confirmed to us that the craft had transported several dozen al Qaeda members and their family members.

"We had them crossing on the 14th and the early morning of the 15th," said a haggard, old boatman with sandy, bare feet. "These were mostly Arabian families and they crossed in a big hurry. Some of the men were missing, and the ones who did cross traded their guns for the ride over." His remarks checked out with the hurried conversations we had on our own twilight drive into Jalalabad; they meant that at least some of the Arabs had crossed that morning, before our afternoon drive in. Leaving L'alpur we retraced our tracks to the main road and turned south in the direction of the Spin Ghar Mountains.

About thirty minutes into our drive through a flat desert patch, we ran up against a United Nations Development Fund truck traveling in the opposite direction. Ten of Hazret Ali's Pashay tribesmen rushed at us in the vehicle, clearly one of their recent acquisitions. We waved each other down almost simultaneously. They wanted to know where we were going, and we wanted to know where they had been. Mashal jumped out and ran over to their door; I got out more cautiously from the other side, pretending not to be overly interested. The truck's commander, Mohamed Amir Shah, whose curly, red hair was billowing in the wind with each new sand blast, said he understood that his men would get twenty-five thousand dollars for each al Qaeda prisoner they killed or captured. "Maybe he is confused with the twenty-five-million-dollar reward that Washington says it is paying for help in the arrest of bin Laden," said Mashal, as befuddled as I was at the talk of new reward money. It seemed a good sign, in any case, that the Afghan proxies had picked up on the idea that there would be real rewards for nabbing al Qaeda fighters. Shah responded somewhat apologetically when asked about the stolen vehicle. "We don't steal cars," he said sternly. "But we need this one to help us capture the Arabs. We'll return it when we are through.

"Yesterday, we had a shoot-out with some of the Arabs around Tora Bora," he continued. A boastful young fighter with a string of brass bullets across his chest interrupted, claiming that his gang had killed some seven Arabs in a gunfight a day earlier. One of his comrades lightly slapped him in the face and said, "No, we didn't, you liar," at which point the bandoliered youngster pointed his Kalashnikov at his accuser's shins and threatened to pull the trigger. "He is asking him to dance," chuckled Mashal, apparently unfazed by the performance. Other fighters wrestled the two men to the sands and disarmed them before Shah gave them each a mighty boot kick to the abdomen.

When asked, the commander said he believed that Arab fighters in and around Tora Bora had left about two hundred pickup trucks in the foothills before climbing farther into the mountains. He estimated that "several hundred" Arab fighters were hiding in the caves. They were protecting those vehicles by shooting down on anyone who tried to approach. He made it sound like the Arabs had simply decided to take to the hills and defend themselves. At the same time, he made it clear that they held the high ground and that it would take far more than his truckload of cutthroats to go after them there.

"Do you have any plans to attack?" I asked.

"Are you kidding? Those are the best fighters in al Qaeda. We can take cover and fire at them, but it would take a major offensive and hundreds of men to attack them."

The blood-red sun sinking in the distance outlined the enclave where he claimed his men had fired up into the hills. As far as he was concerned, "the clash" hadn't produced any confirmed casualties at all.

As we left the commander and his band of unruly and undisciplined soldiers by the side of that remote desert road, I reflected on the information we had turned up on our day trip. Many of the most-wanted enemies could easily be slipping through the grasp of the American military, possibly with our supposed Afghan allies looking the other way, and definitely with the assistance of local civilians. Many of those fighters not making the exodus into Pakistan were congregating in Tora Bora. For the sake of justice and a good story, I hoped bin Laden remained among them. Hunkering down in the backseat, Mashal clutched our could-be-deadly weapon, aka the empty whiskey bottle, stared into the mountains, and suggested that we ask the warlord from Dijon just what he planned to do about all this.

## Insider Trading

Tora Bora. Literally, it meant "black dust." Even the name had a strong verbal thrust—the right onomatopoeia, if you will—to connote a last stand. As the mountains receded in the distance, they resembled inverted snow cones with white caps on the points, brown-and-green bodies beneath. A B-52 etched a trail across the blue sky above and eventually dropped what appeared—from our vantage point some thirty miles away—to be a small payload. We still had no indication that bin Laden or any of his top lieutenants were there, but investigating this story sure beat wading through the chemical warfare formulas we had found in al Qaeda's notebooks a day earlier. I agreed completely with Mashal's suggestion that we start by asking how the Afghan commanders planned to attack the impenetrable redoubt—if, indeed, they did. From the first moment Zaman's convoy had arrived to find Ali's men occupying the Spin Ghar Hotel, I had recognized that tensions would run high between the competing strongmen. In the ensuing time, it became even more obvious that the two were vying not only for dominant control of Jalalabad and its environs, but also for the good favors of their new American "friends."

It wasn't easy to know exactly what motivated Jalalabad's strongmen. First of all, the U.S. play for al Qaeda's flesh and blood was as new to them as it was to the rest of us. I was not convinced from conversations I had had that either Zaman or Ali had deeply considered just how many pickup trucks and goatherds the twenty-five million dollars in U.S. reward money would buy them. I'm not sure they could even imagine it. On the other hand, both men knew from the air power on display overhead that sidling up to the Americans would make sense, for both their own staying power and their future safety. I had the impression, reinforced by Mashal's sixth sense, that both men wanted to be as nice as possible to Uncle Sam without pissing off their local constituencies. If that meant betraying them both—with no one getting hurt by what they didn't know—schmoozing with the Green Berets in the short run was worth it to guarantee that they would still be king of the hill when the fighting was all over. After the war against al Qaeda had come and gone, there would be other deals to make—not least of them for control of Jalalabad's vast poppy fields, some of the most fertile in all of Afghanistan. Keen to exploit their greed to my own advantage, I had an idea to play one warlord off against the other—trying to get everyone to lay claim to al Qaeda "booty" and thus to extract information about what was going on within the secretive network and whether its members planned to fight or to flee.

On the morning of November 19, we began with Zaman, who had moved into his old haunts on the outskirts of town. The compound was several acres square, with a two-story ranch-style home in the middle surrounded by orange groves. From the outside, Zaman's place looked like a fortress with ten-foot-high walls, but on the inside it was a veritable Garden of Eden, with birds fluttering through the trees and weary travelers sleeping in their shade. When we arrived, workers were busy repainting the concrete walls surrounding the compound. Outside the gates, truckloads of bearded fighters had taken up guard duty. Inside, the wily warlord was already holding court with several dozen villagers. Lieutenants soon informed us that the hunt for al Qaeda had already begun. Zaman had bundles of hard cash, Pakistani currency that he was already handing out. His "posse" was growing rapidly. Hundreds of young men of fighting age were now filing through his orange grove, anxious to sign up. The youngest had been sent by their fathers, and the fathers had come too, in hopes of putting food on the table.

Up a rickety flight of stairs, we were welcomed into Zaman's lair. It was after sunset, and his servants had laid out a spread of nuts and dried fruit to break the fast. In those early days, until I recognized that Zaman was a ladies' man, I had the impression that he, like several other warlords, was anxious to impress Americans, any Americans. When we entered, Zaman was sprawled out on the floor with several of his top lieutenants. Apparently anxious to show that he had already begun rooting out the bad guys, he asked his sons to bring in a group of Pakistani prisoners, bound and gagged. He ungagged them and proceeded to interrogate them in front of us; I noticed he was kind enough to offer his charges the same cashew nuts we were eating. Zaman, who spoke minimal English, translated what the prisoners said into French. The frightened young men all looked contrite and quickly confessed to having been "misled" by a rather awful-sounding zealot, a "mullah," over the mountains in the Pakistani tribal areas. Everyone had a big laugh, and Zaman told the prisoners to behave themselves and that they wouldn't have to remain long in his custody.

We knew that Zaman knew more than we did about Tora Bora. It had been his own base of operations for several years during the fight against the Soviets. Even when Zaman had fought there, it had been one of the most extensive cave and tunnel complexes in the country. Since then, however, workers had refurbished and expanded the redoubt. Over the previous years, hundreds of Zaman's own tribesmen had signed up with al Qaeda to carry out the renovations.

Zaman told us that he knew that several hundred Arabs had fled into the mountains only days before his own arrival in Jalalabad. He had already sent a "reconnaissance mission" into Tora Bora to find out just what was going on in the secluded redoubt. Zaman's trusted comrade in arms Gul Amerji had led the mission. A short, slight man, whose large, coin-sized birthmark on his cheek made him look to me like a pirate, Amerji had gone with an unnamed "Arab speaking" interpreter, which in Jalalabad meant one of only a handful of people. Zaman informed us that he had ordered Amerji to ask the Arabs kindly to move out of the region. Over tea and sweets, the al Qaeda members had responded to Amerji swiftly and to the point, leaving no room for negotiation. The Arabs vowed to fight to the death—or as he said they put it, "until we are martyred."

I felt that I was likely getting ahead of Zaman's plans by asking him when he intended to attack Tora Bora, but Zaman winked at the idea and said he was making plans to do just that. "Don't worry, when I go, you can ride right alongside me in my truck," he promised.

With one promise in hand, we set off to find Hazret Ali to see how he would respond to Zaman's professed intention to attack Tora Bora. Ali had moved his office out to the airport; he and his top lieutenants occupied the guardhouse near the front gate of the terminal. When we entered, we saw Ali sitting on the floor fiddling with a new satellite phone, which he couldn't quite get to work. I knew it was customary to sit on the floor in Afghanistan, but the scene somehow struck me as something akin to a kid sitting beneath a Christmas tree trying to figure out a new toy. It didn't look very professional.

Ali welcomed us in and offered us all green tea. We advised him to point the dish of his satellite phone "in the direction of the Indian Ocean," and after a few minutes he managed to get a dial tone. He grinned and asked us if we had anyone we wanted to call. "Say, the U.S. military?" he joked, giggling uncontrollably. His bright mood quickly darkened, however, when we addressed the purpose of our visit to him. Ali became particularly irritated when we informed him that Zaman had vowed to attack Tora Bora.

"What do you mean?" he demanded, abruptly slamming the phone's receiver onto the floor. "All the guns are with me. Haven't you seen all the tanks that my men captured?" Mashal informed Ali that we hadn't actually taken an inventory of what hardware any of the warlords had, so we couldn't well judge anyone's firepower. Ali was put off by what he considered to be a bad joke. "This is my domain, and the world should know it," he snapped. Again, with him sitting on the floor and fiddling with his phone, the warlord's words did not sound as tough as he might have intended them to. Ali insisted that the Eastern Shura, the post-Taliban ruling body of four dozen tribal chiefs that governed the three surrounding provinces, had the final word on what should be done about the Arabs holed up in Tora Bora. He hinted that he would carry out the will of the Shura when the time was ripe.

But the Shura, itself, hoping to stage-manage the growing rivalry between Ali and Zaman, had only aggravated the situation by previously appointing Ali as regional security chief and Zaman as military commander. In most parts of the world, military commanders would control tanks, but in this case the police commissioner had the lion's share. Ali made it clear, in any case, that he would be the one responsible for enforcing the law.

"The Shura has the right to decide what to do with the Arabs. For now, we have the right to arrest them, nothing more. I was going to send religious scholars up there and ask those people to leave peacefully, but we will make a real plan in two or three days time." On that count, Zaman had already beaten him to the punch. Ali, claiming his own inside sources, told us that he believed Osama bin Laden was squirreled away up in Tora Bora. "I'm 80 percent sure that bin Laden is up there. He has mules coming and going from Pakistan to help supply him. If the Shura can't decide what to do, I'll do this thing myself." His vow sounded empty, as though he was making it only because he feared Zaman would make the first move. In the meantime, Ali offered to show us the four hundred Pakistani prisoners he had picked up recently. Mashal rolled his eyes, and we declined.

Self-serving interests aside, Ali had hinted at the real problem that Colonel Mulholland and the U.S. military would soon face in rounding up a reliable posse. More al Qaeda sympathizers than detractors stacked the ranks of the ruling Eastern Shura. Bin Laden and company had brought employment opportunities and commerce that had benefited many tribes in the region, so their loyalties came as no surprise. The Shura's main interests were stability and defending fellow Muslims, including bin Laden himself, from a possible U.S.-led offensive. The newly formed political body would, for the next two weeks, act as a brake on detailed discussions of an attack on Tora Bora.

Political ties dictated the way forward. The most influential player on the Shura was an aging warlord by the name of Maulvi Younus Khalis, a renowned anti-Soviet resistance commander. Anyone of note in Jalalabad, including both Ali and Zaman, had served under Khalis during the fight against the Soviets. Some of them had even dragged his sled through the snow as the old man lay prostrate, giving orders. He was irascible but lovable, and nearly everyone in the community, from moderates to fundamentalists, respected him. Khalis, who had opened the way for the young Taliban revolutionaries in 1996, had taken the key to the city back from the fundamentalist zealots the night the Taliban and their Arab friends left town. He had appointed his own commander, Awol Gul, a short, rotund Islamic scholar, to take control of many of the heaviest weapons left behind by the Taliban. Ali, with his early sweep into the Jalalabad after the Taliban's departure, had seized much of the other weaponry they had left behind. Zaman, the newly appointed military commander, had to scrounge for whatever leftovers he could find.

So, in essence, a triangular power struggle was under way, with Khalis at the top, controlling the Shura, and Ali and Zaman on the other two wings and vying for the upper hand. None of the three factions could possibly move alone to attack Tora Bora, even if it had the will—which none did, at least for now.

Realizing that Khalis likely possessed the greatest power in determining how the military hunt for al Qaeda would proceed, and increasingly suspicious of his motivations and loyalties, we decided to pay a visit to the aging warlord. A week after our arrival in Jalalabad, Mashal and I turned into the gravel road leading to the old man's redoubt, where until recently bin Laden had kept his four wives. Zaman's men had earlier insisted that Arab fighters still visited the abode under the cover of night to stock up on supplies, so we asked Jamal to drive up the road with extreme caution. Near the compound, known simply as "The Families" (read: the rulers), a young Afghan in a black turban manned a large Chinese-made machine gun. From a distance, we could see several other fighters inside a canvas tent sipping tea. Above them was the mysterious compound lined with ten-foot-high mud walls, a few electrical cables, and thick metal doors. It looked both forbidding and impenetrable.

Our do-not-enter warning came soon enough. Someone unloaded a rifle round and Jamal panicked, slamming the car into reverse and jolting us into a state of shock. After some minutes, we calmed back down and convinced Jamal to continue up the hill. As we approached the tent, another lot of guards protecting the road stopped us. The soldiers insisted that Western "infidels" would not be allowed to proceed, so I asked Mashal to go ahead on foot to ask after the red-bearded Khalis. The old man had not shown his face in public in several days. At that time, family members had to carry the ailing patriarch up the stairs of the governor's mansion for the first meeting of the Eastern Shura. Apparently, his chronic illness lingering, Khalis was in bed, flat on his back, but still holding court with his admirers. Mashal's humble entry into the mud-brick room was met with a growl. "Questions?" he snapped. "Well, ask me quick, I haven't got time for your infidel friends."

It was a cue for Mashal to work fast. "What in Allah's name do these people want with Osama?" he asked.

"Osama is a man of peace," Khalis moaned back at him, lifting a bony finger and shaking it at his guest.

Khalis had been there to welcome bin Laden at the airport in 1996 upon his return to Jalalabad in a private jet from Sudan. Now that Osama was "a wanted man," the Afghan elder felt compelled to issue a prediction. "Well, the Americans can bomb all they want, but they will never catch Osama!" Khalis, even on his deathbed, wasn't about to betray his friend.

When Mashal returned down the hill and told me about his encounter, we both recalled what Zaman had told us two days earlier. "The two men are like blood brothers," he had warned. "Khalis invited bin Laden in the first place and now he is reluctant to see him, and the financial strings he pulls, leave forever."

What we learned that day did not bode well for the success of the U.S. military's effort to catch bin Laden "dead or alive." Though credible reports indicated that bin Laden's current residence was in Tora Bora, Ali, the local warlord best equipped to lead an attack against the redoubt had chosen to defer judgment to a Shura being led by an individual who viewed Osama as "a man of peace." Our only other hope, Zaman, for concrete action to go after enemy number one seemed momentarily contented with having advised his Arab Muslim brothers in the mountains kindly to pick up and leave the region. I sighed and wondered if General Franks or Donald Rumsfeld knew something we didn't.

## The Sheikh Plans an Escape

The next day, on November 22, we returned to Zaman to try to pry more out of him. He agreed to take a private walk with me in his orange grove. Shortly into the walk he grew serious, flicked a fly off his nose, and began complaining that the attack he had vowed to make on Tora Bora wasn't going to be as easy as he had initially thought. He outlined a tale of bin Laden's carefully planned "strategic withdrawal into Tora Bora" from Jalalabad, a story he claimed to have picked up on through his own intelligence sources. What he said to me that balmy afternoon in the fruit orchard reminded me that bin Laden still had far more loyalists in Jalalabad than did the United States, which still didn't have soldiers on the ground in the area. In subsequent interviews with other subjects, I was able to confirm Zaman's basic story and add further details that allowed a fuller picture of the events leading up to the terror mastermind's calculated decision to withdraw a bulk of his forces into the protected seclusion of Tora Bora.

On November, 9, 2001, as Jalalabad suffered daily aerial assaults and Kabul teetered on the edge of collapse, al Qaeda operatives in Jalalabad swung into action to organize a meeting to rally support from tribal leaders. The meeting was set to take place within meters of the Spin Ghar Hotel at the Saudi-funded Islamic Studies Institute, which, by no coincidence, had been converted to the Taliban's intelligence headquarters just after September 11. In the entranceway of the institute, behind a glass enclosure, a map display indicated that little inside the radical learning center had changed since September 11. The map showed Saudi Arabia with a large black hand dripping blood across it. The hand belonged, the caption explained, to the "infidel Americans." The sign, of course, had—figuratively speaking—bin Laden's own fingerprints all over it. Removing the black hand of the infidels from his own homeland was at the heart of his global terror mission. As Taliban and al Qaeda front lines north of

Kabul began to crumble, senior network operatives began to congregate six hours east in the Islamic Studies Institute.

Al Qaeda had hatched a plan to garner the protection of regional tribes by playing on and reinforcing long-standing loyalties and by greasing the wheels with money. The Taliban government, in conjunction with its Arab financiers, sent a fleet of minibuses into the countryside on November 9 to collect tribal elders from the region, particularly those controlling clans along the Afghan border. It was not unusual for regional elders to gather for large meetings, or *jirga*s, but this time al Qaeda promised a "banquet" and an important message.

One chief, Malik Habib Gul, from a remote Afghan village along the Pakistan border, sat in the second row in the basement of the institute on November 10, 2001. It was an evening he would not soon forget, a lavish one by Pashtun standards, particularly given the famine and drought that had ravaged the region in recent years. Along with hundreds of other male guests, Gul, a burly fifty-five-year-old Afghan with a long nose slightly askew, stuffed himself on a meal of lamb kebab and rice. Tribesmen were sitting about on the floor talking about the endless U.S. bombing, and they did not pay much attention to a short, pudgy Arab named Ahmadi when he asked the Afghans to prepare themselves for the day's "special guest speaker." Ahmadi, with long black locks that fell in waves down the back of his kamis, told the assembled leaders that they would soon be called upon. "You are the great holy warriors, your names will be etched in gold. We left our families for your cause. The U.S. has destroyed its own buildings and used this as an excuse to try to occupy our Muslim land. You need our help and we need your help."

Ahmadi continued, "And now the Sheikh himself has the pleasure to address you."

When bin Laden, flanked by fifteen bodyguards cradling short Chinese machine guns, walked into the dining hall, the chewing stopped. Osama, known simply as "the Sheikh" by most of the tribals, carried an unmistakable gravitas. Soft but excited whispers swept the dining hall. Several of the tribesmen threw flowers that cascaded about his feet as he walked up to the podium.

Without prompting, according to Gul, all of the about one thousand Afghan and Pakistani tribal leaders rose and shouted, "Zindi-bad, Osama" (Long live Osama!). The al Qaeda chief placed his right hand over his heart, the ethnic Pashtun acknowledgment of being honored. He was dressed in loose gray clothing and was wearing his signature camouflage jacket. His commandos, garbed in green fatigues, had their shiny, new Kalashnikovs specially rigged with grenade launchers. As bin Laden held forth—appearing confident and determined, according to members of the audience—several Arabs shouted from the middle and back of the rooms, "God is great! Down with America! Down with Israel!"

Bin Laden interrupted the cheering to begin speaking, according to those present. "The Americans had a plan to invade, but if we are united and believe in Allah, we'll teach them a lesson, the same one we taught the Russians." Continuing through a short address, the terror chief must have sensed that he was preaching to the choir. He told the assembled tribals that it was "our duty to fight in Palestine, Chechnya, Kashmir, and everywhere that Muslims are being oppressed and tortured by the infidel." Blending his theological and martial message, bin Laden concluded with one final appeal: "God is with us, and we will win the war. Your Arab brothers will lead the way. We have the weapons and the technology. What we need most is your moral support. And may God grant me the opportunity to see you and meet you again on the frontlines."

Support was all bin Laden had ever needed from the impoverished Pashtuns, who, along with the deep pockets of the CIA and the Saudi government, among others, he had helped to finance in the battle against the Soviet Union. Locals in the Jalalabad area still considered the Arab fighters, whom bin Laden commanded, to be elite warriors, allies in the struggle against Soviet aggression. They felt indebted, but also honored, to have the attention of some of the wealthiest fundamentalists in the world. When the West, particularly the Americans, pulled up stakes in the early '90s, it had been the Arabs, with Saudi Arabian and other Gulf state money, who remained, funding institutions like the one that bin Laden was now using as a platform on which to expound his message of hate. Further, the religiously conservative, Pashtun-dominated region around Jalalabad had offered a strong base of popular support for the Taliban during the years of civil war. Since bin Laden had closely allied himself with the Taliban and remained a hero of the anti-Soviet jihad, the outpouring of love and support from the elders came as no surprise. The tribal leaders now saw the Arabs as the most likely martyrs in the new and revived struggle against persons they viewed as "infidel aggression."

The money handed out that afternoon by senior al Qaeda operatives, including Egyptian "jihad" leader Ayman al-Zawahiri, provided even further incentive to support bin Laden's cause. Like the other tribal elders in attendance, Malik Habib Gul received a white envelope full of Pakistani rupees, its thickness proportional to the thirty extended families under his jurisdiction in his village in an area known as Upper Pachir. His "spending money," Gul told us, did not run out until late February 2002. He received the equivalent of three hundred dollars; leaders of larger clans received up to ten thousand. Bin Laden had delivered his message, and his associates now delivered the goods.

Bin Laden remained at the meeting to eat but, according to three sources in attendance, did not remain for more than forty-five minutes. After he finished his meal in the company of his guards and several Taliban chiefs, the Sheikh stepped away from the podium. His guards closed ranks and shuffled out the door behind him. The tribal leaders knew he had gone in the twilight hours when they heard the sound of gravel crunching beneath the wheels of four white custom-made, four-wheel-drive Toyota Corollas.

Bin Laden's address took place two days before the Taliban's final race to abandon Kabul and al Qaeda's move to seek shelter in Tora Bora. I first learned of the tribal gathering from Zaman in his orange grove a little over a week later.

As they rallied support, al Qaeda leaders were aware, of course, that they might have to make a calculated withdrawal from Afghanistan altogether. Even before the U.S.-led war to overthrow the Taliban had begun, the regime's leaders, including supreme leader Mullah Omar, vowed to retreat into the countryside and wage a classic guerrilla war. Al Qaeda gathered the tribal leaders, who were drawn in two polarizing directions—an urge to stay and fight on one hand, and on the other to escape and continue the struggle outside

Afghanistan—and prepared them for both possibilities. But they still did not reveal any specific escape plans. According to two al Qaeda members in attendance at the banquet, bin Laden faced considerable resistance from within his own ranks to the idea of leaving Afghanistan.

## Night Flight

Details of al Qaeda's frenzied flight from Jalalabad and into Tora Bora had been buzzing through the streets since our arrival in the city. Eyewitnesses, however, were difficult to come by. To try to find out more about bin Laden's withdrawal into the mountains, Mashal, Karim Abdul, and I followed a lead that took us down to the livestock market on the southern edge of town, not far from the Khalis compound.

One of the more unusual members of the fourth estate, Jake Sutton, decided to join us in our investigation. The happy-go-lucky Welshman was one of those oddball characters who fall like manna from heaven into any war zone. They make it all worth the adventure. He first introduced himself to us as "a documentary maker"—which was, at the time, more of an ambition than a fact. A freelance cameraman, working for AP TV and anyone else who would buy footage from an old Beta cam, Jake possessed a big eye and an even bigger heart. The wild-eyed Welshman loved the "hunt for Osama," but even more he loved the people he met along the way. Mashal, Karim Abdul, and Jamal, our trusty driver, took to him immediately. His quick smile and easygoing demeanor were a far cry from the gravity of the holier-than-thou network correspondents. He exuded the unusual air of a French painter vacationing in the tropics. Even the locals stopped their shopping and pointed to the strange foreigner when he passed by. He also just happened to be an artist. He sketched landscapes, caricatures, and portraits with amazing acumen. This could be very flattering, but also a little distracting and sometimes even dangerous if a warlord took his depiction the wrong way. Jake was a hard nut to crack. He certainly didn't fit my idea of an insensitive, battle-hardened hack. His wavy red hair and heavy accent made him seem more like a lover boy than a war buff.

Jake had his camera along the day we approached the sprawling livestock marketplace on the southern edge of town. Hundreds of Pashtun tribesmen stood lazily beside beasts of burden that they had tethered to poles. The animal vendors looked each other up and down and preened, trimming their lengthy beards with tiny scissors while looking puckishly into handheld vanity mirrors. Some wore pakols, favored by Afghan "freedom fighters"; others had their heads swathed in thirty feet of silk. The beasts in their midst grunted and brayed, apparently unimpressed with the vanity of their masters. Someone slapped a horse on the rump, and it bucked, kicking its front feet out as onlookers dove for cover. "Sold!" shouted an auctioneer.

We spent the next several hours asking around for an eyewitness to bin Laden's exodus into Tora Bora. Locals pointed us to a guesthouse and small mill beside the market. Several of the farmers told us that the owner, a man named Babrak Khan, had been standing outside the night of November 13 as a large Arab convoy congregated on the southern edge of town.

We found Babrak leaning against a tall metal door that marked the entrance to his "pension," a nice name for a one-room shack with an outhouse across the courtyard. Khan was twenty-eight, but he looked maybe forty. A wiry man of medium height with a face covered in a black, shaggy beard, he offered to give us an account of what he had seen that night. First, in the grand tradition of Pashtun hospitality, he invited us inside for a cup of tea. Jake pulled out his camera and started to film. As Babrak settled himself onto a floor mat next to his friend, Lala Agha, he put on a somber face. A servant poured five cups of green tea as Babrak began the story of November 13.

The streets of Jalalabad had been dismal and flush with fighters for the three nights after al Qaeda's grand banquet. Bombs hammered military barracks on the edge of town as Chechens, Yemenis, and Algerians seized control of major intersections across the city. American "smart bombs" honed in on military barracks and key Taliban installations, but did not pick up on former educational institutions, like the Islamic Institute, which had become a nexus for al Qaeda extremists. Still, the growing uncertainty over security in Jalalabad sparked fears among some residents that al Qaeda had actually overthrown the Taliban militia in a "coup d'état." Indeed, many of bin Laden's top commanders believed after the banquet that their mission would be to dig in and fight for the city, so they had taken up key security posts usually assigned to Afghans. The Taliban had not resisted the moves, though some city elders and elements within the movement did not relish the idea of street-to-street fighting in their hometown. Most residents shuttered their windows, locked their doors, and hunkered down, fully prepared to endure a coming storm.

On the evening of November 13, 2001, Babrak Khan had been preparing to listen to the BBC's Pashto-language news broadcast, just as he had done every evening since the war started. But outside his guesthouse, in one of Jalalabad's only lightly wooded areas, hundreds of cars and trucks had begun to converge. Responding to the rising commotion, Babrak opened his gate and peered out. He couldn't believe his eyes. In the road right in front of him, some thirty feet from his own position, stood an Arab sheikh whose face Babrak knew well. The Saudi had led in the daily prayers several years earlier when Babrak had served as a guard inside the al Qaeda's Tora Bora base. Back then, he had never imagined that "the Sheikh" would become the world's most wanted man.

"I saw Osama in the sixth or seventh car, and behind him were from a hundred to two hundred vehicles. At the end of the convoy there were five armored vehicles. [We saw him] standing here in front of our guesthouse at 9 P.M. on that Tuesday. Osama stepped out of the truck and was giving directions. He was surrounded by sixty armed guards, and he was standing in the middle under that tree," Babrak added pointing to a tree with low branches that stood beside a wooden vending stall. As he spoke, his friend Lala Agha nodded his head in agreement. Also a witness that evening, the slight man with dirty blonde hair, who had suffered a major bout with polio that had disfigured his legs, would later repeat parts of the story. As Babrak described it, bin Laden rapidly exited his custom-designed white Toyota Corolla hatchback, something akin to a small SUV, barking orders to his men. He wore loose gray clothing covered by a camouflaged jacket and cradled a Kalakov machine gun, a shortened version of a Kalashnikov.

Bin Laden was accompanied by some of his Afghan friends. Maulvi Abdul Kabir, the Taliban governor of Jalalabad, was holding his hand, as is customary for Muslim men who are spiritually close. The two men were speaking briskly with Mujahid Ullah, the wispy-bearded son of the same Younus Khalis who was about to become the post-Taliban Shura leader in Jalalabad. Mujahid, who would finally make the U.S. military's "wanted list" in Afghanistan nine months after the invasion, had taught Islamic studies at the Islamic Studies Institute where bin Laden had held his meeting a few days prior. For years, Mujahid had, like his curmudgeonly father, sided with al Qaeda, the members of which he referred to "as our Arab guests." (He later warned us in an interview that the American "crusader war against Muslims" would fail and that local Afghans would not cooperate with the U.S. military to fight al Qaeda.) But also like his father, Mujahid wanted to see Jalalabad spared from street fighting and so had tried to convince bin Laden to take the fight into the mountains. The Yemeni and Chechen fighters, however, had been, even at this eleventh hour, arguing in favor of a "house to house" fight in the heart of Jalalabad. These hardcore warriors insisted that they could trap the Americans on the ground and force them to withdraw after heavy losses, as they had done in Mogadishu, Somalia, in the famous "Black Hawk Down" battle. As two al Qaeda sources later confirmed, bin Laden had sided with his old Afghan friends and turned his powers of persuasion onto his fighters to convince them that the conflict's venue should be moved into the mountains, where al Qaeda's guerrilla tactics would be more effective.

Less than one hour after this rare sighting of bin Laden, the convoy, mostly four-wheel-drive trucks, followed by five armored vehicles, hastily left town. The fleeing al Qaeda and Taliban members snaked their way down a bumpy dirt road that runs through ancient battlefields and tattered villages to the heart of the Tora Bora mountain base. That night, the skies above the convoy of Arabs, Afghans, and Chechens were "filled with fire," according to an Egyptian woman who had ridden in the same car with Osama bin Laden. All the vehicles in the massive convoy, however, escaped unscathed.

By fleeing into Tora Bora, bin Laden had also expanded his options. Jalalabad is nestled in a valley that, if surrounded by the right number of U.S. infantry and weapons, would have surely become a graveyard for al Qaeda fighters. Tora Bora, on the other hand, straddled the border with Pakistan, thus giving the terror chief a more obvious choice of fighting or fleeing.

The al Qaeda convoy, which contained family members as well as fighters, had split up after leaving Jalalabad and moved along on different desert routes leading to the same final destination. This division had taken place, no doubt, to avoid attracting too much attention from American bombers prowling the skies. This we later learned from subsequent interviews with villagers and two al Qaeda members who had witnessed and participated in bin Laden's entry into the complex on the night of November 13, 2001. One group of vehicles entered the complex via the village of Mileva; bin Laden's part of the convoy deployed into the mountains from the village of Garikhil, a few kilometers to the east. Bin Laden did not simply pass through Garikhil, however; he stopped to have a "secret meeting" with several chiefs of the local Ghilzi tribe, whose villages straddle the rugged border between Afghanistan and neighboring Pakistan.

Malik Osman Khan, the village chief in Garikhil, described bin Laden's entourage as "scornful and in a hurry." Al Qaeda military commanders handed over some four hundred Kalashnikovs as "gifts" to the Ghilzi tribesmen, according to both terror network members and local villagers. In exchange for these presents and others bestowed earlier at the November 10 banquet in Jalalabad, the tribesmen promised to help smuggle Afghan and Arab leaders to freedom in Pakistan if and when escape became necessary. The village chiefs watched as al Qaeda leaders sat on a porch and divided up the fighters, handing out their cave assignments before their foray into the wilderness. He added, "Our people were terrified, because we thought the U.S. planes would hit the Arabs as they stopped in our village." But there was an inexplicable lull in the bombing. American military might was, at the time, focused on finishing off the Taliban's remaining defenses in and around Kabul.

Three days later, after al Qaeda and Taliban forces headed into their trenches, caves, and dugouts, U.S. bombing finally intensified.

Wahid Ullah, the sixteen-year-old son of Khan, was one of more than a hundred civilians killed in and around Tora Bora. He had been playing stickball at the foot of Tora Bora on November 16 when a cruise missile shattered the earth at his feet. "At first, we thought that the U.S. military was trying to frighten the Arabs out, since they were only bombing from one side," Khan told us later. The tribal chief provided us with his own wry analysis of the U.S. bombing strategy: "When we round up a pack of stray sheep, we send in shepherds from four sides, not just one." It had the ring of sound logic.

## Bombs in the Air, No Booty on the Ground

In October, a full month before bin Laden's flight into Tora Bora, U.S. intelligence already had a bead on the mountain redoubt. The president had informed his cabinet on October 8 that his best intelligence showed that al Qaeda, possibly including bin Laden, had sought refuge there. While the Western press took little notice of this suspected hiding place, U.S. B-52s were already dropping two-thousand-pound bombs on the warren of caves in the White Mountains. On October 10 and again on October 27, Rumsfeld said in war cabinet meetings that bombs were targeting Tora Bora.

Through late October and early November 2001, leading "hawks" in the Bush administration became increasingly nervous about George Tenet's idea of relying on Afghan proxies to surround al Qaeda and seal the borders. A real victory in Afghanistan—the crux of the matter, as Vice President Dick Cheney kept stressing to the cabinet—was to kill or capture bin Laden. For that, he and others believed, the United States should be prepared to go the extra mile and put "boots on the ground." Cheney, in theory Bush's top adviser, had advocated the insertion of a tough U.S. ground element into the Afghanistan conflict. In late September he had warned, "Air ops without boots on the ground could look weak." On November 1, he had stressed the need to get U.S. soldiers onto the ground as soon as possible: "If we don't get them, they'll get us." In the same conversation he added that Washington should send out "hunter-killer" teams to root out terrorists in Afghanistan. He said, according to Bob

Woodward's account in *Bush at War,* "We need greater urgency. The longer UBL [Usama bin Laden, as sometimes transliterated] is free, the greater the risk of a hit here at home." Judging by the statements that Cheney would later make on record in television interviews with major networks in late November, however, he did not worry much that bin Laden would be "spooked" by what might be coming his way.

Task Force Dagger had begun to settle in for the long haul as soon as Taliban defenses north of Kabul collapsed in early November. Colonel Mulholland arranged his base of operations at Bagram Air Base north of Kabul, but within days he was feeling the heat of a growing debate at the highest levels in the U.S. government about how to move ahead with the next phase of the war. "I'll be honest with you, there was underlying pressure, currents, and a desire to get conventional forces into the fray," the colonel told me a year later.

"The agency [CIA] were basically the ones who came to me and said, 'Hey, look, we believe Osama bin Laden is in Tora Bora.' We were working together and it really became clear that we were going to mount an operation into Tora Bora."

With a rather confusing array of warlords running the show around Jalalabad, the U.S. military had to make a decision—a firm choice—about whom to work with on the ground. "Hazret Ali is the guy who really raises his hand and says 'I'll play ball with the Americans.' And Zaman is also part of the equation, but Hazret was the only one up there who was familiar with the defenses [inside Tora Bora]. At least, he claimed to be. He had a lot of hardware himself, including tanks." Mulholland indicated to me that the CIA had been unable to provide much new insight on the spectrum of warlords ruling the region. "We were still trying to figure out who these guys were, but it was Ali who had the advantage through his connections—having fought with the Northern Alliance against the Taliban for the last several years," he said. "Some of our joint efforts in dealing with the Afghans involved money. It worked, and I wished that I had had more of it."

Mulholland was aware of the discussion taking place at the highest levels involving the possible use of the Tenth Mountain Division, his own backup, a force that he had turned from a mere airport security asset to his own "rapid-reaction force" by mid-November. However, it was his preference—although not his choice—to move ahead with the UW, or unconventional warfare, approach to tackling Tora Bora. "We did not want to be the next Soviets. And right below the skin of these guys there was the possibility of a very negative reaction to the 'foreign invader.' [As far as my own forces go,] we do what they [the Afghans] do. We eat what they eat, sleep when they sleep, and we work with them, and we don't put them aside. One of the concerns I had was that this area was an especially fundamentalist [Islamic] region and so we had to think about, well, what is the greater good, to put a large number of Americans on the ground and yet risk alienating them [the Afghans]. And if you do that, does that then further defeat your ability to go after this guy [bin Laden] or do we try to do this with surrogates? That was the theoretical discussion at the time."

Mulholland also saw the logistics of conventional warfare in a country like Afghanistan as a major impediment. "Everything has to be flown in and at the same time you are fighting, you are resupplying," he said. "It is a logistical nightmare." Still, there were obvious drawbacks to the choice of proxies. From Mulholland's point of view, the emerging situation was a kind of "catch 22." He knew it would be tough to expect the Afghans to enter the fray under the wings of U.S. air power in such a crucial battle without getting to know them and providing them with some basic training in coordinating this kind of attack. Training foreign fighters was nothing new for the Green Berets; their work almost always included quality "getting to know you" time. In this case, having such a luxury of time would likely have permitted the colonel and his men to discern whether or not the Afghans had any intention of taking dollars but hoodwinking them when it came to a battle. Alas, the training had to be scrapped for lack of time. As Mulholland put it, it was a huge gamble to use the Afghans, but he felt that it was worth a shot. Still, as he explained just over a year later, commanders much farther up the food chain made the final call, albeit with his recommendations.

There were other reasons for sticking with UW. Up until this crucial phase of the war, the unconventional approach had served the Pentagon well. It still permitted the U.S. military to put all its best technology on display. Unmanned drones were firing Hellfire missiles, and stealth bombers were hurling their payloads from ten thousand feet. The young, innocent-eyed American teenagers who had paid with their lives in earlier wars were nowhere on the ground—at least so far. Instead, laser wielding, thirty-something U.S. Special Forces soldiers worked as observers, liaisons, and spotters for air power—but not always as direct combatants. The Soviets, who had lost thousands of fighters and five hundred flying machines annually trying to fight a conventional war, would have been astounded by the U.S. tactics, which might never have succeeded without the deadly and intense aerial bombing that went on day and night. So far, no front line that the Americans faced off against had managed to withstand the incessant onslaught by B-52s, F-17s, and unmanned drones firing Hellfire missiles. Not a single American had lost his life in combat up to this stage in the war. Now, perhaps, bringing Osama bin Laden himself to justice would serve as a splendid denouement for a long string of victories in the Afghan war.

# 3

# THE BIG ADIOS

Every one clings to something that he thinks is high and noble, or that raises him above the rest of the world in the hour of need. Perhaps he remembers that he is sprung from an ancient stock, and a race that has always known how to die.

—Winston Churchill,
*The Story of the Malakand Field Force*

## The Itch for Revenge

Toward the end of November 2001 the scene inside the Hotel Spin Ghar was heating up with the untamed egos of leading war correspondents. Quickly nicknamed the Hotel Tora Bora, the wretched dive soon gave rise to a parody of the Eagles' song "Hotel California":

> On a dark Afghan highway, cool wind in my hair
> Warm smell of guerrillas, rising up through the air
> Up ahead in the distance, I saw an F-16 in flight
> My head grew heavy and my sight grew dim
> I had to stop for the night. . . .
> Welcome to the Hotel Tora Bora
> Such a lovely place
> Such a lovely race
> Plenty of room at the Hotel Tora Bora
> Any time of year, you're in danger here.

In an urge to cling to some sense of normalcy, Pam Constable of the *Washington Post* and Jake Sutton took up the task of preparing the press corps a proper Thanksgiving feast. The meal would serve as both a memorial to our fallen colleagues and a reminder of how grateful we should be that we were not flying home in a flimsy wooden coffin. Jake prepared a menu, featuring, of course, turkey. With Jamal back in the driver's seat, we all headed down to the city's sprawling market. Watched over by anxious vendors, we picked out eight of the best-looking gobblers. Behind a wooden shed, the vendors slit the throats of the big, squawking birds and handed them to nine-year-old boys with nimble fingers to do the plucking. If these had been "good times" in Afghanistan, the boys probably would have been slaving away in a carpet factory. Instead, they laughed and buried themselves in piles of down and feathers. We also made a whirlwind trip to purchase oils, vegetables, and, of course, alcohol. Feeling a bit like a drug addict, I waited in an alley with Jamal for a pharmacist's brother to emerge from a back door with a bottle of rubbing alcohol imported from Bombay. Even if every journalist had a life insurance policy, which most of us did not, I wouldn't have risked drinking it. (Later I found out, however, that the Bombay concoction was, in fact, a favorite of locals who dared break the Islamic laws against drink. It mixed well with OJ.)

Pam and Jake advised the hotel's kitchen staff as they assembled in a medieval cookery out back. They meticulously prepared the birds, meant to feed some fifty long-hungry reporters, and placed them in huge pots to simmer above open fires. It was a mess fit for the Ottoman army. The birds looked delectable, and the extras, like the rice with raisins and the strange Afghan berry sauce, made us all salivate in anticipation.

Mashal and I sat down across the table from NBC correspondent Mike Tiabbi. Someone had a bottle of red and a bottle of white saved up. A round of pouring left everyone with a thimbleful of wine. Tim Wiener of the *New York Times* proposed a toast to the four journalists who had died in the line of duty. Someone seconded the toast and suggested a round of applause for the cooks.

Toward the end of the meal, Geraldo Rivera arrived. When Geraldo enters a room, his presence sweeps under tables and along the rafters, landing right in front of you—as it did when he plopped down in the seat beside us. He reeked of self-confidence, the kind that is hard to come by even in a war zone, and it struck me that he so well fit the mold of an action reporter that I wondered how anyone could have cast him as a talk-show host for so long. He reminded me of the dolls that I played with as a kid—the "Action Jackson" GI Joe, a character prepared for anything and everything. You just bought the uniforms and bent him into shape. Geraldo fit the mold.

By the time Geraldo sat down, the big juicy birds we had purchased for our Thanksgiving dinner had been virtually picked clean. That didn't disturb him. He just snapped his fingers, a sign for some of his people to look farther down the table for something with a little more meat on the wing. Responding like grunts for one of the local Afghan warlords, his "help" quickly obliged. I didn't lose the chance to make his acquaintance. Almost immediately, Geraldo invited me to breakfast with him the next morning at 5 A.M. I was flattered. Deep down, however, I suppose I also felt a kind of creeping anxiety. I had been warned from my earliest days as a newspaper reporter to never trust the "TV stars." It may have been that I was also a little in awe, but I suspect that it was more than that. I felt threatened. For sixteen years I had been traipsing around from war zone to war zone, barely scraping by. Now I was confronted with this first-time war reporter with a salary of several million and a budget that multiplied that by a factor of ten. I was, I allow, a little jealous.

From the moment their convoy pulled up to the Spin Ghar, it had been obvious that a new kind of war correspondent had arrived. The two "*GQ* guy" producers—one a "kid brother" named Craig—who shadowed Geraldo around the world had exited their vehicles strapped into flak jackets and what looked like motorcycle helmets wired with microphones for barking instructions to their star when he came under fire. I immediately wished I had that kind of backup on the front line. I fantasized for a moment that I would have a lackey to the left of me and a few spotters to the right giving me instructions. "OK, Philip. Now, they have a bead on you. Duck and roll, and now raise that pistol, you've got old Binny in your sights!" Geraldo's right and left-hand men also held miniature video cameras to film his every move. Apparently, the team had been equipped and assigned to catch everything from Geraldo's poetic asides to his bouts with diarrhea, which made me happy that I was just a lowly print writer.

Clearly, Geraldo was a man worth all the attention Fox could give him, and the ratings would prove it. As we had breakfast the next morning, I found Geraldo to be a jolly, cordial chap with a nose—broken on several occasions by his interviewees—for news. Over tea and cakes, Geraldo was, despite his reputation for having a ten-thousand-pound ego, exceptionally kind and left me with little doubt that he would go out of his way to save my ass if I ever found myself under attack. I felt humbled by both his personality and his firepower, and I left wondering what I could do—on my own, with my humble attire—to bring Osama to justice.

Geraldo brought with him a legend—albeit an American one—to compete with the likes of Osama bin Laden. Also, he knew the entertainment business better than most of us. Someone had to try to counter Osama bin Laden's public relations success, and so Geraldo was preparing to take him on "mano a mano" in the trenches. Just as he had been the king of tabloid journalism in his younger days, Geraldo had morphed now into a new kind of millennium man, a product of America's new patriotic fervor. He was—in this respect—a paradigm of the mood that had swept the country when President George W. Bush had called for the skin of Osama "dead or alive." Geraldo packed a pistol and didn't make any bones about it. That actually put him, I noted, in a long tradition of patriotic soldier-reporters. Ernest Hemingway had angered his fellow journalists when in August 1944 he joined a band of French resistance fighters. Going back a bit farther, Winston Churchill had covered the Boer War with a notebook and pistol. But the war in Afghanistan was a different place and time. Several journalism-protection organizations howled that Geraldo's packing a gun violated the Geneva Conventions and put the lives of other journalists who chose to remain "aloof observers" at risk of being considered combatants. Already, eight journalists had been killed in Afghanistan. None of them had been carrying weapons. Geraldo, however, tried to downplay criticism of his decision to carry a gun. He said, "That makes me feel ill, that suddenly it's become an issue that I'm putting journalists at risk. That is complete bull."

Geraldo was definitely a breed unto himself. He was redefining a profession that few felt needed redefinition. The "Fourth Estate," as we sometimes proudly refer to ourselves, is, with all its obvious faults (which often include a penchant for lechery and an uncontrollable urge to caste blame on others), an excessively earnest profession. The earnestness of the average Western journalist, particularly the American brand, leads to delusions of "objectivity" as a skill, rather than an ideal. The journalist's creed dictates that this "objective view" of events allows an unbiased reporting of the truth (and nothing but the truth) to the public. These puritans of the Fourth Estate, from which I try my best to exclude myself, generally brand anyone who crosses the line into the subjective realm, who engages in participatory or emotional reporting, an outcast. It was an understatement to say that Geraldo blurred the line between soldier-reporter and cheerleader. He knew his public appeal lay in his defiance of the norms of journalism and his embracing of the struggle, the U.S.-led war on terror. His actions, from his arrival in Tora Bora, appeared aimed to disprove the myth that our profession required objectivity. His masters, on the other hand, appeared still to be hiding behind the myth. Either that or the Fox news motto of "fair and balanced" was meant as a provocative "touché" for those of us who didn't like the idea of mixing guns, patriotism, and journalism.

Geraldo's threat to his colleagues—me included—was not his emotional take on the news, but his open revenge-seeking and willingness to use a gun to accomplish his end. My own empty bottle, though I had dreams of wielding it in a final effort to bring bin Laden to justice, was clearly only a pitiful means of self-defense compared to what al Qaeda had in store.

Geraldo had little doubt about his own abilities. He told the *Philadelphia Inquirer* that if he came across bin Laden first, he would "kick his head in, then bring it home and bronze it." This sounded a bit too close to what the CIA's own counterterror chief, Cofer Black, had told his operatives in Afghanistan. They had one mission: "Go find the al Qaeda and kill them. We're going to eliminate them. Get bin Laden, find him. I want his head in a box." At the same time, the CIA probably was more politically correct than to refer to the enemy, as did Geraldo, as "rats," "terror goons," and "psycho Arabs." Geraldo clearly had his own special mission—which made one wonder, though, if some of this posing wasn't just pandering to America's lust for revenge. In Mazar-I-Sharif, for example, Geraldo used the toe of his combat boots to turn over a corpse of an al Qaeda fighter. He offered up the following kernel of wisdom to the viewers back home: "This amigo has taken the night train to the big adios." If any journalist had ever done such a thing in the Balkans, irate colleagues would have run him or her out of town. Warlords, not reporters, kicked corpses. But for Geraldo it had worked—at least so far.

Geraldo played the protagonist in this new, fascinating tragicomedy called the War on Terror. He rode out front in the line of fire, ducking sniper fire ("so close that it parted my hair"), probing caves and peering down rat holes. He was, by his own admission, out to avenge the lives of all those who had died on September 11. "One way or another, we're gonna get him," he would tell the cameras after having tweaked his mustache and brushed down his bushy eyebrows. But Geraldo's worst sin as a journalist, in my own view, was probably not the stroking of his own ego on air. Instead, it was his cheerleading for the U.S. military, his willingness to buy the Pentagon's view of its own exploits that kept him from pursuing the unvarnished truth. Geraldo wasn't quite harmless, and he also wasn't quite alone. His willingness to buy the Pentagon's line on the war in Afghanistan—line, hook, and sinker—put him in league with several far more respectable news organizations that managed to do the same thing early on in the Afghan war.

Geraldo embodied the chauvinistic zeal that sweeps any nation in time of war. As one media critic put it, his network, Fox News, had become a "sort of headquarters for viewers who want their news served up with an extra patriotic fervor . . . in tough guy declarations often expressing a thirst for revenge." The network executives were encouraging their correspondents to engage in Marlon Brando–style method acting by tapping into their hate and letting it guide them as they unloaded their reports on air. Jim Rutenberg, a media critic for the *New York Times,* wrote that it was reminiscent of an earlier age when the old Hearst papers and the ideologically driven British tabloids beat the war drums.

In eastern Afghanistan, the revenge seekers had arrived, but the pictures did not yet add up to a real war. Most of the Western press—in the early days, when we first caught wind of bin Laden's hideout—fell victim to overestimating what was inside the mysterious Tora Bora base. I was guilty of this myself, having used the phrase "Arabesque beauties" to describe the interior of some of these caves. More intriguing than the caves themselves was what bin Laden might be up to inside Tora Bora.

The *Los Angeles Times* did a nice job of putting the "us versus him" showdown in perspective: "The hunt for Osama bin Laden has come down to this: two men in two caves half a world apart, conducting the first subterranean war of the twenty-first century. One commands the most advanced weapons and technology on earth. The other, little more than the ancient tools of the hunted—stealth and cover." The report added, "Vice President Dick Cheney was presiding over the hunt for bin Laden and his lieutenants from a secret command center drilled hundreds of feet down into the super-hard granite of a mountain in the East Coast." The "Veep"—who, having weathered four heart attacks, knew a little about personal survival—had first headed to his own underground redoubt on 9/11 and had continued to revisit the command center ever since. Indeed, it seemed at times that the crick-necked, grandfatherly Cheney had rarely emerged to catch a breath of fresh air. In the honeycombed chambers, shielded by steel blast doors, the vice president was receiving dispatches from U.S. military commands and intelligence agencies worldwide. The United States was constantly spying on cave complexes with unmanned drones that could hover overhead for thirty hours at a time, gazing down like hawks and sending back real-time video of the cockroaches—as the U.S. military sometimes referred to al Qaeda—scurrying for cover below.

Cheney's own pleas for faster action in Bush's secret war cabinet had been to no avail. In late November, two weeks after al Qaeda and the Taliban had cleared out of Jalalabad, U.S. Special Forces still had not arrived at the local airport, which had long been under the control of Hazret Ali.

## Fire in the Hole

After Thanksgiving, confronted by the competition of the entire Western press corps mobbing the lobby of the Spin Ghar, Mashal and I agreed that we would have to do much more to penetrate the "impenetrable" redoubt of Tora Bora, on the outside chance of lining up an interview with Osama and scooping the world's press. We sent Lala Agha, the lively polio victim we had met at Babrak Khan's after listening to his account of bin Laden's flight into Tora Bora, on a reconnaissance mission. I felt that Lala's shining, somewhat cunning, blue eyes held some clues to what we wanted to find. Excited to join our hunt, he headed down the road to ask about the possibility of talking with some of the Arabs inside Tora Bora. He agreed to go for cab fare alone, so we trusted that he wasn't trying to hustle us. When he arrived back after his first foray he brought with him a fellow clan member, Asmat Ullah, a hunchbacked man of forty years with grimy and blackened clothes; Lala explained that he had been working for al Qaeda, carving out new passageways and expanding corridors inside the caves. The "cave cutter" claimed that bin Laden's associates paid him two hundred dollars a week and supplied a jackhammer. An impoverished peasant, he clearly felt in awe of the terror network. "If you saw his [Bin Laden's] caves and his network, you would understand how he could take down the World Trade Center—or even a country. And I've seen boxes and boxes full of hundred dollar bills."

Lala had also managed to set up a meeting with some shady characters at the base of Tora Bora. Mashal agreed to return with Lala the next day to try to make further arrangements. Already, we were hearing that the Arabs inside Tora Bora would not come out to meet us, but that we would have to go to them for an interview. (None of this sounded convenient. I had visions of al Qaeda chaining me down in a cave, and I was sure that no one in Washington or London would be anxious to offer concessions for my release. I recalled languishing in a Balkan jail for a week only to have a senior U.S. diplomat refuse to do anything for me: "We can't let this guy Smucker become the center of a diplomatic row.")

The next day, Mashal left in the company of Lala and a local spiritual leader, a tall and slender man who wrapped himself from shoulder to toe in a brown woolen blanket. The three of them traveled into the forest and slipped through the first al Qaeda checkpoint with the help of the spiritual leader, a respected local elder. Then, at the base of the mountains, the three encountered a "graveyard" of several dozen four-wheel-drive vehicles and army trucks with antiaircraft guns. Like a band of robbers in the Bronx, thieves had stripped the vehicles. On the hills above, al Qaeda fighters and the Afghans they had been working with had set up mountaintop firing posts inside caves and behind cliffs. Fighters had fortified the positions with old Soviet scrap metal, ripped from the sides of destroyed tanks and crashed helicopters. Heavy machine guns, rocket launchers, and antiaircraft guns aimed down at the dirt roads and trails winding through the base. Large boulders had been set in place on mountainsides to roll down the mountain at intruders.

Mashal, Lala, and the spiritual guide continued deeper into the pine and scrub, entering a narrow valley that marked the entrance to the base. As they came upon a second, seemingly unmanned, checkpoint, a fat, jovial Sudanese commander shouted from beneath a cliff ledge. "Halt! Who is that?" Lumbering out toward the party of three, his vest wobbling with grenades and detached Kalashnikov magazines, the commander approached them. As usual, Mashal did not even think of presenting his credentials as a journalist. Instead, with the spiritual leader, he had worked out a cover story. When he later told me the tale he had concocted, I chuckled and remarked that it was almost too far-fetched to believe. Unlike the cover story that had gotten him locked in a shed in Kabul, however, this one did the trick. He explained to the guard that he had arrived in Tora Bora to survey the forests with hopes of purchasing lumber to take back in the direction of Kabul. The befuddled Sudanese commander agreed to let the party pass. Asked about the U.S. bombing, he laughed a little and described a system of decoys that sounded to me an awful lot like what I had seen the Yugoslav military use during NATO's aerial bombing of Kosovo. He said that al Qaeda was employing the strategy of setting up empty tents inside the base to give high-flying U.S. fighter jet pilots false targets. "They can drop all the bombs they want," he told Mashal. "We'll be bundled away inside our caves and waiting for the ground troops." Mashal asked him about a possible meeting with senior al Qaeda figures. The Sudanese thought the idea feasible, but that it would take him a few days to come up with a definite answer.

Having waltzed past the commander, the three were now virtual "guests" inside Tora Bora. After passing through the second checkpoint, Mashal, Lala, and the spiritual leader stopped to pray in a small, makeshift mosque along with a few al Qaeda fighters. In the mosque, they met an Afghan man named Haji Jamal, who claimed to be the local al Qaeda supply chief. Jamal boasted about his close ties to bin Laden. Jamal was responsible to Awol Gul, the commander, who answered to Jalalabad's wily old power broker, Younus Khalis, the leader in the Eastern Shura who had boasted to Mashal that the U.S. military would never catch Osama.

The supply chief sat for tea with the three and revealed a great deal about the activities inside Tora Bora. He claimed that bin Laden was holed up in there with about "four hundred of his elite fighters." Jamal, a lusty-looking, middle-aged man, talked with a touch of pride when he spoke of bin Laden. "I saw the Sheikh [bin Laden] after he returned from a short run to the Pakistani border last week. He went to Tendi village and the chief there, Malek Sorat Khan, gave him assurances for his safety," he said. Jamal boasted that al Qaeda had recently purchased fifty mules to help move food and supplies into Tora Bora, and he openly discussed his own role in the supply chain. He explained that he didn't travel back to Jalalabad himself, but rather picked up necessary supplies from a "safe house" controlled by Younus Khalis. In addition to his matter-of-fact remarks about the al Qaeda supply lines, the Afghan operative expressed noticeable glee at what he claimed several Arab fighters had promised him for his loyalty. Tossing back his head and unleashing a hearty laugh that echoed across the valley, he told Mashal, "They [al Qaeda] have advised me that if they are killed I am authorized to take their wives. They are insisting that the ones I do not want, I give to my fellow Pashtuns." It was easy to be misled by the "religious" nature of the political struggles in Afghanistan, but often when you peered beneath the surface Mashal reminded me, money and lust actually drove the story.

The next day, Lala returned to Tora Bora alone to follow up with the Sudanese security chief on our request for an interview. The commander penned a return note in Arabic that sounded somewhat optimistic. Its only stipulation: "You must meet with us at a place and time of our own choosing." Jake and I discussed the idea and decided, with Mashal's advice, to press for a compromise, a meeting halfway between Jalalabad and Tora Bora. We felt hot on the trail.

The American bombing of the Tora Bora cave and bunker complex, which had begun in early October 2001, intensified in the last two weeks of November. The constant pounding was exacting a heavy physical and mental toll on the al Qaeda fighters inside. Over the weekend, after the Sudanese security commander had promised us access to senior leaders inside the warren of caves, we learned through his lieutenants that a large "bunker buster" had taken his life. We had no way of confirming his death, but we understood it to mean that our interview request had hit a temporary dead end.

## Stuffed Quail

By late November, Tora Bora contained the largest concentration of foreign commandos anywhere in Afghanistan. The fighters at the Tora Bora base were some of the youngest and best educated in the al Qaeda network. Almost all of them were fluent in Arabic, and dozens of them spoke English, often a prerequisite for the network's suicide missions anywhere in the world. Most were prepared, in any case, to die for a cause.

Estimates from Afghans who had traveled inside to meet with the Arabs put the number of fighters at between 1,600 and two thousand. Villagers in the area said the core of bin Laden's close-quarters guard consisted of sixty men. This personal security unit was backed by a four-hundred-man force that acted as pickets on the flanks as the Saudi chief moved from the Mileva Valley in the west to the Tora

Bora Valley in the east and back again. Beyond this, another force of four hundred Chechen fighters, known for their alpine fighting skills, guarded the perimeter of the Tora Bora complex. Afghans fought as gunners, though as talk of an imminent ground assault grew louder their numbers diminished. As a part of a new force-protection policy, senior al Qaeda leaders were welcoming regular foot soldiers into some of their largest caves, whose electricity had been cut to avoid detection by U.S. surveillance planes swarming overhead. The tents that Chechen and Yemeni guards had once slept in became decoys for U.S. bombers.

Al Qaeda fighters, as we later learned in subsequent interviews with network members both at large and in captivity, had not been informed early on about bin Laden's imminent plans to escape from Afghanistan. As far as they understood, Tora Bora would be either the scene of a great victory over the American infidels or their grave-yard. One Saudi fighter had understood from bin Laden's direct orders that he should defend his own cave down to the last man. "When we arrived in the White Mountains, the plan had been to defend Tora Bora to our deaths," said Mohamed Akram, thirty-three, a waif of a man, whose small head was covered in a black-and-white turban wrapped about his jaw for warmth. "We had thousands of men there. The Sheikh himself divided us into the caves and said, 'This is your position, and that is yours.' Then he went to his own cave."

As Akram recounted to us what he had been through inside Tora Bora, his fingers shook and his nostrils, plugged with cotton, bled from a recent beating. Two months after his ordeal and in the captivity of a cruel Hazara warlord, he was still in pain from a bomb blast at the mouth of his own cave that had killed two of his close colleagues.

Akram's story of joining al Qaeda was typical of those of many of the Arab fighters who became mercenaries and followers of the al Qaeda cause. Most of them had been brainwashed into believing that they had to convert the rest of the world into thinking as their leaders did. Akram's tale was not just that of another misguided fanatic. In the middle eighties, Akram had been a curious young Saudi casting about for a mission in life. "I visited a lot of countries, including

Egypt," he told us, relating the excitement and inspiration he had found there. "I wanted to study there. I was fascinated with religion and wanted to become a scholar. But when I started in school, there were young men who said it was wrong to study—and that we should, instead, be fighting for Allah in Afghanistan [against the Soviets]. I was young and impressionable and so I went there."

Akram claimed that he had arrived in Afghanistan when, "I was just a kid, nineteen years old. I came because I had a great devotion to Islam and holy shrines and the idea of fighting for the freedom of Muslims as a holy warrior." But when the war with the Soviets ended, Akram, like so many other fighters from the Middle East, found himself out of a job. Bin Laden's network was a fallback, particularly for fighters like Akram who had seen a lot of action on the front lines, often seeing their idealistic colleagues mowed down by Soviet firepower. Their hate of the outside world and addiction to the intensity of battle had a great deal in common with the "Vietnam syndrome" that swept through the ranks of U.S. soldiers in the wake of an earlier war. Their own post–traumatic stress (PTS) syndromes often led to them to more violence, addiction, and suicide back home. But many remained loyal to the concept of a global *jihad*. Through his vast network of financiers in the Middle East, bin Laden channeled this pent-up anxiety and anger to his own use by guaranteeing the former holy warriors food on the table and a continued mission in life. Their were some perks as well, even medical care, as Akram's experience showed—"When I had a bad heart Osama agreed to have me sent to Detroit for medical treatment," he said.

Training camps for holy warriors started popping up all over Afghanistan and in parts of the Middle East, including Yemen and the Sudan. Not quite fit to serve as a frontline combatant in a place like Chechnya or Bosnia, Akram managed to stay on in the al Qaeda camps anyway. The young Saudi became a religion instructor, with local Pakistani and Afghan boys as his students. They learned Arabic from him, so that they could recite the Koran verbatim in its original verse. In the meantime, with little or no critical appraisal from his followers, Osama bin Laden had shifted his focus from the Russian "infidel" to the American "infidel." In 1998, less than a hundred miles south of Tora Bora in the Zhawar Kili training camp, he made it official: America was enemy number one. His twisted logic allowed an explanation for all the problems in the new world order. After all, the greatest enemies of the Arabs were the Jews, and their biggest backers were in the United States.

It didn't take much of a leap of faith to fall into bin Laden's warmongering trap, and Akram admitted that much to us. He had come to perform his religious duty and fight in the jihad against the Soviets, and had never left. "Most recently I have been a guard in Tora Bora and a cook. My real passion is cooking, and that is what I do best. Some nights, when Osama was in the mood for one of his favorite meals, he would ask me to come around and cook for him." This was only on special occasions, though, he admitted. Akram's detailed account of bin Laden's taste for Moghul cooking had the strange ring of truth to it. "Osama's favorite meal is fowl—anything with wings. He likes quails and if he cannot get his hands on one, he will settle for a chicken. Most of the quails he ate, we hunted. Others came in by road from Iran. Osama often made special requests for the mutton and yogurt Moghul dish that I do best."

However, what Akram remembered most from his experience at Tora Bora was not, of course, his efforts at haute cuisine. He recalled hunkering in his own small cave, a bunker cut with rock tools out of the face of a cliff and extending back into the mountain some fifty feet. When the "bunker-busting" bombs hit, the scrub and pine blew helter-skelter, ripping the earth clean of all vegetation. By the fourth week in November, arms and legs amputated by the blasts hung from trees. While most fighters remained hunkered down in their caves, hoping eventually to see the whites of the infidel eyes, the morale of al Qaeda fighters had slipped under the relentless U.S. air assault.

As for his boss: in the first week to ten days of his arrival in Tora Bora, bin Laden enjoyed relative freedom of movement around the two adjoining valleys that made up the complex. "We saw him outside using his satellite phone around the 20th of November," recalled Akram. The terror chief made one trip south that lasted several days, but by the fourth week in November, bin Laden, probably aware that the U.S. military knew his map coordinates, became far more cautious, said the young Saudi.

As the month progressed, the American military and intelligence services picked up more information on what was going on inside Tora Bora. As early as October, U.S. military officials had pegged Tora Bora as a likely al Qaeda hideout, and now the CIA was picking up more solid intelligence to that end, according to Colonel Mulholland. Still, despite regular aerial bombardments, arrangements for a ground offensive were only just beginning.

As Tora Bora exploded in heat and fire, talk of a ground war heightened inside Zaman's orange grove on the edge of Jalalabad. The cantankerous old warlord, who had readily divulged a few scoops in the first few days of our arrival in Afghanistan, now became more standoffish. He had a new favorite, *LA Times* reporter Megan Stack, an Irish-American sweetheart and rookie war reporter. Stack's beguiling baby-blue eyes were the hook, and she used them with a vengeance. In a land where men hide their women away like bars of gold beneath a mattress, Stack's innocence in a war zone was irresistible even for several of her middle-aged colleagues. But it was Zaman who had the "news," and thus the mojo, so all the other would-be suitors had to drown their desires in Bombay rubbing alcohol. Megan happened to be my neighbor at the Spin Ghar, and when I asked she didn't deny that Zaman had fallen head over heels in love with her, though she made sure to point out that she did not intend to return his affections. By the fourth week in November, he was inviting her around to the orange grove almost every night to break the fast with him in lavish mode, with dates, nuts, baskets of fruit, and lamb roasted on a spit.

Mashal and I both felt a bit put off by this. Zaman never repeated his promise to have us ride shotgun into the battle with him. However, on a warm autumn day, the warlord invited several foreign reporters, ourselves included, to stroll with him through a bombed-out military base on the east end of town. As we walked through the scene of destruction, children crawled over Russian tanks, and fighters squatted under trees in the midday sun. The devastation wrought by the U.S. bombs through mid-November was astounding in its scope. We stood over fifty-foot-wide craters, caused by bombs that had ripped out the barracks and scattered ammunition. Zaman said he could have used the ammunition to mount an offensive against Tora Bora. He stood in a clearing and made a speech, pleading through the Western press for, among other things, gasoline for his trucks and guns for his fighters. Zaman then confided to us that American officials had asked him to take part in a major offensive against Tora Bora. He complained, however, that the U.S. military appeared intent on working with Ali first and himself second. There was a growing sense of urgency in Washington that the battle be joined as soon as possible, but Zaman wanted to know what he would receive in return for his diligent efforts. The twenty-five million on bin Laden's head sounded fine, but most local warlords did not expect to see a cent of the reward. Zaman also openly wondered why, if Washington was willing to pay so much for bin Laden's head on a platter, the military resources that he had been promised were so slow in arriving.

## Our Men in Flying Machines

Colonel Mulholland was almost ready to send his men into the fray, but there was still legwork to do in lining up the allies. As U.S. Special Forces had done in breaking the back of the Taliban north of Kabul, the plan was for them to infiltrate Tora Bora to identify targets for aerial bombardment, clearing the way for Afghan fighters to storm the redoubt. But just as the targeting of Taliban positions had initially lagged behind the actual arrival of U.S. forces to help with the targeting north of Kabul, prior to the arrival of any U.S. forces on the ground in eastern Afghanistan the "precision" bombing left much to be desired.

Only a few days after his arrival in Tora Bora, Geraldo Rivera reported on his own findings: "On the road into Kabul . . . there is eloquent testimony to the devastating effectiveness of our air strikes, awesome and precise, with very little collateral damage." Three days later he let his vengeful, patriotic mood hang out on air again, telling Fox anchor Laurie Dhue, "We've been in various conflicts, and we keep our chin up and keep focused on the fact that we want Osama bin Laden to end up either behind bars or six feet under or maybe just one foot under or maybe just a pile of ash, you know. That's it." Geraldo was doing all the cheerleading he could get onto the air, but like other network reporters, he wasn't paying much attention to the harrowing cost of the bombing.

Some senior news executives appeared almost cavalier about a part of war reporting that goes hand in hand with victory and defeat. Brit Hume, Fox's news director and anchor, shrugged off criticism that his network was ignoring the human cost of the war. "OK, war is hell, people die," he said. "We know we're at war. The fact that some people are dying, is that really news? And is it news to be treated in a semi-straight-faced way? I think not." CNN, which didn't want to be seen as playing catch-up in Fox's game of "get the bad guys," took the bizarre step of ordering its correspondents to mention the September 11 attacks during any showing of civilian casualties in Afghanistan. This struck me as condescending toward the viewer. Why did an informed public need to be led by the nose on questions of cause and effect, if not for some underlying urge to provide moral justification for this war? Or did the CNN executives believe that the situation demanded some moral justification? Indeed, the requirement, written in an internal memo, represented—whether CNN executives would have liked to admit it or not—a mild form of self-censorship. It ordered the correspondent in the field to tell the story and present the facts in the order preferred by some "suit" in Atlanta or Washington.

It was a mistake either to downplay or ignore the civilian deaths in this war—just as it would have been to overlook the horrors of Hiroshima or the bombing of Dresden. As far as I could see, many of the deaths—estimated at well over a thousand in the first six months of the war—were due to a lack of solid U.S. and allied intelligence on the ground. In the aftermath of one errant U.S. raid, Ningahar's governor, Haji Abdul Qadir, invited Western journalists along to see the results of aerial bombing at a village near the Khyber Pass, which his men had controlled for several days. The journey was a crapshoot—the U.S. bombers might strike again. Still, we reasoned that getting killed by "friendly fire" was less likely than getting whacked by the Taliban or al Qaeda. But even so, the governor, killed by thugs in Kabul less than a year later, approached the village of Gluco with extreme caution.

The first sign of a tragedy in Gluco was a set of shattered homes, the beams and buttresses of which had been scattered like an emptied matchbox across the hillside. We drove behind the governor at a safe distance. A wounded white mule brayed in the road as the pungent smell of sulfur and death mingled to produce a stomach-churning stench. It was a testament to the immediacy of the last of three U.S. bombing runs that villagers had not had time to put the wounded farm animals to rest. They had, we soon learned, been too busy with the human casualties.

Though Haji Qadir had sent his own fighters to secure Gluco more than a week before our visit, the U.S. military had not apprised themselves of these developments on the ground. In the last two days, three bombing raids had been conducted against the village, which was on a well-known smuggler's route. After the first attack, villagers had sent word up the road that they had come under attack, but the governor, who was a well-known personality in the region, claimed he had had no means of contacting the U.S. military directly to inform them of their initial error.

When we arrived in the village center, villagers asked us to sit with them in a walled compound. They claimed to have been taken by complete surprise by the U.S. bombs. Villagers described how bombers had circled overhead for several minutes before unleashing their payloads. There were a total of seven villagers dead from the three raids, mostly women and children. The carnage was scattered across a mountain pass normally used to smuggle everything from opium and heroin to Japanese television sets on the backs of camels, mules, and horses. The governor complained that American officials had not bothered to ask details of the new allied positions he had set up in Gluco. This excuse did not placate the villagers. The eyes of the headman, Said Un Gul, narrowed on our small party as the governor now asked me to explain "as an American" through Mashal that the U.S. planes had made a terrible mistake and unintentionally targeted the village.

I knew that had there been U.S. forces on the ground in this already "safe" area, such an accident would have been avoided. This was a case of pure and simple military negligence that I wasn't able to explain. "Well, you see, the planes must have had bad intelligence—they couldn't have known what they were shooting at," I said. The expressions in the crowd only made me feel like an apologist. It was a rather poor explanation, and I was embarrassed to have tried to pass it off as soon as I opened my mouth.

The villagers' eyes soon glazed over, and their headman, Gul, snapped back at me: "How can this be a mistake? Even the Russians couldn't kill us, because we had time to run from them. We have had no way to defend ourselves this time. This is the third time in two days that our village has been hit." So concerned about a repeat after the first two bombings, the villagers had handwritten a ten-foot-sign in English on their schoolhouse. It read simply, "THIS IS A SCHOOL!" Another villager asked the governor, "If the Americans can see a tank from the air, why can't they read our sign?"

The strikes on Gluco, by no means the first or the last human errors of the U.S. campaign bombing, suggested that the U.S. military had less than adequate intelligence on the ground in eastern Afghanistan, where hundreds of Arab fighters were still holed up. This seemed doubly surprising because the CIA had been claiming since October 12 that it had operatives in Ningahar Province.

By conservative and documented estimates, the early wave of U.S. bombing around Tora Bora in November left eighty noncombatants dead. Confronted with newspaper reports of mounting civilian deaths in eastern Afghanistan, U.S. Central Command in Florida shifted into damage control. A Major Brad Lowell said that the command had reviewed all means available and had found nothing. "We had good imagery on these," he said. "We saw the weapons hit their targets, which were cave and tunnel systems. There were no buildings in view to depict or suggest residential areas. The rounds fired in the area were on target and have all been accounted for." Lowell would not say what means of detection had been used. In Washington, Secretary Rumsfeld insisted that no army in the history of warfare had taken as many precautions as the U.S. military in trying to avoid civilian deaths or collateral damage. Nevertheless, the deaths of civilians in eastern Afghanistan was news that even the cheerleading retired generals manning the network "analyst" desks managed to ignore. The bombing might have been "awesome" as Geraldo insisted, but it certainly was not yet precise, and it provided—to use his phrase—"eloquent testimony" not to any accuracy or extra caution, but rather to the utter folly of fighting from ten thousand feet without boots on the ground.

The death of noncombatants was real news for other reasons, not least of which was that it finally goaded our reluctant allies into battle. Ironically, errant U.S. bombing finally moved the proxy fighters to speed up their preparations for an assault on Tora Bora. On December 1, 2001, American planes attacked more villages in the foothills of the White Mountains. The attacks came in four waves, the first being the most devastating. The *New York Times*' Barry Bearak would write after surveying the carnage firsthand that "after that, the living ran into the gully that was left unmolested. The houses were small, the bombing precise. . . . Fifteen houses, 15 ruins."

After these attacks, Zaman's tribesmen besieged the front gates of his orange grove to give him a piece of their minds. They were outraged that while U.S. planes were dropping bombs on their homes Zaman was asking them to hand over their sons for America's battle against al Qaeda, which had, until recently, been bankrolling the community. We found Zaman sitting on his front lawn with a few of these families; he appeared downcast but suddenly adamant that the assault on Tora Bora would commence immediately, ready or not. "The battle may take weeks. My people are ready to fight the Arabs. They want an end to their own slaughter." Gul Amerji, his intelligence chief, who had already been inside Tora Bora to meet the Arabs on two occasions, echoed the words of his commander, telling us, "We have no alternative now but to attack." Amerji's resigned decision to go into battle didn't sound even faintly like the war cry of Rambo, nor did the U.S. military's own chaotic approach to the crucial battle. The slow, difficult movement of U.S. troops into the area and the atrocious coordination with the Afghans did not provide any real sense that Bush's war cabinet was genuinely bent on the final prize at Tora Bora.

As far as the men of Colonel Mulholland's Fifth Group were concerned, they were already on their way to success in Afghanistan— Osama or no Osama. Mulholland later explained to me what his own brief from his superiors had been. "My permanent mission was to bring down the Taliban regime, to destabilize in order to deny sanctuary to al Qaeda, and we did that. We feel we were very much instrumental in liberating Afghanistan. Now, in the course of doing that, my mission was also to destroy as many al Qaeda as I could." He made it sound almost as though the killing of al Qaeda and by extrapolation, the capturing of Osama, was viewed by the Pentagon's top brass as a possible by-product of a far broader mission. Yet, I also knew that the colonel was following his orders down to the last dotted *i* and crossed *t*.

Mulholland, ensconced at the Bagram Air Base and in daily contact with General Fahim's Northern Alliance, was also doing what he could to achieve the proper mass and mix of forces to begin the battle of Tora Bora.

"In the third and fourth weeks of November, we were still fighting some pretty healthy firefights across Afghanistan," he said. Kandahar, the Taliban's spiritual and military stronghold in the south of the country, did not fall until December 7, and the Fifth Group's few hundred troops were tied up with that battle, with the help and firepower of the Marines. "We were trying to conduct a classic pincer move on Kandahar. We've got the Marines down in the desert and we were fighting across the board and we were already—very much—hurting on airlift. In November, I got a team into Jalalabad, but remember that the big fight I'm fighting is Kandahar. The big focus for me at this time is taking Kandahar, which is in the Taliban heartland, that is the heart and soul of the Taliban movement."

Still, Mulholland's own intelligence experts were keeping close tabs on the "rat lines," the movements of senior al Qaeda leaders over roads and goat trails in Afghanistan. A day after Gen. Tommy Franks revealed on November 28 his own suspicions that bin Laden had gone to ground at Tora Bora, Cheney expressed his own views of bin Laden's whereabouts on ABC's *Prime Time Live*. "I think he was equipped to go to ground there," he said. "He's got what he believes to be a fairly secure facility. He's got caves underground; it's an area he's familiar with." If bin Laden hadn't picked up on General Franks's suspicions a day earlier, he would have likely heard about Cheney's on the many wireless radios inside Tora Bora. In any case, bin Laden still had ample time to move out, since neither U.S. forces nor their proxies were ready to mount an attack. Tenth Mountain

Division elements were waiting in neighboring Uzbekistan and could have been whisked by chopper to Bagram in a day or two, but Mulholland claimed that he did not consider this force adequate for the task: "This was a light battalion and they were for providing force protection."

That would not have stopped the Tenth Mountain from fighting if it had been tapped for the job. According to the commander of the Eighty-seventh Battalion in Uzbekistan, his seven hundred light infantry had been ready from the middle of November and could have been summoned to fight anywhere in Afghanistan. The battalion was light, but that made it mobile, particularly in harsh terrain, the very kind that now presented itself in the eastern Afghan highlands. "As the enemy voted with their feet down there in Afghanistan, Mulholland gave us an added mission as a quick reaction force," said the battalion's commander, Col. Paul La Camera, a West Point graduate, who spoke with me over a year later in upstate New York. "From my foxhole, I sat there and watched. We knew. We weren't just sitting there digging holes and looking out. We were training for potential fights because eventually it was going to come to that. And I don't make the decision when. I don't pick targets, I just execute against them. When I'm given my sandbox, I fight against that."

But the U.S. military's top brass decided to keep Tora Bora an almost exclusively Afghan sandbox. Part of the delay in getting a Green Beret A team into Jalalabad was due simply to the difficulty in getting the proper allies in line. Asked why it took until the 26th of November to get any U.S. forces on the ground, Mulholland replied, "Well, I can't answer but—what I know—we were waiting for that Pashtun leader in the area to emerge that gave us kind of an entrée to the region. So as soon as Hazret Ali emerged—and, as far as I know, the CIA were the ones who identified him—we moved in." It would become, of course, a controversial decision. Ali had already gone on record as wanting to follow the will of the Eastern Shura, which U.S. officials should have known to be stacked with al Qaeda sympathizers. On the other hand, it would have been hard to bet on Zaman instead, because many of his own Hugani tribesmen, who lived hard up against the White Mountains, were still on the terror network's bankroll.

From the 26th of November, as the window for bin Laden's capture was already closing fast, Mulholland began making final plans for an Afghan-led assault on Tora Bora. "My forces went in the end of November to do their initial assessment, training some of the Afghan guys and helping them get fitted out with arms and ammunition," he told me. A Green Beret A team quickly set up shop in an abandoned schoolhouse about ten kilometers from bin Laden's base at Tora Bora. The U.S. base was located at the left-hand fork in the road that led around to the villages of Pachir and Upper Pachir, two former enemy strongholds where we had first made our own al Qaeda contacts. When the battle started, the Green Berets would coordinate U.S. air strikes. For this task they had, in addition to their high-powered rifles, sophisticated laser guns capable of zapping beams into the mouths of caves and at any other potential al Qaeda hiding place. Mulholland's fighters made an extra effort to blend in with the local population. Their job was to perform but not be seen or heard. Still, hiding two dozen U.S. servicemen from the Afghans or the world's press would have required a Houdini act of remarkable proportions. Someone had thought to purchase a set of black-and-white bandanas for the team, but since they all matched they made the U.S. fighters appear a little too color coordinated. The fighters' beards were, however, intact and at least provided a semblance of cultural sensitivity in a region where men without facial hair are ostracized oddities if not complete outcasts.

By the first two days in December, the U.S. Army was finally sending in long-awaited supplies at night by helicopter from Bagram, north of Kabul. Ali's men at Jalalabad airport were unloading wooden crates full of weapons and night-vision goggles. The same airport where bin Laden had returned in style to Afghanistan in his private jet in 1996 was now buzzing with construction contractors filling in craters left by U.S. bombing in October. A haggard foreman we met on the runway told us that the Americans wanted the track repaired within seventy-two hours. He wasn't sure he could make deadline.

There was a plan for attacking Tora Bora, albeit a confused one that already had the participants fighting—in their heads, at least—over the spoils. With the Eastern Shura's secret diplomacy inside the mountain redoubt taking place simultaneously with the planning for an attack, the element of surprise had long since been lost.

# 4

## OSAMA SLIPS THE NOOSE

One valley caught the waves of sound and passed them to the next, till the whole wide mountain region rocked with the confusion of the tumult. Distant populations on the continent of Europe thought that in them they detected the dull, discordant tones of decline and fall.

—Winston Churchill,
*The Story of the Malakand Field Force*

### The Backstabbers

It would be difficult to determine which of the two closest U.S. allies, Haji Zaman or Hazret Ali, engaged in more betrayal of the American cause. Both warlords continued to behave, despite Uncle Sam's goading and generous financial support, in keeping with their own Islamic bonds and ties established during the liberation struggle. Al Qaeda had enjoyed long and intimate ties to the Jalalabad area, and our political naïveté probably led us to expect that our money could convince the Afghans to turn suddenly against their coreligionists. We also had entered the fray handicapped by Washington's relative neglect of the region over the last decade. With the accumulated forces of fanaticism pulling in one direction and Mulholland's small Fifth Group attempting to yank them the other, we never enjoyed good odds.

Hazret Ali, who drove around town in a shiny, silver land cruiser and whose fighters saluted him with their bazookas pointed upright, had become well practiced at the double game long before the assault ever took off. On any given day, you could catch his bushy hairdo and wry grin inside the shoddy lobby of the Hotel Tora Bora. His popularity with the Western press corps grew, and his blue eyes sparkled with glee and appreciation. With his ragtag former rebels, flowers in their hair, he became the go-to guy for Tora Bora, and with this came demands that he know more than he really did about the developing situation. To placate his inquisitors, Ali regularly held long, ranting press conferences—with Mashal at his side, serving reluctantly as his translator. As Mashal kept being dragged away from the restaurant or out of his room to interpret, he gained considerable insight into Commander Ali's thinking. After some questions, Ali would turn to Mashal and ask, "What should I tell them now?"

While Ali was obviously cultivating his public image and his relationship with the press by giving us what we wanted regardless of its veracity, one event Mashal and I witnessed indicated that he may have been acting with equal duplicity in his overtures to the U.S. military. One afternoon Haji Hayat Ullah, a well-known philanthropist who ran a string of orphanages in Pakistan and Afghanistan that were funded by radical Saudi clerics, dropped by the Spin Ghar Hotel to talk with Ali. In the full lobby, Mashal and I stood some ten feet from the two, eavesdropping on them as they sat on a couch sipping tea. Ullah, a short, fat man with no aversion to wearing a thick gold watchband and several gold rings, represented a typical al Qaeda sympathizer and also had voting membership in the Eastern Shura, which remained reluctant to strike at its Muslim allies in the hills.

The orphanage manager had come to the Spin Ghar on the 3rd of December to plead with Commander Ali for the "safe passage" of five Arab friends who were cooped up at Tora Bora. "These men are not fighters and they are trapped in Tora Bora," he said, handing Ali a list of five Arabs he hoped would gain safe passage. Ullah asked that Ali allow the men to leave the village of Upper Pachir by mule and car, north toward the main highway that runs from Jalalabad to Peshawar. He wanted the Arabs sent through the province of Kunar, where he said his own family would help them slip over the border into Pakistan. Ali held the list for some time. He appeared torn over how to proceed. Then, after about ten minutes, he pointed to three of the names and said, "That is the best I can do. You'll be able to deliver the money?" Ullah nodded. We were nonplussed but reported the deal in full—without including Ali's name, in case he might decide that we had betrayed him and seek retribution. His deal making had made Ullah's ties to al Qaeda apparent, and we subsequently confirmed Ullah's direct links to the terror network through a senior Pakistani intelligence official. That our "ally" would so willingly assist Ullah smuggle his friends out of Tora Bora vividly demonstrates the shortcomings of trusting locals to fight a proxy war.

In any case, the U.S. military had chosen its ally and could not—or did not want to—retreat from this choice. Despite Ali's reputation as a prevaricator, a double-dealer, and something of a halfwit among reporters who had been in Jalalabad for two weeks, he enjoyed the leading role in the U.S. military's drama. It made one wonder how good the CIA's intelligence had ever been—at least out in eastern Afghanistan.

Col. Rick Thomas of the U.S. Army later told me, "We looked at the entire spectrum of options that we had available to us and decided that the use of small liaison elements were the most appropriate. We chose to fight using the Afghans who were fighting to regain their own country. Our aims of eliminating al Qaeda were similar."

Those aims might have crossed like laser beams in the night, but they were far from similar. Both Ali and Zaman had warned from the start of the battle against using large U.S. forces to lead the battle. They had made it clear in interviews with the Western press that eastern Afghans would not fight alongside the American *kafir*s, or infidels. But important figures with no direct hand in the fighting, and thus no shot at the twenty-five-million-dollar reward money, did not hold this view. Pir Baksh Bardiwal, the intelligence chief for the Eastern Shura, said that he would welcome a massive influx of U.S. troops. He believed that the Pentagon planners were making a grave mistake by not surrounding Tora Bora. It would have been hard for Bardiwal or any other critic to place the blame for this failure on the two dozen courageous U.S. soldiers actually present, overburdened with target spotting and grumpy warlords. The buck stopped much higher up the echelons of power.

## Dancing with the Devil

The U.S.–orchestrated plan to take Tora Bora was straightforward enough. Apart from the highly sophisticated role of American air power, it could have been arranged around a campfire at the base of bin Laden's Tora Bora redoubt with a plot of sand and a few sticks for pointing out the meandering goat trails leading into the mountains. As Mulholland and the warlords later described the plan, it gave Zaman and Ali separate though parallel routes of attack into the mountains. Zaman's fighters would take the western half of the base, moving south; Ali's men would be in the center; and the eastern flanks would be shared—if an arrangement could be worked out with Governor Haji Qadr's son, Haji Zahir. The role of the U.S. soldiers would be to help coordinate this "unconventional" attack, mostly by bringing air power to bear. Lastly, the Pentagon asked Pakistan to move forces close to the border to prevent escapes. The direct attack from the Afghan side, moving south, had already lost the element of surprise, and it was still not at all clear that the Pakistanis could carry out their end of the deal. The request from Washington had arrived with little advance notice. Northwestern Pakistan's tribal areas had been off limits to the regular Pakistani military since independence, and the more experienced "frontier police" worked under the sway of religious leaders sympathetic to the Taliban and al Qaeda.

The plan was designed with the idea that someone other than U.S. forces would fight for Tora Bora. What ensued in early December took on the appearance of a real battle, albeit belated and part of a plan riddled with loopholes—and, as it turned out, several escape routes.

The battle opened with warlords tripping over each other and fighting for turf even in the foothills of Tora Bora. Ali rushed a thousand of his men and Zaman an equal number of his own to the base of the mountain redoubt. Here they would, in theory, go their separate ways up the mountain, but it wasn't long before skirmishes broke out between Ali's men and local villagers in Zaman's tribe. At the time, Mashal and I were drinking tea and eating mandarin oranges with Zaman, who hadn't yet bothered to drive out to the front. I sensed he had completely forgotten his promise to allow me to ride shotgun into the battle to catch Osama. As we sat chatting, a panicked villager rushed through Zaman's front gate with a story about how Ali's men had come in shooting and looting. "The barbarians have overrun us and our people are panicked! Last week we were bombed by the Americans and now we have Ali's men disarming us." Our man Zaman, who always seemed a bit on edge before he met his *LA Times* sweetheart, appeared dumbfounded.

He launched into a diatribe against his rival as we sat uncomfortably at his feet. "Ali, that bastard! He is a stupid peasant and so are his men!" he snapped. "He'll pay for this!"

If Ali had led his men into battle and Zaman had at least sent his men ahead to start without him, one slacker warlord was still sleeping, missing the whole show. The onset of the battle and the now urgent U.S. call to arms sent unexpected shocks through the sleepy bedrooms of Jalalabad. One does not normally roll out of bed in the morning and decide to go after twenty-five million in reward money. But that is how at least one Afghan warlord threw himself headlong into the fray. Haji Zahir, whose seven hundred men would eventually constitute a third force, in addition to the Ali and Zaman contingents, was lying in bed at 7 A.M. watching CNN when an anchor announced that the battle of Tora Bora was about to begin. Zahir had had some advance notice of the plan, and despite Zaman's reluctance to let the governor's son fight, Ali had already asked him to round up as many men as he could. Zahir's recruiting was taking time, however, and no one had bothered to tip him off to the timing of the battle. Realizing that he could make more money from the bin Laden reward than he could from scamming journalists, the balding, clean-shaven Zahir jumped out of bed, brushed his teeth, and began hastily to assemble fighters. None of them had winter gear, but by the end of the day they were racing into the snow-capped peaks to capture bin Laden.

If the warlords looked unkempt and unprepared as they raced to the front on the first full day of battle, December 5, 2001, the press corps, myself included, was in equal disarray. With word of skirmishing in the foothills the night before, we were up early and rambling through the desert at fifty miles per hour. The ride south to the White

Mountains, which could take three hours in a truck, would take only ninety minutes in a low-riding Toyota taxi. We knew a shortcut through Younus Khalis's compound, and we made the turnoff without hesitation. Though winter weather was already blasting a chill through the streets of Kabul, the lower-lying city of Jalalabad still enjoyed ripening fruit orchards and short sleeves. On the outskirts of the city, the fertile farmland turned to desert. The road meandered through parched fields and past adobe homes. Tiny twisters of twigs and sand whipped up in the wind and spun along beside us. In several villages along the way the children, scrubbed clean at dawn, were caked in dust by midmorning. The dust-coated kids resembled small ghosts, with only the shiny white teeth of their smiles rendering them lifelike.

Joining our party—which already included Karim Abdul, Mashal, and a driver—would be a friend, Jon Swain, whom I had met covering an uprising in Burma back in 1988. That conflict had helped addict me to my own foolish profession in the first place. It had seen us dashing about the monsoon-swept streets with a bird's-eye view to the kill. Courageous students in bare feet, bare chests, and white bandanas had put on an amazing show. We had watched, slipping our heads around street corners as they battled government forces using bicycle spokes fired from their slingshots. By night, we would return to the decrepit British bastion of the Strand Hotel to send our stories on an antiquated Telex machine, sip gin, and eat langoustine beneath twirling ceiling fans. During those days, most of my own compatriots paid little attention to foreign news. Fewer still would have recognized my friend Jon of the *Sunday Times* as a key player in the drama of *The Killing Fields,* who tries to save the life of Sydney Schanberg's interpreter and barely escapes a Khmer Rouge firing squad. I considered "Swainster" both a good-luck charm and someone who could dispense solid advice if we ever got into a tight corner. Even as we set out that morning, disheveled and in a good mood for a nasty day ahead, Jon was busy entertaining anyone he met with a series of three photographs he had taken some years back. The first photo showed a young tribesman who looked down on his luck. "This is my good friend Mohamed, from Waziristan," Jon would say in all sincerity. "He is still looking for a wife." The next shot displayed the same tribesman now smiling from ear to ear alongside a possibly voluptuous figure in a blue burqa. Apparently, he had discovered the woman of his dreams. The last picture shows the burqa unveiled and Jon himself snickering and preparing to embrace his good friend like the desperate French Legionnaire that he had once been.

The scenery on the route to Tora Bora was equally amusing. We ran up against a small convoy of competing journalists and slowed down in time to catch a good glimpse of an extraordinarily curious local population. Mothers, fathers, and children came streaming out of their homes by the hundreds on the first day of the battle for Tora Bora. They came to see a parade of Zaman and Ali fighters lining the backs of pickup trucks with their rocket launchers and polished machine guns. The fighters were dressed in drab browns and grays, and most of them had their faces covered by cloth to protect against the dust. The children, standing shoulder to shoulder with their fathers, also watched the strange foreigners in their brightly colored winter coats, naïve Westerners who would travel into a war zone with no camouflage and—most of them—with no guns. The scene of gawking peasants and wealthy Westerners racing toward the front lines reminded me of passages I had read about the similar strange voyeuristic phenomenon in the Civil War, when Virginians and Washingtonians piled into their buggies and mounted their horses to attend a battle. Instead of blankets on the grass, picnic lunches, and fair women beneath parasols, the battle of Tora Bora brought journalists setting up pup tents and a lot of clean-shaven Caucasians— possibly two hundred of us—angling for the best view.

The Afghans also came to see the B-52 bombers, swooping with their white contrails ten thousand feet over our heads. For weeks, they had been flying by, mostly one at a time, dumping immense payloads into the mountains, then circling around and heading off to some unknown land. Only recently, however, had these planes begun to target the villages at the base of the mountains. Curiosity mixed with terror in the eyes of every child—even the ones who waved timidly to us as we sped past. From the start, the battle for Tora Bora had an aura of the surreal. Could it really be that the world's most wanted man was about to try to make a "last stand?" My gut instinct told me that somehow this picture wasn't quite right. As we approached the White Mountains, the road rose and curled into a series of rolling foothills. Our taxi struggled to climb the loose earth as the road snaked over and around mounds in the direction of a barren hillside, the shape of a crouching camel.

The jumping-off spot for the bulwark of the Western press corps looked obvious from the start. The camel's back itself would become a rear base for the Western press for the length of the battle. It had its advantages. As an immense, barren hill set at the base of Tora Bora, it provided semi-flat ground for networks and cable stations to lay out their equipment and set up their vans, their tents, and their satellite dishes. While it presented a magnificent target for the enemy, on the one hand, it was such a large target that, as experienced war correspondents knew immediately, it would serve as kind of bellwether that the tide of the battle was turning and that it was time to hightail it back down the other side of the camel's back. In other words, there would be some safety in numbers. If an incoming mortar round struck, it wasn't likely to kill all of us at once and would provide fair warning for the lucky ones to make their escape.

Ali's own fighters had also taken a liking to the camel's back for their own rear position, which made interviews and picture taking that much easier. When we arrived at the top of the hump there were already several ancient T-55 Russian tanks poised farther up the hill in firing positions. I noticed immediately that several of the young Afghan fighters on the backs of these hulking beasts had earplugs already in place.

Meanwhile, the networks got to work setting up their tents and stringing out their cables. There would be campfires under the stars at night, but the first day of battle was just beginning to unfold. Few war correspondents—seasoned or novice—were disappointed at the fireworks display. Along with Jon, Karim Abdul, and Mashal, our party parked on the camel's back. Very quickly, events began to unfold with a peculiarly Hollywoodesque air to them. We jumped out of our taxi and sprinted up the hill just in time to witness three antiquated T-55s about one hundred feet to our south fire into the pine scrub beneath the snow-capped peaks. Each blast sent dust and wood fragments flying into the deep blue skies. B-52 bombers swept overhead, long, billowing condensation trails emanating from tiny dots of silver that sped above the two mountain valleys that constituted Tora Bora. When their bombs hit, the earth shuddered, and a gaggle of Afghan children on the barren slope on which we stood cheered. It was not clear, however, what inspired them. It made you wonder if many of them, the youngest being three and four years old, knew the difference between the stick guns they fired at one another in the dust and the game before them, in which the stakes were much higher.

One of Ali's battlefield commanders made the opening day battle sound a little too scripted. Surrounded by a crush of microphones and reporters begging for news of the battle, he soon delivered the goods. "The battle for Tora Bora has begun and will continue until we eradicate al Qaeda." As the commander spoke, we stood listening within mortar range of al Qaeda positions, which seemed to have paused for the commander's speech.

In search of a story beyond the official line, Mashal accosted one of Zaman's men who was struggling up the camel's back in our direction. The skinny young fighter Gohar Ali, seventeen, with a rocket launcher on his shoulder that just happened to be also seventeen years old, claimed he had fired the first shot of the battle for Tora Bora. That would be a tough one to confirm. He also said that his commanders had met with an "Arab envoy" just before the shooting began. Courteous words had been exchanged, and the al Qaeda envoy had explained, "You are our Muslim brothers and we will not fight with you, we are waiting for the infidels [non-Muslims] to arrive with their own ground troops." After that, the Arabs and Chechens had withdrawn farther into the mountains to hunker down and await the expected "arrival of the Americans."

By late afternoon, however, it became clear that many of the al Qaeda fighters intended to make a stand, no matter who the enemy happened to be. They withdrew into bunkers fortified with scrap metal in hopes of drawing their attackers into the mountains and into the trap of their crossfire. Cornered by several dozen members of the Western press, Sorhab Qadri, a short and rather clever-looking intelligence official for Ali, admitted that his men had still taken no prisoners. He gave the first hint, however, that bin Laden might well have vanished from the scene. His words, as Mashal interpreted for most of the Western press corps, left the issue of the al Qaeda chief's presence in Tora Bora open to speculation that would grow and grow in the coming days. "He [bin Laden] was here a few days ago, but we think he has now gone underground." Did that mean he was in a cave or had fled the scene? Qadri wasn't saying, probably because he didn't know. In Washington, though, U.S. officials, following the leads of the confident General Franks and the vice president, stuck to their guns. They announced their strong suspicions that bin Laden remained in or around Tora Bora. They said that their efforts to capture him remained focused on the cave complex.

After a warm night spent back at the Spin Ghar, calming our nerves with a bottle of Johnny Walker, we piled back into our Corolla and sped to the front lines again on December 6. On the second morning, the crowds of children were again out in force. We left Karim Abdul off on a side road and asked him to try to walk as close to Tora Bora as he could, moving in the direction of a village, Upper Pachir, situated on the eastern perimeter of the fight. He did this on his own as we headed back up the camel's back. His mission was to try to reestablish the contacts we had made earlier inside the redoubt.

As we passed into the hills, scores of fresh fighters were crouched around campfires sipping green tea before their own forays into the mountains. At the crest of the hill, the T-55s were again hammering the hillsides. We soon encountered a curious Afghan gentleman who called himself "Bomber Khan." Khan claimed to have been a repairman of Russian tanks for the last two decades. Ali had ordered him to get the T-55s in working order, and he was now displaying his profound pride in his own accomplishments. Each time the tank let loose a round into the nearby hills, Bomber would first plug his ears, then begin to dance, a little circular jig that proved him quite agile on his feet. "That is the sound of music!" he shouted to us so loud that we were tempted to plug our ears again. Apparently, Bomber could no longer hear the strength of his own voice. He tried teaching Jon to perform the Bomber jig, but the efforts were soon lost in a haze of dust and cannon smoke.

The Arabs had begun the morning by firing mortars and machine guns back down the mountain, though none of their bullets had hit

U.S.-allied Afghans. Rather than spend the entire morning with the tank repairman, Mashal, Jon, and I decided to try and work our way closer to the action. To do this we had to retrace our tracks and double back beneath the camel's back along an exposed ridge, in view of al Qaeda positions. After the road moved back around a bend that blanketed us from the firing line, we came up to another T-55 tank; it was firing about a round every ten minutes into the surrounding hills. Several of Zaman's men on our left flank hunkered down behind large boulders. Another round echoed forth, and the chassis of our car quaked. We decided to take cover, ducking behind the tank.

After an hour down in the dirt with the fighters, we watched as a red pickup whipped around the bend and skidded to a halt. A young fighter, maybe seventeen, standing in the bed let out a sorrowful wail, "We have a martyr, commander!" A weary officer strolled over and despondently lifted up a flannel blanket, its gray threads stained burgundy with the blood of the fighter beneath. The commander shook his head. We also stood up from behind the tank and walked over to look. Riddled with bullets, the body had already stiffened, its eyes closed and the face waxy and blue. I wondered if he had a mother down the hill and whether she would understand the cause he had been fighting for. Would she have known anything about the World Trade Center, or for that matter the al Qaeda network?

The same commander was kind enough to provide us with access to his radio. We listened as bin Laden's fighters chatted back and forth. Mashal tried to make contact with them by querying them in Arabic, but they made no direct reply. They were apparently standing at the mouths of bunkers or caves much deeper in the heart of Tora Bora. We could hear them loud and clear. "OK. You can come out shooting," said one Arab to another. "The planes have flown past." Bin Laden's fighters were taking a beating, but at this point they were shrugging it off. It sounded as though they were relishing their first taste of battle with their U.S.-backed Afghans. They may still have been hoping to see the whites of American eyes. The al Qaeda fighters repeated in Arabic what they said had been an order from Osama bin Laden himself: "The Sheikh says keep your children in the caves and fight for Allah. Give guns to your wives as necessary to fight against the infidel aggressors." That didn't, of course, mean bin Laden was directing the battle on the front lines himself. A messenger on foot or horseback could well have delivered the order from across the mountains in Pakistan. In any case, it sounded like an excellent news lead—"Osama's Burqa Brigade Enters the Fray!" The image of Osama's wives taking up arms to defend him did not mesh well with anyone's idea of what we had expected from the al Qaeda chief.

Mashal, Jon, and I spent much of the afternoon listening in on the terror network's radio chatter. It was amusing, to say the least. At one stage Mashal managed to get a word in edgewise, and a response back from an Arab commando. "What are you fighting for?" Mashal asked. The reply: "We are fighting for the right to live in our homeland free of the long and bloody imperialist hand of George Bush!" After that, Arabs switched channels, and we did not hear from them for the rest of the day.

Having lost our source of entertainment and possible news, we decided to skirt around a hillside and collect leaflets dropped from the skies by our own bombers. The fliers, created by psychological operations teams back at Fort Bragg, North Carolina, told Afghans that the U.S. military was fighting "terrorists," not local Afghans. One side showed the face of bin Laden, the other his top Egyptian lieutenant, Dr. Ayman al-Zawahiri. The goal, written in English and Pashto, was to rid Afghanistan of Osama bin Laden and his cohorts, who had attacked the Pentagon and the World Trade Center. The fliers called on the Afghan inhabitants of the region to support the U.S.-led efforts. But not everyone on our side of the lines was taking the American efforts seriously.

Later in the day, back up at the press corps's headquarters on the camel's back, a slender figure with a new beard of soft, brown fluff proudly announced to us that he had worked on the caves with a jackhammer to help al Qaeda prepare for the showdown. His handiwork complete, he too had fallen back into the role of a voyeur, curious as we were about who would come out on top. He scoffed at the idea of switching sides and doubted that the Americans would or could carry out their vow to capture or kill bin Laden. "We want to see how brave the Americans and British really are," he announced. "Osama is not our enemy, he is yours. We want to see the U.S. soldiers [come down and] fight, not just wear baby coats and fly about our skies." I had informed the young man through Mashal that I was an American. His words came across as a taunt. I looked over at Jon as he gave me an "I told you so" glance. I hung my head in embarrassment. I couldn't help but wonder myself where the GIs were. I had seen former Taliban, new allies, pretending to chase after bin Laden in the hills, but none of our own elite fighters had yet appeared. It disturbed me for several reasons, not least of which was that I really wanted to see bin Laden strung up by his toes. The Western press corps had swelled to the size of a small battalion in the last two weeks. The U.S. military had no barriers to entry; it certainly had overflight rights in Pakistan, as well as landing rights in Afghanistan. With the continuing gunshots and tank blasts, empty words, and unrealistically low casualties, the battle we were covering was looking increasingly like a charade.

## Geraldo Bites the Dust

The next day, December 7, I had a partial answer to my quandary about where our men were hiding out. American forces had already taken up positions with Afghans, but since they numbered first a dozen and later only two dozen, they were difficult to keep tabs on. They worked diligently, but, as their commander, Colonel Mulholland, later explained to me, they were not in Tora Bora to engage in cave-to-cave fighting. They were tasked exclusively with marking targets and providing both logistical and tactical advice to the Afghans.

That morning, we had caught our first passing glimpse of U.S. fighters on the ground. At the base of the camel's back, near the entry of the Mileva Valley, two trucks with what looked like three bearded Western military advisers rushed past. The sunglasses and light hair and skin behind the tinted glass was a dead giveaway. They were headed toward the front lines. Later, at the end of the day, as we retreated back to the Spin Ghar, we overtook three more U.S. soldiers, one with blond hair, a rough beard, and a pakol. They were racing back from the front line in a red pickup truck, indistinguishable from those used by the warlords, but this time we weren't going to let them get away without grilling them a bit on the fighting. We ordered our driver to brake and put a tail on them, hoping that they might grant us a short interview. Like the elite British SAS, the Green Berets are a particularly secretive organization, though, and their orders at this juncture certainly did not include talking with confused reporters. Their driver quickly recognized that someone was in hot pursuit and picked up speed. We did the same, and our efforts soon turned into a wild chase with clouds of dust blinding our driver, who still somehow managed to negotiate the potholes and had no trouble keeping up with the bouncing, less stable pickup truck. Several miles into the race, we passed through a dust cloud and suddenly found ourselves facing a half-dozen of Hazret Ali's boys, who were lowering their guns at us and beckoning us to stop. The Green Berets, we could now see through the settling dust, had stopped to alert Ali's men that they were being chased by unknown elements. The warlord's fighters, in tennis shoes and the ubiquitous flowers behind their ears, now stood between us and our quarry. The chase was over. A gruff soldier told us to back away. "The Americans think you are trying to kill them. Please slow down." Another said the U.S. soldiers were his "true friends. We'll never win this thing without them. They've been down with us on the front lines within two hundred yards of the Arabs." Indeed, while the U.S. forces had made contact with Zaman, they operated in close coordination with Ali only. This had the effect of stoking anger in Zaman's camp; his men thought the Americans were not providing them the same kind of air cover. When several of Zaman's men were killed by errant U.S. air strikes three days into the fighting, the situation grew graver than ever.

On day three, al Qaeda harried Zaman's fighters, drew them into a cross fire, and then opened up with mortars. Over a dozen had already been killed in U.S. "friendly fire" bombings before the ground war; this attack took three more of Zaman's fighters. Zaman had finally journeyed to the front lines for his first full day, and after spending ample time with two of his favorite female correspondents, he granted us an interview, in which he raged against U.S. strategy— one he had both encouraged and approved of earlier—because it essentially put Afghans in charge of the attack on Tora Bora. "The

Americans are in the skies and my men are on the ground," he shouted. "We have been providing them with our best intelligence but the help has been too little. They prefer to work with that peasant Ali and his band of barbarians." Zaman insisted that he had offered the U.S. military the idea of using his own forces in a "siege of Tora Bora," but that the United States opted in favor of his rival, Hazret Ali, who, he said, wanted to pay others to do the real work. Notably, he was not yet accusing his rival of outright betrayal of the American cause. That would come later.

Despite Zaman's litany of complaints, the U.S. bombing in and around the Tora Bora redoubt had become far more accurate—almost overnight. On the front lines, tanks mottled the crisp blue skies with dust clouds that burst beneath the snow-capped peaks and reporters dove for cover behind bushes. Among the Afghans, fresh rumors circulated of "the Sheikh," Osama, prancing through the snowdrifts on his favorite stallion and inspiring his minions to keep fighting through the darkest nights. Editors were begging for any bone of information on bin Laden's whereabouts, prompting queries when Hazret Ali's brother, Kahlan Mir, gave an impromptu press conference. "Has anyone seen bin Laden?" someone shouted as a T-55 throttled the mountainside. Mir smiled optimistically, stroked his red henna beard, and said that he had been spotted a day earlier, "riding on horseback with about forty bodyguards" away from the front lines. Richard Lloyd-Parry, the *Independent* correspondent, who had earlier been lucky enough to snag a pair of bin Laden's briefs from a clothesline in Jalalabad, led his paper with this line. The story made waves in London and heightened the mood of anticipation around the world for the possible capture of the al Qaeda chief.

With bin Laden dashing through the drifts and calling al Qaeda wives to arms, the battle in the White Mountains had all the drama of a blockbuster. But a sideshow had become difficult to ignore—Geraldo Rivera. He traveled with an entourage of about a dozen producers, makeup artists, and cameramen. If Tora Bora lacked any real American war heroes, Fox News appeared out to supply one. His two producers represented the perfect contrast to the fearless front-line reporter. They wore helmets and flak jackets, while Geraldo preferred a mere bandana that came down nicely over his full head of hair and contrasted well with his bushy mustache. The image was crystal clear—"What, me worry?"

Already chummy with the "muj," Geraldo wanted his audience back home to view them as simply the best allies a man could ask for. "And these are great fighters, by the way. They don't have sleeping bags or uniforms, but they got courage, and they've been fighting these bad guys for years all on their own without any help from the rest of the world," he blustered, framed between bursting bombs with his back exposed to the al Qaeda front lines. "Now, they are truly the enemy of our enemy, so they're our friends," he commented, proving that analysis in a nutshell remained alive and well on the cable news networks. Geraldo's words provided simple logic for viewers back home, but within the Afghan context of shifting allegiances, duplicity, and betrayal, they pushed the envelope of veracity to all-time limits.

Rivera was brave. Whatever you said about him, he was more daring than many of us. From day one of the battle for Tora Bora, he had insisted on sleeping in the hills with his crew. Rita Cosby, an extremely attractive anchor, appeared enamored of Geraldo and impressed with his exploits. She felt his courage went far beyond the call of duty. "No reporter has the guts to stay and report from that very dangerous location tonight except for our very own Geraldo Rivera," she said.

Late on the third day of fighting, Rivera faced down what a *Wall Street Journal* editor would refer to as "the perfect moment," or "the money shot." There was a popping sound, a bullet flew past his bandana, and the brave reporter dove to the ground as the camera continued to roll. It was vintage comic-book action. "Poof!" Geraldo bit the dust, and "whoosh!" the fire blazed overhead. Back on his feet, eyeball to eyeball with the camera, our action hero shrugged it off. "I won't say it parted my hair, but it was close."

But Geraldo wasn't the only reporter in the field too involved in the story to question the motives of the warlords or U.S. military tactics on the ground, tactics that would soon have Osama lovers the world over gloating and chuckling. Other far more esteemed members of the Western press blandly repeated the Pentagon's line without daring to question battlefield tactics. In this way, the American public suffered a double hoodwinking. For not only were they watching our top brass present the charade, the Fourth Estate was selling them one in the disguise of a real battle. Had the Western press expressed more doubt about the viability of the Afghan warlords as proxies in this war, the battle for Tora Bora would likely have been viewed with far more skepticism as it unfolded in living rooms around the world.

Not long after his brush with death, we ran into Geraldo as we climbed up the side of a mountain. Jon Swain and I were also covered in dust. We had been under the false impression that we had been the targets of an explosion that ripped the skies some three hundred meters above us and just beneath a B-52 bomber. We were cowering facedown in the dust before we recognized that one of Ali's men had fired a rocket that had exploded early. It had been a false alarm. I kept thinking how embarrassed I would have been had my terror been caught on camera. Just about then, Jon saw Geraldo sauntering down the slope and insisted that I introduce him. It just so happened that Jon worked for the same boss as Geraldo, the media magnate Rupert Murdoch. Jon had long since put away his photos of the "wife from Waziristan." His new shtick—like a broken record—was repeating Rivera's now-famous line about kicking the corpse at Mazar-I-Sharif. "This amigo has taken the night train to the big adios!" he would say, kicking his foot over an imaginary corpse. Geraldo strolled down the hill toward us in his rose-tinted glasses and put the first word in. "Jon Swain, well finally! Your reputation, sir, precedes you," he said like one who knew what that meant. Huffing still to catch my breath, I let the two of them walk off together, considering which one would be remembered most for his exploits in this world or the next.

Geraldo's own battle with the demons of Tora Bora had already put him in hot water with the so-called respectable press. Our hero had made the unusually embarrassing mistake of confusing a "friendly fire" incident in the Tora Bora area with another such incident in the Kandahar area that had left three U.S. servicemen dead. In fact, in what Colonel Mulholland would later describe to me as the worst day of his life, three Green Berets had been killed and twenty American fighters had been wounded several hundred kilometers to the south of Tora Bora when a B-52 dropped a one-ton bomb on their flank. Geraldo, who had been in Tora Bora with us at the time of the attack, told his viewers that he had walked over the "hallowed ground" where the killing took place. It certainly qualified as an apocalyptic on-air experience. "It was just—the whole place— just fried, really, and bits of uniforms and tattered clothing every-where. I said the Lord's Prayer and really choked up." It all sounded a little too biblical to be true. Faced with steady accusations of dis-honesty and recalling that he had not had the services of a helicopter in recent days, Geraldo took a step back from the precipice and chalked his simple mistake up to "the fog of war." That wasn't enough for the scowling media critics back home, who, short of the capture of bin Laden himself, needed more heroes and villains to write about. When the *Baltimore Sun*'s television writer David Fol-kenflik, the first to point out Geraldo's blatant error, questioned his honesty in a couple of jeering columns, the Fox correspondent shot back with what sounded like an offer of matching six-shooters and an eighteenth-century–style gentlemanly showdown. "He has im-pugned my honor," he told the *Washington Post*'s own media critic, Howard Kurtz. "It is as if he slapped me in the face and challenged me to a duel. He is going to regret this story for the rest of his career. The time has come to stop Geraldo-bashing."

Geraldo was unfazed by the hullabaloo over his reporting. He had not yet begun to fight. He continued to crawl, belly down over scrap metal and bomblets while dodging increasingly unfriendly fire. He forged ahead in his ever more comic mission to expose the "rats" and "bad guys," commenting the day after his unfortunate "friendly fire" story that "the rat can still bite. . . . We're undaunted, though. We're going back up the hill. These guys are getting ready to mount their third straight day of assaults on the Tora Bora complex and then, you know, then it's going to get really ugly. Then it's going to be brutal hand to hand, eyeball to eyeball, bayonet to bayonet fight-ing to root the rats our of their nest." Geraldo was slowly but surely reverting to the super-hype and purple prose of his days as a tabloid exposé reporter. War—or possibly just the altitude—was definitely going to his head. He started behaving like a twelve-year-old at his first boxing match. I preferred to think of it as possible overindulgence in Superman comic-book fare as a youngster.

"How's this, Osama?" he shouted on-air as a bomb blast ripped the mountaintops overhead. He sounded a little like Batman—or was it Robin? He continued, "Remember September 11th!" The fiery half–Puerto Rican now set his eyes again on his mission to take down the dastardly bin Laden, reciting a Sting lyric that did not appear to reflect the Pentagon's own ability to keep track of the terror chief: "Every move you make, every step you take, we'll be watching you!"

Geraldo, like not a few other reporters on the scene, appeared to convince himself that Osama bin Laden was still in Tora Bora. How did he know that? Well, he claimed he felt the "vibrations." A couple of days later, echoing an "OK Corral" gunslinger fantasy, he made a bold prediction for his viewers, some of whom had grown increasingly skeptical of his insights. "Osama will be caught at high noon tomorrow."

"Was this the wild, wild West?" I asked Jon in a fit of confusion.

"No, my friend," answered Jon, setting me back on course. "This is the crazy, fucking East. Where nothing is as it seems."

Only six months after the battle for Tora Bora, a toy company named Dragon Models came out with a new line of U.S. soldier toys. The line was named "American Freedom Fighters: live from the Afghanistan front line." The line came with individually named figures, the most popular of which soon proved to be "Tora Bora Ted," a Delta Force special operations soldier. He was, as the company's promotion, explained a "fully posable" action figure. It said that "'Ted' is a member of the Delta Force Night OPS Tora Bora and comes with an M16, night-vision goggles, a hand grenade, a walkie-talkie, an MK23 Carbine, an M4 Submachine Gun with an M4 SR5 sight scope and more." I judged this a clever takeoff on the farce that went on in Afghanistan during the month of December 2001 and called Jon in London to get his take. We both agreed that it would have been far more appropriate to have come up with a "Tora Bora Geraldo" figure, since he had been a far more visible, albeit less than heroic character during the battle. The marketing of this new version of "GI Joe" made Jon wonder, however, if the young boys playing with Tora Bora Ted in their sandboxes would ever grow up to learn "the real story of how bin Laden gave the Yanks the slip at Tora Bora."

## Chic Friends of the Sheikh

By the fifth day of the battle, December 10, all the terrified creatures that could flee the battle had done so or were about to make their move. Afghan villagers captured two panicked monkeys stranded beside a rushing stream at the base of the front lines. Fighters had spotted tigers and wild boars fleeing the U.S. strikes. Jon and I, however, spotted some of the most elusive creatures, Green Berets, making their way toward the battle. On our way down one mountain and headed up another, we ran smack into a dozen of Mulholland's men, their faces swathed in checkered black-and-white—Palestinian style—bandanas. The U.S. soldiers lined the backs of shiny, new pickup trucks, washed by village boys that morning. Rather than have us chase them, as we had done once before, the Americans pulled off on the side of the mountain, hoping, I suspect, that we would ride past them without needling them or attempting to take their photograph. It was easy to understand their desire to be left alone, but we still wanted a word with them, which was, after all, our job. It might have been useful to the readers back home as well to take notes on what their laser guns actually looked like, I thought to myself.

At this stage in the battle, the Pentagon's hype had already begun sounding stale, and we wanted a quote or two "from the ground" to put the fighting in perspective. Jon shouted across a fifty-foot swale between the road and an imposing rock face where the U.S. troops now milled beside their trucks, anxiously awaiting our departure. He asked if they believed any senior al Qaeda leaders were still inside Tora Bora. No doubt he wanted to hear word of bin Laden's elusive movements. His question was met with utter silence, as though the Green Berets had been ordered not to say a single word. It felt as though he had addressed his query to the rock face, not the men in black-and-white bandanas. The U.S. fighters were up against the mountainside and didn't have anywhere to go, unless they wanted to jump back in their vehicles and tear off past us. If they had wanted to do that, they could have tried that already. We decided to approach them cautiously, maybe offer them a cigarette and a drink of water in exchange for a "hello." We also wanted to make clear that we were not the "enemy." Then we heard the unmistakable release of a safety on a machine gun. I looked to my right and noticed that a Pakistani or Afghan driver, standing alongside several Green Berets, had raised his weapon and was pointing it at the two of us. In retrospect, it might have been wise to slink back to our taxi, but the prospect of friendly fire goaded us on. "That would make a good headline, 'Osama Flies the Coop and Green Beret Allies Take Down Overzealous Reporters,'" I said, addressing the Pakistani. Jon had a more appropriate line: "Go ahead, make my day!" he shouted as we gave up our hunt for a good quote. We turned and left them to their duties.

As we rumbled farther into the mountains later in the day, the real Afghan winter had already begun to descend on the White Mountains. The wind howled as a flutter of light snow carpeted the dusty foothills. When we came upon Zaman, he was strolling up toward the front lines on foot with a contingent of some forty armed men. He had his usual brown blanket wrapped tightly around his woolen pakol. His face had an unusually pained expression, his jaw so swollen that he seemed to have a ping-pong ball lodged in his lower cheek. Toothaches were something that Afghan warlords endured, not something they treated. Our favorite warlord didn't appear to be in a mood to talk, but we hit him up anyway. He responded in nearly incomprehensible French, *"Ils font fes fous, ils font fes fous"* (They are fools, they are fools). It sounded as though he was chewing a rather large candy bar and talking at the same time.

Despite his obvious misery, the unexpected arrival of his favorite female reporter, Megan Stack, cheered Zaman momentarily. The crusty old man had kept up his end of the bargain and was still hoping for more. Like clockwork, he had been providing the *LA Times* reporter with all the information he could for her late-night deadlines. But Stack had recently gotten some competition for the old man's heart in the form of Janine "The Machine" Di Giovanni, the swashbuckling American star of the *London Times*. Janine is quite possibly the most aggressive female war reporter on the international set. She has considerable talent, and she knows how to use it.

Hounded for news by his favorite ladies, Zaman offered the entire Western press a chance to tour his front. Few of us had the horsepower in our own vehicles to blast up the rock and gravel of the road's steep incline. Zaman's party was leaving, however, and so several dozen journalists attempted to leap into the beds of pickups along with the young fighters. Annoyed at the extra weight, Zaman ordered his soldiers to throw several hacks, Jon and me included, off at gunpoint. Janine, however, had another idea. She opened Zaman's door and thrust her ample derriere into his lap. Instantly, the warlord's ping-ponged cheek broke into a jagged grin as he set his foot to the floorboards and ripped off up the mountain with his new interest soundly in his lap. For Janine, all was fair in love and war. Her charms only made those of us with fewer assets jealous of her talents.

Jon, Mashal, and I decided to march ahead on foot in an attempt to reach Zaman's forward positions. We set out walking along a goat path in the shadow of a dirt road as al Qaeda fighters hidden behind the next mountain shot down at anyone foolish enough to take the high road. Nearby, T-55 tanks were moving along as U.S.-backed Afghans seized one mountain after another. Shots pinged around the base of a tank we slipped behind for cover. Just over the next mountain, we could see a B-52 homing in on its prey. I hadn't gotten much sleep the night before, and this may have contributed to my vision of the plane as a giant eagle emptying its bowels. The bomber unleashed its load with a thunderous roar that rocked the earth a mile away.

As the ground settled after the massive explosion, we continued along, running low, almost touching the ground with our knuckles as we sprinted across a hill exposed to enemy fire. On the now-barren hillside, U.S. bombs had ripped shrubs from their roots and cut small trees in half. Huge metal shards had torn the ground. The casings of two-thousand-pound bombs littered the barren slope. One of the empty shells carried a rare message from an American crew member, Gary. It read: "This bomb is going to shine like a bright light in the goat's ass." Mashal judged the message to be a little more pointed than the psy-ops leaflets denouncing the "evil" bin Laden that littered the ground beside the casing. During the battle of Tora Bora, you sometimes needed to be reminded that angry and determined beings aboard U.S. ships floated somewhere out there on the Arabian Sea or Indian Ocean. This was a war fought from afar, but not without the gusto of real warriors.

As we approached Zaman's forward position, one of his men waved to us to get down and take cover with him behind a large boulder at the top of a hill. He held a walkie-talkie, and again we had the opportunity to listen to the al Qaeda fighters. Their boasting of a few days earlier had been replaced by far less optimistic talk of caring for the wounded. "Call the doctor," chirped an Arabic voice over the radio. "Call the doctor up the hill as soon as possible." The same dispatcher then warned in familiar language, "London calling. Danger. More planes. Watch out and get back in your caves." More precise U.S. bombing now permitted our Afghan allies to crawl forward and follow up the immense bomb blasts with the chatter of their Kalashnikovs and crashing whooshes of their rocket launchers.

Vague and uncertain talk of surrender began the next day, December 11. As we listened in, though, we realized that the negotiations reflected earlier calls from the Eastern Shura aimed at securing the peaceful departure of the Arabs rather than a handover of weapons and presumed surrender to Washington. The Arab fighters used an Afghan translator to convey their wishes carefully. "Our guest brothers want to find safe passage out of your province," said an Afghan negotiator from behind al Qaeda lines. He was talking to Zaman, who stood on a peak just out of our eyeshot, jabbering back at them. Zaman replied, "Our blood is your blood, your wives our sisters, and your children our children. But under the circumstances, I am compelled to tell you that you must either leave or surrender." It was the same old talk of "give in or get out," and it reminded me of how little the CIA or Green Berets had managed to persuade Zaman of the real goal of his fight.

That was not to say that killing wasn't taking place. The Afghan fighters had just overrun a Chechen machine-gun position and killed four al Qaeda fighters. Machine-gun fire had riddled two of the corpses, but the Afghans had executed two others—damn the Geneva Conventions—who had been in their custody, or at least that is what they happily claimed. Beneath the scene of mayhem, I stood with Mashal and Jon on top of a bunker beneath snow-capped peaks just a few hundred meters in the distance. Off to one side, standing near a grove of pine trees, Hazret Ali was sending up orders to his own men. He had overheard Zaman's manner of negotiating with the al Qaeda fighters, and he probably knew that it would upset his American friends. He shouted into his own handset that "no deals" were to be made. "There will be surrender or death!" he snapped.

Zaman had a quick reply for Ali. "Hey, if you want to hold this ridge, send your own men up here! You are down there with the press and the pretty ladies, and I'm stuck up here." Both men chuckled. It was all in a day's pay, but—as we learned from Zaman's lieutenants much later in the day—the Special Forces team leader, an anonymous forty-something gentleman with a touch of gray on his temples whom we had spotted a few days earlier entering the mountain redoubt and disappearing behind a ridge, was outraged. He had orders, of course, to capture or kill the al Qaeda fighters. The mere suggestion that they could "leave" the area stank of betrayal. Zaman continued for some time to banter back and forth with the al Qaeda translator. They still had given no definite indication that they planned to surrender. Still, it did not seem possible that al Qaeda could hold out in the White Mountains much longer. We sensed— and were looking to prove—that they were already taking an easier way out.

As we stood listening to the lively negotiations, Mashal noticed that another Jalalabad-based warlord, one who had remained in the shadows for weeks, had joined "our side." It was none other than Awol Gul, the commander for Younus Khalis, the frail, red-bearded Eastern Shura leader who had earlier unleashed the nastiest sneers of all at the U.S. efforts to capture bin Laden. Zaman and his sometimes ally Hazret Ali had persuaded Gul—mostly through cash installments, as they latter explained—to hand over several dozen tanks that the Taliban had given him when they fled the city on November 13. This did not mean that Gul had taken the bait, though; he made it clear that his sympathies with the al Qaeda network were as solid as ever. He joined us on top of the bunker, the roof seemingly about to collapse under the combined weight of two correspondents, one interpreter, and the hefty commander.

Gul, I must say, looked nothing like I had expected. He wasn't fat or athletic or mean looking, but rather diminutive, with a caved-in chest and a small potbelly that appeared to have consumed what his upper body had lost. The warlord sounded mild mannered and almost professorial in his speech. He delivered a tantalizingly cryptic analysis of the evolving situation. "They've been under quite a bit of pressure inside there," he said, sounding as though he now pitied his old friends. "It is likely that they have made a tactical withdrawal. They have good roads, safe passage, and bin Laden has plenty of friends. We are not interested in killing the Arabs. They are our Muslim brothers."

There it was, my "quote of the day." Of course, it was hardly worth including in a dispatch. Who would know one Afghan warlord from the next, especially if even the U.S. military could not distinguish the good guys from the bad guys? It was a disturbing prospect. Within two weeks, Ali would have Gul arrested and blame him for betraying the Americans, when in truth they were equally guilty. Rival Zaman, at Ali's urgings, would pay the price that same evening for his lackadaisical negotiating approach of "give in or get lost." With the nod of the Green Berets, Ali blocked Zaman's fighters from roads leading to the heaviest fighting. This diversion left hundreds of fighters looking down the barrels of their machine guns at their erstwhile allies. Colonel Mulholland had put Ali in charge of contacts with the enemy, and Ali, standing on a mountain peak, informed the world that there would be "no talks with terrorists."

This boast did not hit home. For Ali, the aiding and abetting of al Qaeda went on behind the scenes, as we had witnessed in the lobby of the Spin Ghar Hotel only days before the opening of the battle for Tora Bora. Closer to the Pakistani border, Ali's deal making was as much about hard cash as it was about loyalty to religion and tribe. Ali's lieutenants, who later claimed to have been "double-crossed" by so-called bin Laden sympathizers, refused, however, to take the blame. One of Ali's top commanders, Musa, sitting cross-legged in a loft above a garage full of fighters, told us later that a wily commander named Ilyas Khel, whom Ali had assigned to guard the Pakistani border, had acted as an outright escort for al Qaeda. "Our problem was that the Arabs had paid him more, and so Ilyas Khel just showed the Arabs the way out of the country into Pakistan," Musa moaned unconvincingly. Khel, a tall and limber forty-year-old commander with a reputation for summary executions in the war against the Russians, had done more than escort the enemy to safety. Indeed, Afghan proxy fighters, Zaman loyalists from villages on the border, told us how they had engaged in running battles with Khel's fighters, who, they claimed, had been "firing cover for escaping al Qaeda." Khel, who turned out to be a very successful double agent, had entered Ali's ranks after having served Awol Gul, Younus Khalis's commander.

That Ali had trusted a junior commander of Gul—even before making deals with him to draw him into a temporary pact on the front lines—suggested to us that the escapes were part of a much broader conspiracy to assist al Qaeda right through to the end. While concerns about other warlords led the U.S. military to rely primarily on Ali, he may just have been the smoothest talker of the bunch. He knew, in terms of financial and military assistance, what being an "ally" to the United States would mean for his good fortune, and he was willing to say whatever was necessary to maneuver himself into that position—his actual intentions aside. His successful ouster of Zaman from the Jalalabad area, with American complicity, some weeks after the battle for Tora Bora, bore witness to his unchallenged success as a slick operator.

As gun smoke drifted from peak to peak in the mountains, it became clear that the fight for Tora Bora had a shadow battleground thousands of miles away in the halls of U.S. power, where Rumsfeld and his top brass still couldn't decide how to tackle the world's most important manhunt. Publications that took Pentagon spokesmen at their word prepared their stories following the official line. Terry Atlas, the national and foreign editor of *U.S. News & World Report*, asked me to think about what I could add to bin Laden's obituary—or capture—in a day or two when the battle wound down and the results were in. At the same time, the *New York Times* reported a confident-sounding senior U.S. military officer in Washington describing the terror chief's dwindling chances. "He's in a shrinking area," he said. "And the sense is, he's going higher and deeper into his complex of caves and tunnels." Despite the officer's assertion that the U.S. and Afghan troops had contained Osama in an ever-tightening noose, such a maneuver only works if the noose forms a complete circle. Since the military operation had failed to secure all sides of the redoubt, trying to push al Qaeda deeper into the cave complex simply pushed them toward an easy escape route leading into the lawless tribal regions of Pakistan. Though Pakistan had promised in late November to move forces up to the border, they arrived only in mid-December, due both to logistical headaches and to resistance from tribesmen in the Northwestern Frontier Province, who lived along a long-disputed border and did not even recognize Pakistani hegemony. At the same time, Pakistani authorities had continued to reject the idea of allowing U.S. forces into their country in a combat role. Only small numbers of Americans were allowed to operate out of Pakistan for "search and rescue" missions. Those obstacles left the Pentagon with a tough choice: placing hundreds of more conventional U.S. forces on the ground in a "siege" inside Afghanistan or leaving the heavy lifting to our erstwhile allies.

# 5

## OPERATION VAMPIRE

Dynamite in the hands of a child is not more dangerous
than a strong policy weakly carried out.

—Winston Churchill,
*The Story of the Malakand Field Force*

### Voices from the Inferno

With surrender negotiations seeming to have reached an impasse,
Mashal and I decided to redirect our efforts. Our mission, apart from
capturing or killing bin Laden—which was really more of a joke
between friends—was to get some kind of inside scoop on the secretive undertakings inside Tora Bora. Was bin Laden fighting or fleeing? What were the hardcore fighters inside Tora Bora thinking?
Were they panicking or fighting as determined martyrs? For answers
to these daunting questions, we returned to our original al Qaeda
liaisons in Jalalabad to try to reestablish contact with the terror network. We had only thin leads, but Mashal and Karim Abdul had
picked up on intelligence about several "safe houses" supposedly situated not far from the fighting. These houses, we understood, provided refuge for the families of escaping al Qaeda members and other
important "friends of the Sheikh."

In the late afternoon of December 11, on our way back to Jalalabad from the front, Mashal and I returned to a fork in the road,
drove past the NBC house and the U.S. Special Forces base, and con-

tinued for another hour in an entirely new direction. A smirking Lala Agha rode in the backseat with us that afternoon, his shrunken frame contorted as always by polio. In addition to Karim Abdul's enterprising investigations along the eastern flank of Tora Bora, Lala had helped us reestablish contact with the Afghan tribal sources who had introduced Mashal to the Sudanese security chief two weeks earlier. Now he was pointing to the bends in the road and directing our driver back to that same village. We crossed out of the main battle zone, driving along the base of the mountains toward Pakistan for a few kilometers and then into a valley that led directly into the most important warren of caves inside Tora Bora. Our driver negotiated a rock bed and forded a stream. It was a strange drive, not least because we saw no armed men along the way. We could barely hear the chatter of machine guns farther to the west. Afghan fighters allied with Washington had never bothered to move into Upper Pachir, leaving the village in the control of al Qaeda sympathizers, who, as we would soon discover, had long since organized an "underground railway" to move family and fighters out of the fray. It was a dangerous area, and villagers had warned us that we should think twice about going farther. As we neared the village, we decided as a safety precaution to back our taxi down the long, narrow dirt road leading into the village, so that we could flee at top speed if necessary.

Once safely inside Upper Pachir, Mashal exited the taxi and walked up a small hill, where he rapped on the door to which Lala had directed him. Meanwhile, I ducked down in my seat and pulled my pakol tightly around my ears. A small, hunchbacked man answered, and another man in a black turban soon appeared behind him. Makmud, the rough-looking character in the black turban, had been an al Qaeda machine gunner and still served the network as a sympathetic Afghan with great sway in his own village, Upper Pachir. Makmud told Mashal that he had someone for his Western reporter "friends to meet." The three talked for ten minutes before Mashal returned to inform me that he had managed to set up an interview tomorrow morning—which he had been led to believe would be with several Arabs. As before, Makmud insisted on a meeting in "a place and time" of al Qaeda's choosing. He also wanted two hundred dollars for his trouble, a fee that sounded exorbitant on the surface, but was in fact minimal in view of the wartime inflation that had hit all standard "fixing fees" once the battle started.

We knew we could not trust Makmud, a serpentine man with hollow-set, dark eyes. However, since we knew from our Jalalabad sources, including Babrak Khan, that he remained in the employ of al Qaeda, he was at least close to the action about which we wanted information. As he had explained to Lala weeks earlier, he no longer fought, but rather acted as a security agent in Upper Pachir. When we returned to the Spin Ghar, we chased down Jon Swain, who was in the restaurant trying to digest a plate of rice and a single chicken wing. I had long since decided to rely on Jon to make the final decision on any potentially life-threatening scenario. He had twenty-five years' experience as a correspondent and a three-month-long kidnapping episode in Africa to steel his decision making. Though we seriously weighed the possibility of going to this meeting on our own, Jon advised that we send Mashal as our envoy and squeeze as much out of the interviews as possible. Mashal, ever the intrepid mole, agreed, of course, to go forward into the dark abyss the next day. As Mashal's experience would ultimately prove, had Jon and I returned to Upper Pachir, we might never have escaped to tell the fascinating tale that emerged.

The morning of December 12, Mashal dropped me off on the front lines and doubled back with the driver in the direction of Upper Pachir. When they arrived, they turned down a narrow dirt road and parked in the marketplace as Makmud had instructed them to do the day before. Next, two vegetable vendors told them to wait in the confines of a shuttered shop. About fifteen minutes later, two thugs showed up with blindfolds and a promise to escort them to "a secret location." One of the men had a large, bloody gash in his chin, and another carried a curved dagger in his belt. Both held shiny new Kalashnikovs and spat tobacco juice in the dirt as they spoke. The driver, a young family man of some twenty-five years, had not bargained for either a blindfold or a secret meeting. He panicked and tried to jump up and run for his taxi.

"Not so fast," said the thug with the scar. The men told the driver he didn't have a choice and hit him in the shoulders with their rifle butts, pounding him back down to his chair. For good measure, one of them also whacked Mashal across the back of his head. The thugs fixed blindfolds across their eyes and threw them in the bed of a truck. They drove around the hills for fifteen minutes before depositing Mashal and his driver at Makmud's home. Since Mashal recognized the inside of the house from the day before, the necessity of the blindfolds escaped him. Makmud stormed in.

He was steaming. "Where are the foreigners?" he demanded. "What did we agree to?" He was decidedly annoyed that Mashal had arrived on his own. "You said you had an American and a Brit. What is this?" He bore down on them and instructed the guards to beat the pair again with their rifle butts. The thugs slapped and beat them for five minutes. Mashal felt terrified for one of the first times in his adult life. He pleaded to be allowed to leave, but Makmud just scowled and asked for the money, holding out his hand.

Mashal handed over the cash, believing that it would not pay for any interview, since he had apparently become a prisoner. Makmud appeared to confirm this notion as he stormed out the door with the uncounted wad of money, the two guards in tow, demanding that Mashal and the driver remain there until he returned. The two heard a truck engine start as Makmud and his guards drove back down the hill.

Only moments after Makmud left the room, Mashal heard the groaning of someone in pain. The moans, which sounded like those of an older gentleman, grew louder, and then a door connecting two rooms swung open. A small child peeked out from the cracked door before disappearing back into the dark. Though still terrified, after waiting twenty minutes Mashal stood up and walked over to the door. He swung it open. Attended by two children and a woman, a short but hefty man of about fifty years lay stretched out on a couch. Mashal could immediately see that the gentleman's leg had been amputated or blown off at the shin. The leg, swathed in bandages, had turned a burgundy color, saturated with dried blood. The man grimaced as his wife wiped beads of perspiration from his forehead.

When he saw Mashal, the man sat up in his seat. He appeared flustered and asked Mashal in Arabic to identify himself. Searching for common ground, Mashal quickly dropped a few names of al Qaeda sympathizers, including Younis Khalis's military commander,

Awol Gul. This seemed to ease the discomfort of the man, who slowly warmed to Mashal's presence, apparently thinking that he might also be a sympathizer. With some mild urging, he gave his name as Abu Jaffar and said he was not a warrior but a "financial supporter of the Sheikh," bin Laden, and that he had arrived in Jalalabad with a donation for al Qaeda some six months earlier. He described strong ties with the clerical community in his own country.

Mashal recognized that Makmud had left him to conduct the promised interview, but he wasn't sure if the Saudi had been informed of his interest, so he began casually, asking the gentleman how he had come to such pain.

"I was in the cave and the U.S. planes had been bombing out front," the Saudi told him in a gruff, weak voice as his rotund Egyptian wife stroked his forehead. "I stepped out to see what was happening and stepped on a mine that exploded and splintered my foot."

As the Saudi began his story, his wife moved away and caressed the forehead of a young boy, who stood with her near a potbellied stove in the corner. Over the next two hours, Abu Jaffar related a tale that dovetailed with what we had heard from al Qaeda members and sympathizers, though he offered far more details concerning the movements of bin Laden.

His religious studies at Cairo's renowned al Ahzar University had prepared him, he insisted, for a life of rigorous devotion to Allah. "I came to Jalalabad with nearly three million dollars, which had been collected from charities in Saudi Arabia," he said. "Osama asked me to stay on with him and then this trouble started." The Saudi had ridden in the same vehicle with bin Laden on November 13, the night the convoy had entered Tora Bora. Jaffar described the night in some detail—including how tense the evening had been when the cars gathered on the southern edge of Jalalabad. After the drive south through the desert and to the foot of the White Mountains, the convoy had stopped in a small village in the foothills. Bin Laden's men had given the local Ghilzi tribesmen four hundred Kalashnikovs in exchange for a promise to transport bin Laden to Paracinar, a bustling tribal metropolis well inside Pakistan, when the time was right. After the meeting, the fleeing Taliban governor, Maulvi Abdul Kabir, who had accompanied bin Laden's convoy to the Ghilzi village, bid his own farewell to Jaffar and bin Laden, and headed off to Pakistan with a large entourage.

Upon hearing her husband relating the details of their flight into Tora Bora, the Egyptian woman began to sob. "I've seen my sweet brothers and sisters killed by fire from the sky. Alas, I've begged them to leave [Tora Bora] and they have refused. They want to die back there for the sake of Allah."

When they arrived at their final destination inside Tora Bora, Abu Jaffar and his wife had moved into a cave with bin Laden. "We were deep in the mountain, but we had everything we needed to survive," said Jaffar. "But when the bombing started, all my wife and I could think about was how to get out alive."

Jaffar said that bin Laden left Tora Bora for one week, almost immediately after they arrived in mid-November, for a meeting with the Taliban ruler, Mullah Mohammed Omar. The Saudi contended that Dr. Ayman al-Zawahiri, the terror chief's top adviser and number two, never returned from that meeting. Jaffar confirmed an additional detail that had appeared in an Egyptian newspaper only a week earlier—that U.S. bombs had killed most of al-Zawahiri's immediate family.

Mashal, anxious that Makmud would return soon in a wrathful mood, quickly steered the conversation to the whereabouts of bin Laden. The Saudi said that bin Laden had followed up on the promise by the Ghilzi tribesmen, who were loyal to the Taliban's former governor in Jalalabad, Maulvi Abdul Kabir. He said simply and somewhat convincingly, "Osama left again just over a week to ten days ago and headed to Pakistan, where he was helped across the border by tribesmen." The Saudi did not claim to know where bin Laden had ended up, but his account suggested that the terror chief had planned to remain within several hundred miles of the Tora Bora base and that he had also taken a strong interest in the outcome of the battle.

Several days after his departure into Pakistan, bin Laden sent a replacement—his young, married son, known by the nom de guerre Salah Uddin. Three or four days after his departure, Osama had called back into Tora Bora with a message, said Jaffar. "He told us not to fear and that 'tomorrow my son will be in Mileva [inside Tora

Bora].'" said Jaffar. The young son traveled with "thirty Arabs and fifty Afghans" from Ghazni in central Afghanistan, through the Gardez and Asrow areas, into southeast Afghanistan in Paktia Province, and finally on to Tora Bora. The Saudi added that the arrival of bin Laden's son had lifted spirits inside the mountain redoubt just when they had hit a low point of fear and indecision. Further, he insisted that Salah Uddin had acted as the sole representative of the bin Laden family inside the Tora Bora terror base.

Jaffar's own strong ties to bin Laden's family meant a lot to the Saudi. "Osama is my good friend," he said, adding that his own son had worked closely with Salah Uddin at an al Qaeda camp in the Ghazni area. "Yesterday, Salah Uddin told me [I could] to leave [and he gave me money] because I will likely need another operation on my leg." The Saudi financier reached in his pocket and pulled out a wad of British banknotes. "We had doctors and nurses in our hospital, and they helped me. But they amputated it at the shin and told me that I had complications and recommended I try to leave."

Despite his injury, Jaffar, as a respected elder within the network, had been involved in the surrender talks with Zaman. The Arab view from inside Tora Bora, as he described it, went some way toward explaining why the talks had faltered. He claimed that most of the fighters left inside Tora Bora had been prepared to end their defense of the enclave after the departure of bin Laden ten days earlier. But just as the ground offensive had begun to unfold, al Qaeda loyalists learned erroneously through their spies in Jalalabad that "scores of British and American commandos" had arrived at Jalalabad airport. These rumors were based on sightings of choppers landing with supplies under the cover of night. Excitement at the prospect of facing off against the infidels swept through the mountain redoubt and inspired the fighters to hunker down and fight on. Abu Jaffar said that Chechen and Algerian fighters had resisted surrender more resolutely than had Saudi, Yemeni, or Egyptian nationals. The Saudi financier, who had left the Tora Bora camp only the previous afternoon, said that the idea of a genuine "surrender" was now acceptable only to a small segment of the remaining al Qaeda fighters, most of whose families had already fled. He gave a rough estimation of their numbers: on December 11, there had still been 250 Yemenis, 180

The author stands in a field near Kandahar with three cheerful Afghan boys. (By Lutfullah Mashal)

Trusted guide and interpreter Lutfullah Mashal. Mashal managed to infiltrate three al Qaeda terror bases with only a smile on his face and a twinkle in his eye. Belatedly, the CIA sought to obtain his services. (By Philip Smucker)

*Afghan warlord Haji Zaman returned from Dijon, France, to do America's bidding. In the end, his efforts came to naught and he was sidelined by his rival, Hazret Ali. (By Robert Harbison/© The Christian Science Monitor)*

*Haji Zaman and several fighters sit for tea on the lawn of a home in the Pakistani city of Peshawar, awaiting their opportunity to retake their old fiefdom near the Afghan city of Jalalabad. (By Robert Harbison/© The Christian Science Monitor)*

Afghan warlord Hazret Ali, whose fighters wore flowers in their hair and tennis shoes on their feet, became the American favorite during the battle for Tora Bora. Officers working under Ali's command betrayed the American cause and helped escort al Qaeda leaders and fighters to safety in Pakistan. (By Robert Harbison/© The Christian Science Monitor)

*Small-time Afghan warlord Haji Zahir holds an impromptu press conference. The Afghan warlords working with U.S. forces during the battle for Tora Bora relished the publicity and profited from the media feeding frenzy. (By Phil Hannaford)*

*U.S. B-52 bombers at 10,000 feet rain death on the mountains in the distance as Afghan fighters observe the fireworks from the "camel's back" ridge. (By Phil Hannaford)*

*An Afghan fighter hired by U.S. forces to help flush out al Qaeda leaders at Tora Bora looks on. Many of the fighters had switched sides only days earlier after defending Kabul and other Afghan cities from invading U.S.-backed forces. (By Phil Hannaford)*

*An Afghan fighter praises Allah just before going into battle against al Qaeda near Tora Bora. Afghans divided their loyalties between their own God and their new paymasters, the Americans. (By Phil Hannaford)*

*Fighters loyal to Afghan warlord Hazret Ali ride high on a rusting R-54/T-55 Russian tank as they charge headlong into al Qaeda's redoubt. (By Phil Hannaford)*

*American Green Berets wrapped in pakols and scarves moved in and out of the battle for Tora Bora disguised as locals. (By Phil Hannaford)*

*Pliable Afghan villagers with dubious loyalties helped al Qaeda fighters escape to Pakistan and Iran before, during, and after the battle of Tora Bora, most often using donkey or camel trains. (By Philip Smucker)*

*Fox News' frontline star Geraldo Rivera yuks it up with a British journalist at his base camp near Tora Bora. Geraldo ducked bullets and stumbled over "hallowed ground" on his way to providing high entertainment for his colleagues and the world. (By Phil Hannaford)*

*Al Qaeda prisoners on display in the aftermath of the battle for Tora Bora. A mix of Arabs, Uzbeks, and South Asians, the prisoners were shipped off to Cuba. (By Phil Hannaford)*

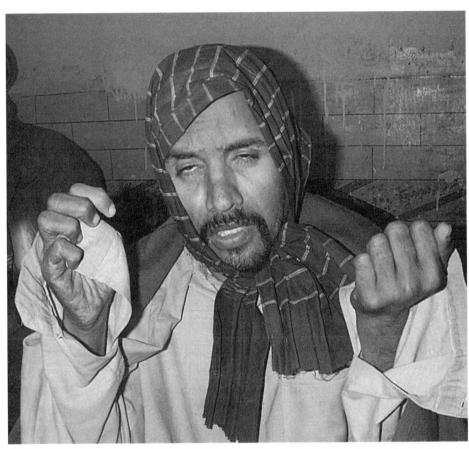

*Appearing bruised and battered by his Hazara captors, Mohamed Akram, who confessed he had worked as bin Laden's chef, gave a credible account of his master's flight from Tora Bora. (By Philip Smucker)*

*American psy-ops specialist (far right) wrapped in a black turban seeks intelligence on al Qaeda's whereabouts from friendly Afghan villagers. (By Philip Smucker)*

*A U.S. military surveillance shot of al Qaeda fighters preparing for battle in the mountains around Anaconda in March 2002. The black and white photo does not show that, either stupidly or fearlessly, both fighters are wearing red. (U.S. Army)*

*American fighters watch as a Chinook sets down on a ridge above the Shah-I-Kot Valley. Al Qaeda fighters took advantage of the Chinook's lumbering flight by shooting several of them down. (U.S. Army)*

*10th Mountain fighters deploy with heavy loads to hills around the Shah-I-Kot Valley as they prepare to flush out al Qaeda fighters. (U.S. Army)*

*A column of American foot soldiers snakes through the Shah-I-Kot Valley as forces go after dug-in al Qaeda fighters. (U.S. Army)*

*American fighters climbing into the mountains around Shah-I-Kot arrange their gear and keep a sharp eye out for the enemy. (U.S. Army)*

*101st Airborne fighters use high-powered binoculars to look into snow-covered mountains at enemy positions near Shah-I-Kot. (U.S. Army)*

10th Mountain fighters fire down from a ridge overlooking the Shah-I-Kot Valley. (U.S. Army)

U.S. fighter eyes the enemy through a sight. American soldiers weren't there to render justice, just (as one duly noted) to "arrange a meeting" for the enemy with "their maker." (U.S. Army)

Algerians, and from 350 to 400 Chechens. He said that there were Egyptian and Saudi fighters as well but provided no numbers. In any case, it appeared that at this point well over a thousand healthy fighters were left inside Tora Bora. The Saudi told Mashal that he would be leaving that evening along with two family members and one Yemeni orphan on the same "underground railroad" others had used to escape Tora Bora. The small clan intended to continue their journey to Pakistan by mule, boat, and car. "We'll go to near Khyber [Torkham] and take a wooden boat at L'alpur across the Kabul River, where a truck will be waiting for us."

Toward the end of the conversation, Mashal informed the Saudi financier that he had been working with foreign journalists. This didn't seem to bother him, leaving Mashal to believe that Jaffar was so traumatized by his ordeal that it made him happy just to have someone listen to his story.

Oddly, or perhaps as planned, Makmud never returned to his own house that day, and Mashal and the driver slipped away down the hill. Fearing the return of the thugs with the eager fists, they slipped into the waiting taxi and peeled out through the gravel, traveling swiftly across the riverbed and back to civilization.

Mashal, whose journalism experience prior to our lucky meeting three months earlier had been writing features about musical performances and archeological sites for the *Kabul Times,* had pulled off a splendid scoop. Nearly 147 publications around the world picked up the story. It just went to show that amid the fog of war any and all hints at what might truly be going on behind the scenes was of immense interest.

If it had not been for the Pentagon's diligent efforts to deny that bin Laden could have slipped out the back door, the story might well have been lost among all the other stories, rumors, and propaganda. Instead, the Pentagon's denial mode boosted interest in our story of bin Laden's slippery moves. Rear Adm. Craig Quigley, the chief spokesman for U.S. Central Command, went out of his way to cast doubt on our report; he said he viewed it with a "healthy dose of skepticism." Pentagon officials were convinced they still had Osama in the crosshairs and stated that they believed bin Laden remained inside Tora Bora. Even Donald Rumsfeld, who had continually warned Bush not to be seen by the U.S. public to be focusing too narrowly on the hunt for one man, now made it clear that he had his own bead on bin Laden and that it wasn't in Pakistan. "We think he's in Afghanistan," he told a press briefing. "We're chasing him."

## The Sick, the Foolish, and the Damned

As the battle for Tora Bora wound down, it became all too apparent that our cherished Afghan allies were working on the principle that a payoff in the hand is better than a captive in the cage. With the money from both the CIA and al Qaeda that they were swimming in, they had won the battle of Tora Bora long before it started. Ali, Zaman, and Zahir had divided up the mountains into equal parts and "cleared" the enemy out of their respective territories. But while our "allies" fought up one valley, they knew that their supposed enemies were being smuggled down another valley on their way out to Pakistan. Makmud, who had ties to religious radicals in Jalalabad's Eastern Shura, operated the "safe house" in Upper Pachir where Mashal talked to Abu Jaffar. Jaffar himself had mentioned how two prominent members of the Eastern Shura, including Younus Khalis's scholarly son Mujahid, had been so kind as to deliver him a "box of dates" inside Tora Bora even as the bombing intensified. The flight out of Tora Bora had been difficult only to the extent that the terror network's own fanatical Chechens tried (unsuccessfully) to prevent healthy al Qaeda fighters from fleeing. Guards did nothing to prevent the flight of the wounded, the lame, the women, or the children, let alone the terror chief himself.

Malik Habib Gul, paid once by al Qaeda for his services at the November 10 banquet in Jalalabad, had eventually reached his hand into al Qaeda's coffers for a double dip. In March 2002, he boasted to Mashal and I that he had prospered by arranging mule trains for their escape from Tora Bora. He described al Qaeda's needs as a "golden opportunity for our village," adding that "the only problem for the Arabs was the first three to seven miles northeast from Tora Bora to our village of Upper Pachir. The bombing was very heavy. But after arriving in our village, there were no problems. You could ride a mule, a bicycle, or drive a car into Pakistan." Over a two-week period from November 28 to December 12, he and other villagers escorted, by their own estimates, six hundred people—both wounded fighters and their families—out of Tora Bora and then out of Afghanistan. He said that bin Laden associates paid, depending on their individual means, the equivalent in Pakistani rupees of from five hundred to five thousand dollars per fighter and family for the use of mules and Afghan guides.

The escape route Gul described began in the valley where Jaffar found Makmud's safe house and wound through Afghanistan for some fifty miles. Moving under the cover of night along the base of the White Mountains, most of the mule trains traveled inside Afghanistan over the same major highway we had all driven in on from Peshawar four weeks earlier. After that, many of the Arabs caught barges or individual rowboats at L'alpur, supposedly secured by Zaman's fighters. This was, to be sure, not a direct route over the snowy peaks of the White Mountains into Pakistan, but a longer, though less physically demanding one.

Though al Qaeda's money certainly offered a great incentive to Gul and his villagers, he insisted that he felt assisting his fellow Muslims to be a duty assigned to him by Allah. It went back to the age-old question of tribal and religious loyalties, which had obviously trumped the efforts that the U.S. military and intelligence services had made to win the villagers over.

Often, however, the aiding and abetting of al Qaeda was as much about hard cash as about loyalty to religion or tribe. Ali's lieutenants, who later claimed to have been "double-crossed" by so-called bin Laden sympathizers, refused, however, to take the blame, citing Ilyas Khel, Ali's commander who had doubled as an escort for al Qaeda, as a "mole" who had infiltrated Ali's otherwise diligent efforts to assist U.S. interests.

There were other telltale injections of hard cash to assist the escape. Mohamed Akram, the sometime chef for bin Laden, claimed that on the day he fled Tora Bora, November 28, he had already grown weary of bin Laden's "master plan" to defend the mountain redoubt. Only days earlier, an infusion of Iranian money had arrived inside the mountain redoubt, he claimed. The source of the money, said Akram, as confirmed by Jaffar, was Shia Afghans with ties to Iran's infamously anti-American Revolutionary Guard. "We received a lot of Iranian currency and the commanders distributed it to the soldiers," said Akram, who pocketed seven hundred thousand riyals ($1,400), as did his fellow foot soldiers. But the young Saudi's decision to flee was also helped along by the intensifying U.S. aerial assault. "I had been cooking with a large pot that evening and a bomb hit directly at the base of our cave," he said. Akram's frail body flew fifteen feet into the depths of the dark cave, and two of his closest mates died instantly. Akram was himself knocked out and couldn't move for some time. When he awoke, he quickly decided that enough was enough. Akram's flight was not simple, however, because hard-core members of the network had vowed to kill "defectors." Rather than walk out a well-trodden goat path, Akram and two associates had to cling to the side of a steep cliff and skirt around Chechen guards on the perimeter of the base. Moving on foot at night over narrow paths, Akram walked over the White Mountains from Ningahar Province into Paktia, stopping first in the Gardez area, where many of Akram's fellow fighters, including a contingent of young Moroccans, met with al Qaeda instructors about plans for future terror operations. After receiving their marching orders, many of the al Qaeda fighters fled over mountain paths in the direction of Iran, according to Akram.

## Doin' the Tora Bora Shuffle

Osama bin Laden, who had paved his exit route with hard cash two weeks before his final departure, had begun his farewells and flight out of Tora Bora almost to the day that Vice President Dick Cheney and Gen. Tommy Franks announced to the world that they believed he was hiding there.

Jalalabad's own intelligence chief, Pir Baksh Bardiwal, gave us access to the transcripts of interviews he conducted with other al Qaeda foot soldiers and junior lieutenants, who later spoke with Green Beret and CIA interrogators. Bin Laden's own trusted Yemeni fighters, many of whom had not seen their leader since entering the cave complex on November 13, told Bardiwal and several other local Afghans that bin Laden had joined them on November 26, the eleventh day of Ramadan. He had sat with them drinking a warm glass of green tea. Instead of inspiring them with anything fresh, however, he merely repeated the "holy war" diatribe that he had delivered on so many earlier occasions, they said. Around him that day sat three of his most loyal fighters, including Abu Baker, a square-faced man with a rough-hewn scruff on his chin. "Bin Laden said, 'Hold your positions firm and be ready for martyrdom,'" Baker later told Afghan intelligence officials. "He also said, 'I'll be visiting you again, very soon.'" Then, as quickly as he had come, Baker said, bin Laden vanished into the pine forests. Though earlier accounts of bin Laden's movements in and around Tora Bora had him on horseback and in the company of several dozen fighters, several of his own fighters insisted that the escape was on foot. The decision to travel in a small group and without large pack animals was likely a precaution to limit the ability of U.S. thermal tracking devices to pick up the escape party. In the weeks following bin Laden's departure from Tora Bora, a vast amount of speculation about bin Laden's actual escape route would emerge.

A year after the battle, though, the U.S. commander in charge of the Afghan proxy war said he had little doubt that bin Laden left in early December in the direction of Paracinar. "Well, Mulholland's take on this is that he went straight south," said Col. Mulholland, shaking his head in the confines of his own office on a chilly Kentucky afternoon at Fort Campbell. In his wood-paneled office, hung with daggers and maps of his "patch of the world," the burly colonel sounded something like a nineteenth-century sheriff, resigned to the fact that he had done his damndest. He had rounded up the available guns and the best horses in Jalalabad and gone after the bad guys, but in the end his efforts at Tora Bora had been to little avail. After a quiet telephone conversation with his wife, apparently dismayed that he was now headed off to northern Iraq to fight another war, the colonel, added, "It was the easiest thing and it makes the most sense that he sought the sanctuary of Pakistan, a very, very friendly place."

Bin Laden's great Houdini act had almost been predictable. Though some optimistic analysts and military minds had hoped that bin Laden would fight to his death in Tora Bora, the strategic think-ing behind his flight became apparent a few weeks later when a Lon-don Arabic-language newspaper published a treatise titled "Knights under the Prophet's Banner: Meditations on the Jihadist Movement," written by his top lieutenant, Dr. Ayman al-Zawahiri. It declared that when faced with certain military defeat, "the movement must pull out as many personnel as possible to the safety of a shelter," to continue the fight at another time and place. Al-Zawahiri, who had escaped at least a week earlier than bin Laden, made the point that even "suicidal" *shaheed*, or martyrs, should apply limits to their self-sacrifice.

## The Immaculate Battle

The final days of the battle for Tora Bora, between December 13 and December 17, garnered massive press coverage, largely due to the

## Al Qaeda Escape Routes

NOTE: Black arrows indicate al Qaeda "rat lines" of escape from Tora Bora.

Pentagon's insistence, mostly through "anonymous" defense officials, that it still had bin Laden in its crosshairs. The reports kept the world on the edge of its seat, waiting to see the grand denouement. The CIA had—according to Bob Woodward's account in *Bush at War* of the internal discussions within the war cabinet—an icebox in its Langley headquarters prepared and waiting for Osama's head. Field operatives had already ordered reinforced cardboard boxes and dry ice as a preservative. On December 14, General Franks reiterated his firm belief in the tactics his fighters and their allies were using in the field. He claimed that al Qaeda forces were between "a hammer and an anvil," with Eastern Alliance fighters on one side and Pakistani troops on the other. Green Berets with laser beams and their "trusted allies" had, in his words, "contained" several hundred al Qaeda troops—and possibly the group's leader, Osama bin Laden—in an increasingly small area. He added, like a commander on the verge of victory, "We will maintain pressure on this pocket of al Qaeda until they are ours." The same day, U.S. warplanes dropped an estimated 235 bombs on area caves and tunnels. While the CIA boasted of spending only seventy million dollars on greasing the wheels of the warlords, the Pentagon was busy paying hundreds of millions over the course of this battle and the entire war for misspent ordnance. Television and some newspaper reports relied on the notoriously inaccurate Hazret Ali as he insisted that bin Laden probably remained in a "special place"—a bunker or a cave. On December 15, U.S. officials had even more "good news" for the public. The Pentagon asserted, despite having no actual recording, that they were "reasonably certain" that one of the voices they had heard on battlefield radio was that of Osama bin Laden. Most news organizations failed to mention that the unrecorded—and, therefore unanalyzed—voice intercept was already over a week old. (If it was real, the transmission may well have been bin Laden speaking from on or just across the border in Pakistan. This would jibe well with Abu Jaffar's contention, when he met Mashal, that a week earlier bin Laden had called into Tora Bora.)

From Hazret Ali, who had first arrived in Jalalabad to plunder humanitarian aid agencies, to the son of the governor, Haji Zahir, who ran a war-zone tourism business on the side with him, the war-lords in Jalalabad had proven themselves to be some of the most despicable and unreliable allies in the history of U.S. efforts to fight proxy wars.

Pure avarice turned out to be a crucial factor in the betrayal of the American cause. Emoluments from the CIA did not go far enough to satisfy the warlords' spiraling greed. Haji Zahir had cleverly linked up with Ali to take advantage of the situation in Jalalabad. Prior to Tora Bora, the short, proud, thirty-four-year-old warlord, with a bit of peach fuzz on his lower chin, had been experienced in the heroin trade but not in battle. When he wasn't entertaining pretty, young American freelance reporters on the second floor of a Western-style ranch home, he was running a well-oiled racket for late-arriving news organizations, one that reflected the entrepreneurial spirit that had long made eastern Afghanistan famous for smuggling high-grade heroin and Sony television sets. Zahir's entire family cooperated in the scheme. It began at the Khyber Pass with charging journalists for a "package deal" to get in to cover the war; the deal included transportation, lodging, and, of course, the all-important "safe passage" down the road to Jalalabad. For organizations arriving too late to get a room in the packed Hotel Tora Bora, Zahir arranged expensive beds in posh villas. As correspondents readied themselves for the two-hour drive south to Tora Bora, a price-gouging arrangement offered them a choice of four-wheel-drive vehicles for $150 each, normally hired in the area at a rate of thirty-five dollars a day. It was nearly impossible to get around the markup by going to the local market, because Zahir and Ali's men controlled the marketplace and refused to rent to any foreigners. (Mashal and I had managed to work our way around the rackets by somehow lining up an unaffiliated driver who ran us up and back from the front lines for just fifty dollars a day and the promise of a slaughtered sheep for Eid, the post-Ramadan Muslim holiday.)

On top of the package deal, both men ran virtual armies of "interpreters and guides," most of whom did not speak even passable English, but nevertheless charged a hundred dollars a day. They would approach their unsuspecting clients with phrases that gave away their uselessness from the start. "You want see Tora Bora?" or

"We go battle, get Osama!" Ali, Zahir, their family, and friends reaped quite a profit from an eager Western press corps that had little alternative if it was to get into the mountains on the hunt for al Qaeda. Some of the networks were already preparing to pay ten thousand dollars to tour bin Laden's bedroom. Even if he had already flown the coop, at least they would be able to look for telltale signs of his lechery and scrape for DNA samples. Others put in their bids for an interview with the terror chief, bound and presumably ungagged. Producers piled up stacks of hard cash for greedy warlords, providing them with yet another motive to keep "the hunt" running as long as humanly possible. A longtime Balkan colleague, Harry Dornbas, known as the "Flying Dutchman," complained, "We are all hostages to the Afghan warlords. The United States and Europe are paying them money to find Osama, Osama is paying them not to fight and the way this thing is going, we won't ever get home for Christmas." These realities appeared lost on the Pentagon even down to the last few days of the battle for Tora Bora. Its officials were quoting—almost verbatim—the words of Commander Ali that his fighters had bin Laden trapped in a cave. In reality, the "laughing warlord," busy with his wartime money-making schemes, had little time to organize and fight a real battle, even if he had wanted to.

Just as confused and discombobulated as the Pentagon, however, was the Western press corps, the behavior of which demonstrated both the lust for a "good story" and the power of wishful thinking. By the weekend of the 14th to the 16th of December 2001, the media frenzy at Tora Bora had reached a crescendo of chaos and overkill. No one wanted to be absent if an Afghan fighter dragged bin Laden's dead body over a mountain ridge—or better yet, if he was carted out alive. The Western press—unlike our Western military allies—had mounted a full-scale invasion and were partying in a way that made our Thanksgiving Day feast in the Hotel Tora Bora look like a soup kitchen giveaway. Afghanistan, a "dry" state until the flight of the Taliban, now had a vast market in the foothills of Tora Bora that offered Johnny Walker Red and Black, single-malt scotch, gin, Russian vodka, and an endless supply of Budweiser beer. Western journalists reveling in their anticipation of bin Laden's capture made the enterprising liquor dealers relatively wealthy men. The mad Welsh artist Jake Sutton, who had finally secured a two-hundred-dollar-an-hour retainer as a cameraman for CNN, while also working as their short-order cook, still managed the time to sketch everything in black-and-white. His sketches brought the press corps's gluttony and lust for hard news into sharper focus.

Few of the Afghan peasants that had been on the al Qaeda payroll just two weeks earlier had any complaints about their new paymasters. They rented out adobe homes with no electricity or running water for five thousand dollars a week as studios for the U.S. and British networks. Afghan laundrywomen in burqas formed a domestic maid brigade. They hung laundry from electric cables, spit-polished tennis shoes, and begged for extra tips. Some of the news organizations hadn't forgotten to pack their Christmas lights, and one had even erected a pine tree topped by a shining silver microphone. When I dropped into the headquarters of NBC for an interview on the Chris Matthews *Hardball* show, a producer from another show was screaming bloody murder into the phone at his executives back home, whom he accused of working the staff to the point of utter exhaustion. "This is worse than the Gulf War! We are all dying here," he moaned as he reached for a shot of whiskey. The conditions were difficult but made easier by a woman's touch. Ashleigh Banfield, the alluringly bright and bespectacled star of MSNBC's twenty-four-hour coverage of the war in Afghanistan, made her entire crew of a dozen grumpy men eggs and Spam for breakfast every morning.

By day, most of the network correspondents stood for their "live" shots on the camel's back, pampered by makeup artists and picayune producers. The stunning backdrop allowed the cameramen to pan out over the snow-capped peaks and watch the B-52s rock the mountainsides. On the surface, the world's most powerful military was doing a bang-up job, and most television correspondents couldn't think to suggest otherwise. At this stage of the war, the U.S. military tactics—everything from the decision not to put hundreds of troops on the ground to the problem of actually surrounding Tora Bora and blocking escape routes—went virtually unquestioned. It was the final, expected prize alone that drove the story line. The greater the press frenzy became, the more bombs the U.S. aircraft appeared to unload. It was war fever and overkill to the $n$th degree, but what was it accomplishing?

The warlords' men were chasing al Qaeda deeper and deeper into its warren of caves. Hundreds of al Qaeda fighters fled, a handful surrendered, but the rest were determined to fight on—especially now that they could get a few infidel journalists into their sights. Zaman's subcommanders agreed, when pressed, that their positions could not stop al Qaeda from simply fleeing out the back or down another side of the mountain. Nevertheless, on December 15, the U.S.–backed Afghans cut off a group of several dozen Arabs on a high ridgeline. An intense battle broke out between the Arabs, finally cornered, and Ali's men.

That afternoon, Jon, Mashal, and I had clung to the bed of an Afghan pickup on our way back into the fray. We jumped out and sprinted across a mountain, all but decapitated by repeated B-52 strikes, and crouched down with other members of the press beneath a ridgeline where Ali was directing a firefight between al Qaeda and his own fighters. The battle was utterly lopsided, in that every time the Arabs fired down, their gun flashes gave away their positions, permitting Green Beret ground spotters to home in with their laser pointers and call in strikes. With Berets on the ground directing the targeting, the United States achieved near-pinpoint precision in its strikes, as compared to the earlier and messy carpet bombing of villages in the foothills of Tora Bora. The shoot-out continued for an hour, and—for a time—it appeared that most of the Arabs had died or had fled down the other side of the ridge.

Taking advantage of a lull in the fighting, one brave network correspondent, dressed in black and wearing a ski cap, looking almost like a commando, crawled out from behind a boulder, grabbed a cordless microphone, and rose to his feet for a standup "at the base of Osama's lair." Jealous that the competition might get a money shot, several more correspondents also scrambled out from beneath trees and crouched beneath a wall with their own mics in hand. Almost perfectly timed to the start of the "takes," a U.S. bombing run dropped five two-ton bombs smack on the ridgeline, blowing everything beneath to smithereens. Deafening blasts rocked the air, and huge mushroom clouds of dust billowed up into the crisp, blue sky. It sounded as close as you could come to a knockout punch, but almost as soon as the dust had settled a barrage of machine-gun fire from the al Qaeda positions on the ridge ripped down into our pool of several dozen absentminded reporters. I was standing beside Janine "the machine" Di Giovanni as a rocket-propelled grenade whipped over our heads and landed in the pine trees to our rear. I dove in slow motion—as it always feels in a war zone—and belatedly for cover, knowing that if that one had even nicked me it would have beheaded me. Pulling myself up out of the dirt and rubbing my eyes and lips, I realized, much to my chagrin, that "the machine" had merely ducked her head.

Mass panic ensued: the press corps and Afghan fighters turned to run back down the mountain for cover. The sudden charge grew into a stampede. A terrified female correspondent working for *Newsday* stumbled beneath the crunch of army boots and camera equipment. A panicked network commando stepped on her back as she came up for air with her palms bloodied and her face covered in dust. Her face reminded me oddly of those of the Afghan children who stood begging on the road to Tora Bora every day we as drove to work. For the Afghan fighters, who had never seen women on the front line—and indeed were slightly offended by even the idea of it—the scene of a woman groveling in the dirt caused intense amusement, and they broke down in hearty laughs. With no other chivalric types in sight, Jon, ever the gentleman, dashed over, pulled her up, and dragged her to safety behind a boulder. Fearless Janine, standing tall with her lovely mane of dark curls flowing behind her, strode over to offer a few words of advice. "War reporting isn't for all of us—you have to really enjoy getting shot at," she cautioned, blowing the dust off her shoulders as a cowboy might do after a long, grueling ride. The injured correspondent broke down and sobbed; the Afghans cracked up in a fresh round of snickering giggles.

No sooner had the world's anticipation of bin Laden's capture reached a crescendo that the networks and the warlords brought it all crashing back down to earth. On December 16, Afghan warlords announced they had advanced into the last of the Tora Bora caves. The governor's son, Haji Zahir, who had first entered the battle when he caught wind of it on CNN, could not have been less pleased with the final prize—only twenty-one bedraggled al Qaeda fighters were taken prisoner that day. "No one told us to surround Tora Bora," Zahir complained to us. He creased his eyebrows, cast his eyes down, and tried, I judged, not to be more vindictive than he felt necessary. "The only ones left inside for us were the stupid ones, the foolish and the weak." He might have said the same for the ones left standing on our own side, particularly the Western reporters.

Gen. Tommy Franks, on whom the press inappropriately heaped much of the blame for the failures at Tora Bora, sounded befuddled by bin Laden's escape. He expressed uncertainty that bin Laden's voice, as first reported in the *Washington Times,* had been heard on short-range radio picked up in the Tora Bora area. "We're not sure whether it's [bin Laden] or not," he said of the transmission. "Is it really true that bin Laden is in Pakistan? We simply don't know right now." Despite the growing angst at having to face up to bin Laden's escape, even after it became absolutely clear that he had flown the coop, the resolve of the U.S. government to catch bin Laden remained apparent. Colin Powell told NBC television: "There's some information that suggests he might still be there, and he might have got across the border. We don't know. But you can be sure he is under hot pursuit. We'll get bin Laden. Whether it's today, tomorrow, a year from now, two years from now, we will not rest until he is brought to justice or justice is brought to him." The mission remained the same—only, one undeniable opportunity had now vanished in the gun smoke.

## Rummy's Redux

On December 16, news organizations that had closely mimicked the Pentagon line on Tora Bora dutifully allowed defense officials to climb down from their earlier contentions. Donald Rumsfeld had arrived in Afghanistan, but he wasn't headed anywhere near the Tora Bora follies. Rather than lead with stories on bin Laden's whereabouts, several networks and cable stations now reported on what sounded like a minor sideshow—the seizure of a suspected chemical and biological weapons center in southern Afghanistan. Rumsfeld insisted the story should garner the world's attention. It also looked to me like a smokescreen for the failures at Tora Bora. The secretary of defense had switched cycles on his internal washing machine and would air no dirty laundry to the press. Inexplicably, however, he allowed for an interesting new scenario when he told reporters in Bagram, "We do believe it's going to be difficult [for al Qaeda] to get out of there, not impossible but difficult." One could almost see the curtains closing in on the immaculate battle for Tora Bora. It had been a perfect, Pentagon-driven storm, but the sun was just starting to peer through the dark clouds, a glimmer of hope for the evildoers. The secretary of defense was anxious to move the story ahead and away from the Pentagon's earlier, often wild, speculation that the good guys had the bad guys cornered. Those loose-cannon "anonymous" sources would now listen closely to what the "Sec Def" had to say. Ironically, on December 23, a week after the sad conclusion of the battle, Rumsfeld readied himself to order hundreds of additional troops into the mountains around Tora Bora. This raised the glaring question, "Why now?"

On April 17, 2002, facing growing criticism for the planning failures at Tora Bora, Rumsfeld sought to quell conjecture that the United States had not committed enough troops to bin Laden's capture. With damning conclusions already drawn, however, by other principals in the Bush war cabinet, the public relations drive also strove to cover up internal rifts about just how and why al Qaeda had—for the most part—already slipped the U.S. noose in Afghanistan. Six weeks after a lengthy March article that Mashal and I wrote for the *Christian Science Monitor* detailing bin Laden's moves through Jalalabad into Tora Bora and back out, the *Washington Post* ran a front-page story headlined "U.S. Concludes Bin Laden Escaped at Tora Bora Fight." It reported that the Bush administration had determined that by failing to commit U.S. troops to hunt him, military planners had committed the gravest error in the war against al Qaeda. The report added that "though there remains a small chance that he died there, the intelligence community is persuaded that bin Laden slipped away in the first ten days of December."

Rumsfeld responded to this scathing indictment of U.S. military strategy with vintage "Rummy." He seemed to suggest to an increasingly skeptical press corps that it had made up or misunderstood the Pentagon's original statements about bin Laden's presence in and around Tora Bora, though they had been quoted verbatim at the time. "We have seen repeated speculation about his [bin Laden's] possible location," he said, adding that the pieces of information "haven't been actionable, they haven't been provable, they haven't resulted in our ability to track something down and actually do something about it." Rumsfeld's response was more than mildly disingenuous. In truth, the nation's highest civilian defense official was using a kind of Orwellian double-talk to obfuscate the reality of bin Laden's escape from beneath the wings of the world's most powerful military.

Indeed, public statements from the days preceding the Afghan ground battle to take Tora Bora leave no doubt that the U.S. military's top brass believed they had a good bead on bin Laden. After the battle, Rumsfeld contended that no one had actually proven to him beyond a shadow of a doubt that bin Laden was present during the U.S.-backed offensive. By this he tried to suggest that he and the generals he commanded bore no ultimate responsibility for not having captured him. It is difficult to think up a precise analogy for this equivocation. If the FBI received credible information indicating that a mass murderer had likely holed up in a particular building, even if it could not be verified, bureau chiefs would certainly surround the place with as many agents as they could round up. If not, and the murderer escaped, the public would never accept the FBI director's excuse that he had decided to not surround the building because the murderer's presence had not been established with absolute certainty. To put the Pentagon's decision in perspective, the local law enforcement agencies and the FBI mobilized several times more officers and agents to converge on the sites of the D.C. sniper shootings in October 2002 than the Pentagon sent into Tora Bora to catch Osama bin Laden.

Rumsfeld had begun reporting to Bush in early October on U.S. bombing runs over Tora Bora. By the end of that month, the warren of caves in the White Mountains had become a focal point of America's aerial assault. Rumsfeld himself had expressed his own strong suspicions about Tora Bora as a bin Laden hideaway since early

October. After President Bush told his war cabinet on October 10, seven weeks before a single U.S. soldier set foot in the area, that intelligence showed that senior al Qaeda operatives, possibly bin Laden, were hiding in Tora Bora, Rumsfeld told the cabinet, "We pounded Tora Bora. We don't know to what effect." The statements, revealed in Bob Woodward's *Bush at War*, prove beyond doubt that top officials had suspected Tora Bora as a hideout for at least two months before bin Laden's escape. In this early phase, when suspicions of bin Laden's presence in the region first surfaced, most al Qaeda fighters in eastern Afghanistan, later including bin Laden, remained in or near to Jalalabad, just forty miles from the key mountain redoubt. Bin Laden himself did not move into Tora Bora until November 13, so the early assessment may have simply expressed an optimistic speculation following from accurate intelligence that indicated the presence of other senior al Qaeda operatives in the caves. General Franks's assertion of November 28 also doesn't mesh with Rumsfeld's later contention that the United States never knew that bin Laden had been in Tora Bora. Franks asserted that Tora Bora was one of only two locations in which bin Laden could be hiding: "These are two areas that we are paying very, very careful attention to," he said. (The other was a wooded area near Kandahar.)

Military intelligence can move fast, but when it comes down from a top commander, it certainly passes through several channels and over numerous desks before being publicly asserted. In other words, for General Franks to posit such a statement meant that the intelligence to back it up had almost certainly been circulating at Central Command and inside the Pentagon for days. (The decision to publicize the information represented a controversial strategic decision in itself, as it signaled to the enemy that we knew of his movements.)

Rumsfeld's attempt to avoid taking the hit should not surprise anyone. The *New York Times*'s Michael Gordon ruffled feathers in early 2002 when he wrote, "The very idea of an occasional lapse of judgment seems to have been banished from the briefing room at the Pentagon." The secretary of defense's own public relations team was grasping at straws when they tried to back up his position that sending in ground troops to root out bin Laden would not have achieved its goal. "Senior defense officials," keen to disguise their identity, told the Associated Press that "to act, the military would have needed to know bin Laden would be at a certain place, at a certain time. The interrogations [prisoner's stories] weren't done until after Tora Bora." This logic was equally unhelpful. After all, the United States had mounted an effort to capture bin Laden at Tora Bora, albeit belatedly and with far too few of its own troops. The prisoner interviews had never been the basis of the U.S. military planning for operations and, therefore, do not have the least bit of relevance.

Capturing or killing bin Laden at Tora Bora—or anywhere else the terror chief had decided to take up in late 2001—would have required a daring, risky, and well-thought-out plan of attack involving far larger U.S. conventional forces. No doubt, the secretary of defense's ability to get infantrymen into a position to take part in the Afghan war had been hampered early by basing problems. General Franks was also struggling to come up with a conventional "Plan B," President Bush having agreed in September and October to move ahead with CIA director George Tenet's plans to win the war as fast as possible and in an unconventional way. But what held up the arrival of a major U.S. ground contingent in mid-November was less a logistical choice than a conscious effort to rely on an Afghan proxy force instead of U.S. fighters.

Within Bush's determined and tight-lipped war cabinet, the only major doubter of the idea of an Afghan-led proxy war had been Vice President Dick Cheney, who made his views known early on. By late November, Cheney appeared convinced, judging by his own press statements, that bin Laden had gone to ground at Tora Bora. Though the window of opportunity was closing even then, the immediate aerial injection of the several hundred Tenth Mountain Division troops waiting patiently a few hundred miles away in Uzbekistan would have served to tighten a real noose around the Tora Bora redoubt, an area less than six miles square. On this point, the *New York Times*'s Michael Gordon argued correctly in a critique of the Pentagon that the issue was not a major switch in strategy, but rather the insertion of adequate force. "After the battle of Tora Bora, Mr. Rumsfeld defended the strategy by arguing that the United States was right not to saturate Afghanistan with large numbers of American ground forces," wrote Gordon at the height of another major battle with al Qaeda in which U.S. conventional forces were used. "But that was never the real alternative. The real alternative was to reinforce the largely Afghan force at Tora Bora with a potent force of American troops who had the will and the firepower to prevent the al Qaeda fighters from escaping."

The Pentagon's subsequent attempts to overlook this failure are troubling for broader strategic reasons as well. The choice of tactics in Afghanistan after the fall of Kabul, a question that came to a head at Tora Bora, presented a "high risk" gamble from both a practical and political standpoint.

In March 2001, long before the battle for Tora Bora, Rumsfeld had written a memo that included his own principles of protecting U.S. citizens from emerging threats. It promised his own commander in chief that he would not shirk his commitment to use U.S. forces when necessary to secure American strategic interests. To this end, he had come up with a personal set of guidelines for committing forces to combat in order to foil any attack on the nation. It encouraged the U.S. military to "act forcefully" and "early." He wrote that the nation's leaders should never "dumb down" a mission to obtain public or UN support. Specifically he added that leaders must avoid "promising not to do things (i.e., not use ground forces, not bomb below twenty thousand feet, not to risk U.S. lives, not to permit collateral damage, not to bomb during Ramadan)." This last sentence referred back to the Clinton administration's internal moral struggles about how hard to strike and whether to use ground troops against the Yugoslav army and Serbian paramilitaries in Kosovo. It was another shot at Clinton's foreign policy for not being decisive enough. Rumsfeld also wrote that American lives should be put at risk only when a clear national interest was at stake, when a mission was achievable, and only after the nation's leadership had marshaled public support. These demanding criteria prevailed early on in the Afghan campaign. Bush himself had stated plainly that the successful capture or killing of bin Laden would be a first major blow to the network. In the wake of the massive attacks on New York and Washington, few doubted his view.

Given that al Qaeda fighters steeled themselves for a fierce fight only after hearing rumors that American troops had landed nearby, a larger insertion of American troops could have produced a bloody showdown. This was a battle, however, that a patient American public was ready and waiting for. A CNN and *Washington Post* sampling of U.S. public sentiment revealed that a vast majority agreed that they would be willing to accept "considerable military casualties" to hunt down bin Laden. Elite and conventional U.S. troops had trained to fight, and being ordered into Tora Bora to catch or kill the man who had caused such heartache in their homeland would have been a dream mission.

In eastern Afghanistan, where warlords had warned the United States not to step into the fray lest they suffer the fate of the Russians, the postbattle clamor concerned what could have and what should have been done to get bin Laden. While putting together our retrospective on the battle for Tora Bora in late March 2002, Mashal and I dropped in to see Pir Baksh Bardiwal, an erudite, bespectacled intelligence chief for the Eastern Shura. He had played a behind-the-scenes role with both the CIA and the two leading warlords in town. His large offices on the outskirts of Jalalabad bustled with impoverished villagers keen to know how they could trade information they had on al Qaeda for seed money for the new planting season. Bardiwal, a tall, soft-spoken Pashtun with a tightly cropped beard and a polished manner, was one of the best-educated officials in town. He contended that the U.S. officials he had dealt with had never taken his advice on putting together a proper "siege of Tora Bora." Bardiwal expressed certainty that CIA operatives working undercover in Jalalabad knew of bin Laden's movements into Tora Bora as soon as word of his November banquet for tribal chiefs escaped the mouths of eyewitnesses on or about November 20, just one week after the gathering and roughly two weeks before bin Laden fled Tora Bora. The local spy chief explained that he was astounded that Pentagon planners, with their extensive aerial surveillance and mapping abilities, didn't think of the most obvious exit routes and put down light U.S. infantry to block them. "The border with Pakistan was the key, but no one paid any attention to it," he said, leaning back in his swivel chair with a list of the al Qaeda prisoners. "And there were plenty of landing areas for helicopters had the Americans acted decisively. Al Qaeda escaped right out from under their feet."

Not only had U.S. officials possessed solid, "actionable" knowledge—albeit not beyond a shadow of a doubt—that bin Laden was in Tora Bora when he was actually still there, but they had, ironically, continued to believe he remained in the area well after he had escaped. Much of the "intelligence" that led the Pentagon to believe it still had a chance at bin Laden in mid-December was only speculation. Pentagon officials contended that there were "signs" that bin Laden was still present—specifically, that al Qaeda was "fighting as if they're protecting something very important." However, at that point, it was only the network's staunchest holy warriors who remained holed up in Tora Bora. Until they packed up and abandoned their ideals, they had been fighting with the expectation that either victory or "martyrdom" would bring them many of the same rewards. In their strictly religious interpretation, death would also ensure them a place in Paradise and a choice of dozens of virgins.

## The Tombs

In a sense, the greatest fears of the U.S. military's civilian leadership came true at Tora Bora. The world's greatest military had bin Laden in its sights but failed to kill or capture him. Rather than "pounding sand," as many in Bush's war room had wanted to avoid, tens of millions of dollars in U.S. ordnance had blasted snow, trees, caves, and dry riverbeds. Whatever happened in the coming months and years, the strategic mistake at Tora Bora would still resonate. From Cairo to Amman to Kabul, in tribal meetings and teahouses, the chatter was disturbing. Many Arabs and Afghans that I spoke to somehow doubted that the U.S. military's leaders had genuinely wanted to capture bin Laden. They just were not convinced that the world's greatest military power, with a budget equal to the next twenty national defense budgets combined, could have failed if it had been truly committed to the task. Ironically, these foreigners I spoke to appeared to believe in the myth of U.S. invincibility more than many Americans.

The battle for Tora Bora was arguably one of the most exciting battles I've ever covered as a correspondent. In the end, however, it left me with a bitter distaste for top brass bluster and Afghan betrayal. Mashal, who headed home for a respite in the Pakistani tribal areas, was equally dismayed at what he had seen. I sensed that, as a loyal Afghan, he had wanted bin Laden's scalp a little more than anyone I'd met so far along the terror trail. We bid farewell and spoke about hooking up again in the New Year. As he headed home to his family and kin, I managed to hire an armed guard to head over in the direction of Upper Pachir. A turbaned chief with a sparkle in his eye now arranged four mules to accompany me up the mountainside as we followed in reverse the route used by these same villagers, who had helped spirit bin Laden's fighters to freedom. It was a credit to Pakhtunwali (Afghan Pashtun) hospitality, possibly also to expertise in chicanery, that the tribesmen could go from aiding and abetting al Qaeda one week to helping a confused and disheveled Western journalist and his bodyguard the next. As the villagers saddled up the mules with brightly colored blankets that had little balls of wool dangling off the edges, I immediately noticed that the beasts of burden, for which I had just forked over fifty dollars each, were looking a bit haggard, as if from forced labor in recent days. Upper Pachir itself exuded an air of prosperity unlike most Afghan villages. The village had done well for itself, living off the crumbs of al Qaeda.

My trek began with about twenty villagers running alongside and a guide for each mule. A small plain fed into the parched hills that, though worked over in the last twenty years by Russian and U.S. bombs, still held their rough-hewn, undulating form. The first village that we entered moving toward Tora Bora was Garikhil, which, along with Upper Pachir, had been the stopping-off spot for nearly two thousand al Qaeda members on the night they fled Jalalabad only two days before the fall of the Taliban in that city. Osama bin Laden had arranged a meeting here that starry night of November 13, 2001, with members of the Ghilzi tribe, a subtribe of the Pashtun, whose villages straddle the Pakistani border.

Small children played in the rubble, and as we dipped into another valley and climbed higher into the White Mountains, our guide, Marmine Khan, a chummy type with a beard down to his belt buckle, explained that it was in the next village, Nasar, that Arabs hoping to escape the inferno of Tora Bora had usually spent their first night in the underground railroad out of Afghanistan. "Of the six hundred Arabs who escaped with our help, most of them were men, though there were also fifteen complete families, including their children," he said. Nasar, I noted, was about one mile as the crow flies from the hill that still hosted the tents that made up the "media circus" where the world's major networks had filmed the two-week-long "siege" of Tora Bora. As we entered a narrow stream bed that cut into a vast gorge, we spotted, from a distance of one hundred meters, three fighters loyal to Hazret Ali, one of the "stars" of the battle. The once lowly woodcutter must have made his own people very proud, I mused. When my bodyguard spotted Commander Ali's men coming toward us, he turned and ran down the mountain, only to explain later that he was afraid he would have been disarmed. Abandoned to my own devices, I left the panting mules in a stream bed and continued up the gorge on foot.

Above us in the clear, blue sky a white Predator drone circled. It buzzed us for about five minutes, hovering with its Hellfire missiles like a bird caught in an updraft, then zipped off to unleash its load—I suspected—on a less fortunate fool than I. Within thirty minutes we came out of the gorge and saw the first sign of the vast network of caves and bunkers that is known as Tora Bora. On a hillside, twelve-year-old boys lifted thirty-pound boxes of antiaircraft shells and tossed them down the hill into a pile of ammunition. There were thousands of boxes in two caves. These caves had been the redoubt of the Sudanese al Qaeda chief, who a month earlier had written us a note in Arabic welcoming us for an interview inside Tora Bora "at a place and time of our choosing." A new "security chief," an Afghan named Commander Nozubilla, reluctantly agreed to provide a "tour of the caves." He charged me a minimal fee in green paper for what he described as "an historic tour." At least, I thought, he wasn't pretending to show me Osama's "bedroom."

Just across the ravine were two truckloads of plainclothes Green Berets, who were frantically combing the area. They looked, I judged by their appearance, to be belatedly obsessed with an expired mission. Indeed, Col. John Mulholland, commander of Task Force Dagger, which was now engaged in the spelunking exercise, would complain bitterly to me months later about the Promethean mission handed down by the Pentagon's top brass. "They wanted every cave searched at Tora Bora," he would tell me. "Well, there aren't enough people on earth to search every cave up there. This was the great cave hunt which I started to refer to as 'Operation Vampire,' because we could never kill that fucking thing." Though he left it to my imagination, I'm sure the irate colonel was referring to the lingering spirit of Osama bin Laden.

Both of the caves I crept into resembled the portals of pharaonic tombs I had entered a year earlier in Egypt's Valley of the Kings. The booty inside was not nearly as mesmerizing—only boxes upon boxes of Chinese antiaircraft shells and Russian rockets, a few spent milk cartons, and a box of Cheerios. "This was once a great base for Osama and al Qaeda," said Nozubilla, who claimed to have only recently switched his allegiances from one local warlord to another—obviously the one with the access to the booty.

When we arrived back in Upper Pachir, a gaggle of Afghan children surrounded us—a good sign for our own safety. They scampered around our mules and kicked up the dust. They laughed and shouted: "Osama, Osama, Pakistan!" I think I knew what they were getting at, and I pointed across the snow-capped Spin Ghar as they nodded and leapt in the air. One young ruffian rolled on the ground laughing and then did a series of somersaults, standing up dizzy and keeling over—as though he had been asked to perform for a stranger.

I couldn't help but wonder what mysterious forces had stage-managed everything down to the last act. A few weeks later, bin Laden popped up again on another one of his videotapes, looking rather gaunt and frail, and holding the microphone in the wrong hand. His backers insisted that he had been through quite an ordeal, which was probably true. Within the month, the U.S. military put out new leaflets, which appeared to descend from heaven, fluttering down to earth from what looked like little bugs buzzing around at about ten thousand feet. The U.S. military's psychological operations division had a new idea for winning hearts and minds—or for maybe winning a few defections. The latest leaflet had the standard shot of bin Laden in a white turban looking austere and devoted to his mission in life. On the reverse side, however, the terror mastermind had shaved his beard and was sporting only a finely trimmed mustache above his coat and necktie. He bore, if I judged correctly, a genuine smirk. He looked handsome, though slightly comic—like an impersonator of bin Laden on *Saturday Night Live*. The message at the bottom charged, "Your leader has abandoned you." The flier suggested that bin Laden had run away, flown the coop, left his fighters in the lurch—an argument that was, I judged at this stage of the hunt, at least half true. On the other hand, I suspected that a few of the most loyal network members would have scoffed at the suggestion that a new face, the very kind of mask they learned to apply in their own terror manuals, could be taken as any kind of betrayal.

# 6

# THE EYE OF THE STORM

Trust in the young white men who led them, and perhaps
some dim half-idolatrous faith in the mysterious Sovereign
across the seas, whose soldiers they were, and who would
surely protect them, restored their fainting strength.

—Winston Churchill,
*The Story of the Malakand Field Force*

## Tracing the Rat Lines

After the battle of Tora Bora, my editors kindly unleashed me to run
back to Egypt to be with my wife, Ivana, for a quiet Christmas and
New Year's on the Red Sea. The war on terror had only just begun,
though, and by early January 2002 I was back in eastern Afghanistan
with Mashal, who regaled me with tales of fleeing al Qaeda fighters
and Taliban officials regrouping across the border in Pakistan, where
his wife and children still lived.

Meanwhile, at Bagram Air Base and at the secretive "K2" Green
Beret base in Uzbekistan, there was frustration, but also a sense that
the U.S. military had begun to pick up good human intelligence on al
Qaeda's movements. Col. John Mulholland's best troops had spent
most of the month of January spelunking through the myriad of
caves and tunnels in the Tora Bora area, picking through garbage
bins and the occasional overturned filing cabinet. Most of the clues
he was getting, however, on al Qaeda movements came from Green

Beret units on the ground; rival warlords were now anxious to report to them about enemy movements, with the hope of getting a piece of the American pie, served up mostly in squares of Ben Franklin notes. Officers collected, collated, and analyzed information on enemy movement inside the frigid confines of Task Force Dagger's Bagram quarters. Mulholland received steady progress reports.

"I had officers who were tracking the flow of these bad guys and they developed what we call 'rat lines,' the paths of these guys, and they all begin to flow from the White Mountains into the Paktia area," he told me months later, pointing to a rugged mountain range south of Tora Bora. "We were developing a pretty good intelligence picture of the entire region. We saw a movement into the Shah-I-Kot Valley, an area that had been a classical 1980s resistance area for the Afghan mujahideen during the Soviet occupation."

Shah-I-Kot was just over a hundred miles southwest of Tora Bora. Al Qaeda forces that slipped away from the fighting in the White Mountains streamed down into the provinces of Khost and Paktia. Some of them were regrouping to fight, while others were just trying to get out of the range of U.S. bombers. As Colonel Mulholland explained, Khost and Paktia were logical provinces for al Qaeda to try to regroup in. They offered vast, wooded mountain ranges and rugged terrain accessible only by foot in many regions. In addition, the local population had an elusive "favorite son," Jallaluddin Haqqani, who was believed to be working hand in hand with the al Qaeda network.

Our own investigations suggested the same. Early in January, we ran into a small group of fleeing al Qaeda fighters camping out on a mule-and-camel path leading from Tora Bora to the Shah-I-Kot Mountains. We had driven into the mountains on a tip from our driver, a local, who had told us that everyone in his village was aware of the presence of al Qaeda fighters. When we arrived at the base of a large, pine-forested enclave, a local villager offered to take us up farther into the mountains, where he said some Arabs had been billeted for the last two days. The villager said that Mashal should go and I should stay behind, but I managed to follow their party at a safe distance, shadowing them behind large boulders on the way up. The turbaned elder shouted up at two stone huts at the crest of the mountain, asking their inhabitants if they wanted to meet with a stranger who might be able to help them. Someone dashed out the side door of one of the two huts, knelt behind a large rock, and pointed his gun down the mountain. Even from my remote vantage point about 150 feet below the huts, I could see that the Arab fighter meant business. He was poised to shoot. Behind him emerged two more al Qaeda fighters hung with belts of grenades, enough to blow up a fleet of trucks. The gunner, a tall, thin man with a wavy, black beard, shouted down, "Who are you? If you can help us, we will talk, but if you can't, just go away and leave us!" For the next ten minutes, the three young fighters in the nomad's village threatened and begged for help to escape Afghanistan. They asked for transportation into Pakistan by car and seemed to calm down considerably once they realized our party had no guns. Mashal's shouting was interrupted by the sound of a U.S. fighter jet overhead; then came an unexpected confession.

"The enemies of Islam have broken our backbone, our people are abandoning us and we have dispersed like orphans in the valleys," said the gunner. It wasn't clear how desperate the Arabs really were, though—or whether they were just feeding us a line. Mashal had nothing to offer and turned back when after a short while they spat into the wind and waved us away.

After achieving their narrowly focused goal of "regime change," which lasted through 2001, the U.S. military mission in Afghanistan began turning into a broader manhunt and an effort to root out al Qaeda fighters, who were in some cases on the run and in other cases regrouping for more fighting against the Western infidel. The massive bombing of suspected targets had nearly vanished. To be sure, new targets were emerging, but they were fewer and farther between than in the early stages of the war. Secretary Rumsfeld had said in the second week of January that he believed bin Laden was still hiding in Afghanistan, despite conflicting reports from the State Department and, more notably, the CIA. Some of the tribal chiefs in the village where Mashal's family still resided said that bin Laden had doubled back into Afghanistan and taken up near the town of Jadji in Khost Province, where he had fought his first major battle with the Russians in the spring of 1986. In addition to his role as a fund-raiser and recruiter for the Afghan Arabs, bin Laden, under the nom de guerre Abu Abdullah, had held out for an entire week in the mountains around Jadji and with the battalion under his command fought the Russians to a near standstill. The talk fueled our own suspicions, though we doubted that bin Laden would have so quickly ventured back into his old Afghan stomping grounds.

In the first two weeks of January 2002, the number of U.S. forces in Khost leaped from twenty-five Special Forces troops living in a school to about two hundred soldiers in all. Already on the ground to greet the new arrivals was a man the Afghans knew simply as "General John." One night, after dining with a local Afghan tribal leader, Mashal and I were treated to a videotape of General John's own visit with the same warlord. The video showed General John seated cross-legged on a floor as attendants rolled out a long mat before filling it with plates of food—enough for a small army. The Pakhtunwali customs we all enjoyed knew no bounds. I noted that this didn't necessarily mean the tribesmen felt any great affection for the American officer, for the Pashtun heartland did not distinguish between a "good" guest and a "bad" guest. Thus, a mysterious mass murderer—like Osama bin Laden—passing through town will be provided for in nearly the same manner and style as would be suspect Americans. The code of conduct made common sense. Only when the Afghans got caught defending their guests—good and evil—did their local traditions create global difficulties.

The young, bearded American's efforts to make friends in Khost appeared to be going well. He quickly extended promises to assist the local Afghans, who were more than happy to sign up for "the hunt for al Qaeda," a job that had proven to be both entertaining and lucrative for any warlord who had joined the fray at Tora Bora. We noticed, however, that General John, who was actually only a midranking officer, was markedly unspecific about what plans he had for the locals. Wary of his hosts, he kept his cards close to his chest.

The Green Beret unit based in Khost was typical of the A teams based across Afghanistan. The unit consisted of weapons experts, medical personnel, intelligence officers, and engineers. In addition, it had air strike controllers, both forward observers and targeters.

On January 4, 2002, just a day after General John's dinner, the new A team in Khost suffered the U.S. military's first death by contact with the enemy. (That it had taken over three months for such a death to occur was due to the Pentagon's cautious use of combat teams, as well as to the relative inability of Taliban and al Qaeda fighters to inflict serious casualties.)

The Khost A team's troubles came about after a fateful decision by Green Beret officers and CIA officials to visit the scene of a mosque destroyed by American bombs back in November. When the mosque was struck, Taliban and al Qaeda leaders had been massing there to plan an attack on U.S.-backed Afghan forces. Though the U.S. military later said—for purely diplomatic reasons—it had targeted the mosque in error, the results of the smart bomb right through the concrete dome had been spectacular. Some sixty to seventy "worshippers"—every man inside the mosque at the time of the strike—had been killed. The incident had inspired locals to build a red-brick mausoleum to the Arab and Afghan "martyrs" who had died. It looked like a small house with no roof on top, only red, pink, and blue flags waving in the brisk desert wind on wooden poles stuck between the bricks. In Khost, the mourners who visited the new mausoleum by the dozens every day were well aware that bin Laden's Arabs had been inside the mosque when it was hit. They readily told us so. What they objected to was that U.S. bombers struck these persons as they had been in the act of praying. Such a death was not only in contravention of the strict Pashtun codes of martial conduct, but was considered a one-way ticket to martyrdom. Even with their relatives in "paradise," though, local tribesmen were not resting easy.

On January 4, U.S. forces accompanied by Afghan escorts had moved carefully around the perimeter of the mosque to have a look at the damage, as a crowd of locals gathered in the surrounding fields. Suddenly, a lone villager opened up on the U.S. forces with an automatic machine gun. A CIA agent was injured, and the first U.S. soldier to die in the Afghan war, Sgt. First Class Nathan Ross Chapman, a thirty-one-year-old Special Forces soldier, fell to the earth. Chapman, who had begged his commanding officers for the Afghan assignment, had been an elite fighter cross-trained as a sniper and light-weapons specialist. A day after his death, Gen. Tommy Franks said that Chapman had been present in Khost to "facilitate cooperation between our forces in the region and the local tribal elements."

Yet even as U.S. forces sought to work closely with tribal sources, experiences from Tora Bora were hard to ignore. After the blunders that had characterized the hunt for al Qaeda in and around Tora Bora, the U.S. military had shifted from a "light footprint" to a noticeably heavier posture. If the bad guys poked their head out of a cave again any time soon, the Pentagon wanted to be sure that it had its own eyes on the ground and far more firepower to go with them.

Khost bustled with U.S. forces, though in early January Mashal and I were the only journalists camping out on the doorstep of the local governor. We watched from the edge of the local airport in the company of a young Afghan warlord as U.S. Marines and Green Berets jumped off Chinooks, the large helicopters used by the military to move goods and men. They were part of a new force sent to Khost to root out remaining al Qaeda fighters believed to be lurking in the mountains of eastern Afghanistan. The soldiers, in light brown camouflage and jet-black uniforms, sprang into action. Several new yellow-and-orange tents had sprung up on top of the airport terminal, as well as along its side in a small wooded area. Helicopters opened hatches to unload spanking new four-wheel drives and a fleet of all-terrain motorcycles. Food, guns, and camping equipment also fell off the back of the Chinooks in bundles near the airport's front entrance. Local Afghans arrived with supplies for the Americans. One fruit truck entered the terminal with a monkey on a chain inside the cab. U.S. soldiers decided that the frisky primate would make a nice companion and so bought him from the driver and tied him up near a set of sandbags that served as a sentry post.

This wasn't, of course, the first foreign invasion the region had seen. Locals liked to boast about their "Soviet Museum" at the far end of the Khost airport terminal. Someone had done a lot of work to create the museum, lining up some three dozen downed Russian transport helicopters side by side. All of the Soviet aircraft had immense gashes—signs that Afghans or Afghan Arabs wielding shoulder-fired rockets had knocked them out of the sky. Several shoeless, dirty-faced children, looking over at the newer, greener American versions now landing on the tarmac, were climbing through the cockpits and wandering through the cavities of the craft.

Though General Franks was anxious to bring the might of the regular army to bear, the Green Berets and the CIA still had the lead along the Afghan–Pak border as Pentagon planners developed sharper intelligence and devised strategies to interdict the flow from one side of the border to the other.

To get the job done, the Americans still needed a few good Afghans, preferably Pashtuns, to help them. Mashal's cordial demeanor and excellent translation caught the CIA's attention one day as he stood at the gates of the airport base translating the wishes of a local warlord. That evening, Mashal arrived back at our base inside the governor's guest house to inform me that he had been "invited to tea." I immediately suspected foul play. At the height of Tora Bora, major American and British networks had attempted, without success, to poach Mashal's services, offering daily fees doubling what I could pay; I had had to remind him that the networks would be in and out of Afghanistan in a few months but that I would be around all year. I now had a new challenge on my hands, and I feared that Mashal would abandon me for the "big bucks."

Mashal arrived on base the next day at noon, just after a U.S. helicopter had crashed nose down, not far from the old Soviet Museum. Soldiers and medics were scrambling to get a dozen injured soldiers out of the wreckage. One died in the mishap, and the injured left for Bagram Air Base near Kabul for emergency care.

CIA officials—all dressed in civilian clothes—were waiting for Mashal in a small tent set up alongside the terminal. Inside, backpacks and MREs (meals, ready to eat) were strewn on the floor along with several satellite phones and two laptop computers. As Mashal took a seat inside, an officer named "Bob," whom he had met the previous day, entered the tent and greeted him. One of the men ran his index finger across his throat to make the point that there could be retribution if the secret ever escaped the canvas flaps. "Let's be clear from the start, none of this goes beyond our base," he warned Mashal.

It soon became apparent that the plainclothes officers were looking for Afghans to go under cover with them in their hunt for al

Qaeda. To that point in the war, the Americans had experienced great difficulty finding people knowledgeable in both English and local languages willing to assist them. One official launched into a brief example of obstacles he had faced. "We ask people to 'please go up that mountain' and they translate it like an insult; 'please go climb a mountain." Mashal, fluent in English, Farsi, Pashto, and Arabic, looked like a better catch than most.

The offer they made surprised Mashal, who had genuinely believed he was only accepting an invitation to tea. "You'll be paid $250 a day—and do you have a car?" asked one of the officers, a tall, blonde gentleman of about forty years.

"No."

"No problem. We'll give you one."

Yet Mashal had never driven a car before, and that idea alone worried him. A tall, bearded recruiter who sat against the tent wall switched back and forth between Arabic and English as he explained the nature of the work. "We must warn you, some of the work is rather dangerous." Mashal had been musing at the crashed chopper on the runway and felt concerned that his duties might involve hopping around the country at night in some kind of U.S. flying machine or other. This caused intense worry at the thought of accepting the men's offer. Mashal took another sip of his tea and said nothing.

"I suppose you know why we are here, don't you?" asked another intelligence official.

"Well, it must be to hunt al Qaeda," he shot back.

"That's right."

The officers, who sat cross-legged drinking tea inside the tent with Mashal, sought to make it clear that the United States had no imperialist intentions in Afghanistan. "We are not here to occupy the country," said one. "We'll hire you for at least three months."

Thirty minutes into the interview and after three separate mug shots, another man, in plain clothes but carrying an M-16 assault rifle, ducked into the tent to inform Mashal that he had been "found out." He had been surfing the Internet and entered the tent with a grim look on his face. "We've discovered that you are currently working with a reporter." The tone of the conversation changed, and the three men reminded Mashal again that nothing was to go beyond the tent.

But Mashal hadn't even nodded his interest. He had long since decided, even before he had dropped in for a chat, that he had no desire to work with U.S. intelligence. He would have liked the money but couldn't imagine flying around in helicopters, possibly getting caught up in a mistaken attack on civilians and then having to live in Afghanistan with the thought of that. I flattered myself that his loyalty compelled him to stay with me, but I knew better.

## Close Encounter with a Hellfire

After Mashal's personal meeting with the new powers-that-be in Khost, we made a decision to shadow the Green Berets, the CIA, and the U.S. forces in Khost and neighboring Paktia Province as closely as we could. We thought that maybe they would lead us in the right direction in our own hunt for the bad guys. Al Qaeda's own strategy was difficult to figure. My own instincts as a reporter suggested to me that most of the network—including its senior leaders—believed it wise to leave Afghanistan, if only to travel as far as the remote tribal areas and concrete jungles of neighboring Pakistan. Most of those who were interested in still fighting the Americans were straddling the border in platoon-sized units. Of course, a guerrilla army doesn't have to hold ground in the classic military sense; it only has to disrupt and terrorize to achieve its ends. This meant that the U.S. efforts, a necessary means of ridding the region of the al Qaeda scourge, would be—by their very nature—an often expensive and fruitless game of cat and mouse.

Teams of Green Berets spread out like cops on a massive manhunt. They searched from apartment to apartment in areas that embraced the Pakhtunwali code of honor, which carried a strong element of hospitality toward outsiders but also protected the inviolability of the home. This was problematic, to say the least. In the Pashtun areas of Afghanistan, you never saw a woman except from a distance of several hundred meters away. Even then, their heads were covered and faces obscured. Searching from room to room for stray al Qaeda cells in such an environment was daunting. Even a local Pashtun who managed to sneak a surreptitious glance at a neighbor's wife could find himself dead within the hour. A complete stranger was even less likely to save himself from the wrath invoked by the Pakhtunwali code.

In late January, we managed to catch up to a group of Special Forces soldiers and Afghans as they combed through homes in search of the enemy. American officers were giving orders in a small Pashtun village just outside the town of Zarmat. They donned state-of-the-art communications equipment with headsets that allowed them direct communication with their men in the field. These were Tajik soldiers alien to the region, and they now fanned out through an adobe village, ducking behind crumbling sandstone walls as some of their colleagues knocked on doors. We cracked the window of our Corolla while waiting in line at a roadblock, listening to an anxious Green Beret with a thick, dark beard bark orders in a southern drawl. After about five minutes of silence, a villager cocked a bird gun as several Tajiks dove into a ditch and assumed the firing position. A Pashtun elder approached the Americans and complained through a translator that the Tajiks had already confiscated over a dozen four-by-four jeeps that had nothing to do with al Qaeda.

The U.S. Special Forces officers understood that they had to let someone else do the looking for them. But if there was a dangerous flaw in the American plan, it was that ethnic Tajiks from the Northern Alliance were being asked to do the dirty work. Southern Afghans hated Tajiks far more than they did Western "infidels." The Afghan capital, now "occupied" by the "northern invaders," had served in recent centuries as the seat of government for a Pashtun king. We were witnessing a delicate game of hide and seek played out in the highlands of central Afghanistan. The more the U.S. forces employed Tajiks to do their hunting, the more likely it was that the locals would hide something from them. If, however, the U.S. officers decided to use the locals, they faced having to trust them, something they were not yet willing to do.

An American officer in full communications headgear walked over to our driver's window and warned us to be careful. "The situation is a little confusing," he said. "It is hard to know who is who."

He put a good face on a hard day's work. After he spoke, a turbaned man who bore and uncanny resemblance to Osama bin Laden pushed his bicycle past in front of us, looking over at the Green Beret with a sneer. At the next checkpoint a local Afghan reminded us of what the U.S. forces already knew, that "even for an Afghan it is difficult to know an Arab when we see one."

Later that day, our armed guards had no difficulty recognizing three Chechens as we stopped in a small village on our way home. The Chechens, immediately identified as former residents of Ghazni during the Taliban's rule, exited a four-wheel-drive jeep and headed into the market to buy supplies for their mountain redoubts. Our guards pulled the clips on their Kalashnikovs, "snap, snap," lifted them slightly in their laps, and prepared for a shoot-out. Fortunately, our standard white taxi did not draw their attention; we departed quickly and without incident.

On January 21, 2002, following up on a tip-off about a U.S. raid on a local community, Mashal and I traveled to the nomad village of Bak, escorted by a group of seven pro-American tribal fighters from Khost. It had been an hour's drive out to the remote, desert area, thick with undulating hills, deep ravines, and the occasional sagebrush as cover from the blistering Afghan sun and wind. We arrived at the scene only to have our eyes dusted by the "whap-whap" of the giant rotor blades of U.S. choppers just departing the scene. The six large Chinooks, dropping from the sky and surrounding their village, had stunned the nomads. About two hundred U.S. infantrymen, guided by Green Berets, had begun crawling up the sandy hills to peer down on the village, ready for escape attempts or sudden attacks. The operation, which went on for two days, was in essence a large-scale "search and seize" operation meant to root out stray al Qaeda cells.

The Pashtun herders didn't quite see it that way. The first sign that it was going to be a difficult forty-eight hours came when one elderly nomad, still watching the U.S. soldiers crawling on their bellies like sand crabs, decided to slip over a sand dune and drop behind his usual sagebrush to relieve himself. He had just squatted down and dropped his pajama-like pants to his ankles when two linebacker-sized Americans leaped on his back and tackled him, rolling him, sans pants, into the dust. The old man told us that from what he could see, the soldiers had been as surprised as he was when the tangle settled down a bit. The soldiers drew their guns—he drew his drawers—and the confusing face-off continued, until the soldiers relented and allowed the elder to complete his mission. Afterward, U.S. soldiers dutifully escorted the kind old man back into the village amid numerous heartfelt apologies. This event, we were informed, repeated itself twice over the course of the next two days. Meanwhile, U.S. forces went from tent to tent searching for clues. The American soldiers hunted and hunted but found nothing. Even a massive al Qaeda weapons cache that al Qaeda loyalists had buried only a few weeks earlier remained hidden.

When we arrived, the bewildered nomads were in a tizzy. A band of old men, including the gentleman who had been tackled, hastily led our own commander to the arms cache, on the side of a ravine. We stood with the nomads for four hours as they dug up the weapons and anxiously handed over antitank guns, rockets, and box after box of antiaircraft munitions to the royalist commander. "We don't want to give the Americans any more excuses for raiding our village," the old gentleman said with a resigned voice. If nothing else, the U.S. forces had certainly frightened the daylights out of the nomads. They were now ready to comply fully, no questions asked, with the U.S.-led war on terror.

Like any extended military campaign, the war in Afghanistan had incidents of overkill. On February 6, 2002, hard against the Pakistani border, a CIA drone equipped with a color daytime camera and infrared night vision spotted a group of men not far from the mouth of an immense bunker at Zhawar Kili, in Khost Province, where Osama bin Laden had first declared his "war on America." It was a site that Mashal and I knew well, having been the first reporters to explore the abandoned cave complex in early January 2002. One of the men, U.S. officials later insisted, stood significantly taller than the others. The drone, with a wingspan of fifty feet and with a U.S. soldier at the controls on the ground, fired a Hellfire missile with a Multispectral Targeting System (MTS) into the crowd, killing three men, including the tall man. This strike soon caused immense speculation in Washington, based merely upon the thin correlation with the fact that Osama bin Laden is also a "tall man." Again, the bin Laden hunters lurched into the realm of wishful thinking. Major news agencies quoted U.S. officials, who did nothing to dampen the speculation. An apparently overzealous Pentagon official boasted "the central figure had a close encounter of the worst kind with a Hellfire missile." It wasn't, of course, impossible that the drone controller had correctly identified Osama bin Laden. That Osama bin Laden had suddenly appeared back in his old haunts, though, appeared about as likely as the queen of England paying a visit to Kabul.

Mashal and I at the time were in Khost, where we had only recently reunited with Jon Swain of the *Sunday Times* and were introducing him to the local warlords. Even as we made the rounds, the relatives of the Afghan dead from the Hellfire strike arrived in Khost to mount a protest outside the governor's mansion. That evening we ran into the *Washington Post*'s Doug Struck, who was in town to investigate the snowballing "Hellfire incident." Earlier that day, when Struck had made it up into the mountains at considerable risk to his person, U.S. soldiers had cordoned off the area to conduct their own searches. When he tried to enter it, Struck found himself looking down the barrel of a machine gun. "They threatened to shoot if I took another step, even after I had identified myself," he later told us. In his published account Struck mentioned the unfortunate incident but, as we read his detailed account, he did not highlight it. He managed to get some excellent reporting done that day, skirting around the cordon to secure interviews with relatives of those killed by the U.S. strike. His story about scrap-metal collectors checked out with what irate villagers had said their relatives were doing when the Hellfire struck them.

The *Post* story dampened speculation in Washington, but the reaction of the Assistant Secretary of Defense for Public Affairs, Ms. Victoria Clarke, to a copy of the story laid out for her on her desk spoke volumes about the tensions growing between the press and the Pentagon. According to a correspondent for the cable network MSNBC, who called me a couple of days later, she flew into a tantrum and shouted to an assistant, "Get this shit off my desk!" The *Post*, which does not dodge controversy, had Struck write a follow-up the next day; it made the Pentagon's version of the deadly accurate air strike appear even more unlikely. Several senior U.S. officers quickly came to the rescue of the Pentagon and the CIA, however, saying that the military was examining DNA evidence to determine the exact identity of the "tall man." That would solve the problem once and for all, they insisted. Indeed, what that tactic served to do, by intention or otherwise, was take the issue out of circulation for several weeks, allowing a tragic civilian casualty controversy to vanish into an abyss. Alas, when the DNA evidence came up negative, neither the Pentagon nor the CIA sought to revisit the stormy issue.

Even as the U.S. forces hunted around Khost, a band of several hundred al Qaeda members was massing in the nearby Shah-I-Kot Valley in anticipation of mounting a fight against the Americans. As the next major showdown with al Qaeda approached, the Pentagon began to recognize that aerial bombing from ten thousand feet was no more likely to pacify the country than it was to liquidate the bad guys. Indeed, their new "boots on the ground" strategy, which combined conventional and unconventional forces in the same missions, made only limited use of aerial bombing. Instead, it took advantage of the U.S. military's superior airlift—mostly helicopter—capabilities.

## The Bear Trap

The Shah-I-Kot Valley, just a hundred miles as the crow flies south of Tora Bora in eastern Afghanistan, lies beneath a range of two-mile-high mountains and is linked by a key pass with a supply and escape route into and out of Pakistan. The immediate region had been the graveyard of four hundred Soviet troops who had dared challenge the Afghan fighting prowess in the highlands back in 1986. Though al Qaeda and Taliban fighters had taken up positions at Shah-I-Kot as early as November 2001, Colonel Mulholland believed that the lion's share of fighters streaming into the region had fled the battle of Tora Bora. Many of them, he suspected, had taken the same escape route into Pakistan as bin Laden and had doubled back through low valleys into Afghanistan. In mid-December 2001, Pakistani authorities had managed to round up over a hundred al Qaeda suspects; some later escaped, but many were handed over to the U.S. government for incarceration in Camp X-ray. Thousands more remained on the lam.

The planning of the U.S. military assault on the Shah-I-Kot began on February 13, with Mulholland in the driver's seat. "The football was to be mine, so to speak. Our initial assessments of the developing situation had been made in January, but because of the weather, we were unable to mount the operation we wanted at that time." Despite vehement Pentagon denials that "lessons" from Tora Bora had been applied to the development of the Anaconda battle plan, Colonel Mulholland made clear to me in an interview in his Kentucky offices that the idea of using a large contingent of conventional forces in the assault was "a lesson learned from Tora Bora," one that he agreed with in full.

"My assignment was to clear the Shah-I-Kot Valley, but as we did our target assessments, it became clear to me that this was a mission bigger than capabilities of the forces that I had available to me. It was big, too big for Special Forces alone. Fortunately, by this time nearly a thousand Tenth Mountain Division fighters, commanded by Gen. Franklin "Buster" Hagenbeck, had moved down into Afghanistan from Uzbekistan where they had been based since early October. We already had a great personal friendship and I said, 'Hey, sir, we think that this is something your division ought to take on because it clearly requires conventional forces to seal this area. I was thinking that, if you really want to seal this thing right, you really have got to put a first team U.S. infantry on the ground.'" Mulholland's account contradicts the contention of Robin Moore in his book *The Hunt for bin Laden* that the Green Berets resisted the idea of working with conventional forces. Both he and Hagenbeck gave early briefings to senior commanders, including Gen. Tommy Franks, who quickly approved the new force structure. Colonel Mulholland then became a subordinate in the task force commanded by General Hagenbeck. If things went belly up, Mulholland could not be singled out as the "fall guy."

This did not mean, however, that Colonel Mulholland would play a secondary role in the upcoming battle—dubbed "Operation

Anaconda," after the South American snake that surrounds and suffocates its prey. Indeed, the battle plan would be a classic "hammer and anvil," with Green Beret–trained Afghans supplying the "hammer" and U.S. forces, blocking the enemy's mountain escape routes, as the "anvil." In this respect the battle plan somewhat resembled Tora Bora, except that it gave American forces the responsibility of closing the back door on al Qaeda, a task that had been assigned exclusively to Afghans and Pakistanis in the earlier battle.

In January, Mulholland's forces had begun training Afghan fighters across the region. U.S. soldiers held training sessions in Khost, Logar, and in Paktia Province, just a few hours' drive by jeep from the Shah-I-Kot Valley. Each new Afghan fighter was to be paid two hundred dollars per month for his martial services. There was little that their forefathers had not taught the Afghans about guerrilla warfare, but the idea of a conventional attack was another tactic entirely, one that put them in the unfamiliar and awkward posture of the Soviet forces they had defeated a decade earlier. As we drove through the region, we could see the U.S. trainers putting their Afghan friends through the motions, demonstrating proper gun safety, crawling in the sand, and cocking machine guns.

"They were working with us hand in glove," said Mulholland, who chose a well-known warlord from Logar Province, Zia Lodin, to carry out what in military parlance is known as the "sharp end" of the operation. "The Afghans were at once very aggressive and at the same time very anti-Taliban. But they weren't from the immediate area, they were from nearby Logar Province, and so they were not operating in their homeland."

Colonel Mulholland supplied the Afghan fighters with pickup trucks for transport and promised close air support. The plan was for Zia's men to leave first in a large convoy accompanied by a few dozen Green Berets. The Afghan fighters would enter the Shah-I-Kot and push their way through the valley in an effort to flush al Qaeda fighters out of their bunkers and higher into the towering mountains, where U.S. forces would capture or kill the fleeing quarry. Other Afghans would attack three small villages in the Shah-I-Kot where al Qaeda and Taliban fighters had taken up, and yet others, mostly from the border regions near Khost, would be used to reinforce the

U.S. military's own blocking positions farther to the rear to ensure that no one slipped into neighboring Pakistan.

The terrain of the Shah-I-Kot was steeper than Tora Bora, and the mountain's that lined the Pakistani border shot up to well over two miles high; however, there were recognizable landmarks that could be used as military objectives. As the battle plan developed, Mulholland, Hagenbeck, and their staffs marked helicopter landing zones (HLZs) on a map and gave them women's names. From left to right in alphabetical order and facing the highest mountains as a backstop, these included Amy, Betty, Cindy, Diane, Eve, Ginger, and Heather. In front of these landing positions was a gargantuan and barren hump, much larger than Tora Bora's "camel's back," which planners quickly dubbed "the whale." Between the whale and the mountains were several small villages where Mulholland and Hagenbeck both hoped—banking on the element of surprise—they would find the main al Qaeda fighting force.

No one really knew how many of bin Laden's men remained in the valley. Intelligence estimates had small groups moving in an out of the region for weeks; figures ran from two hundred to a thousand or more. Beyond that, doubts still lingered about how well the Afghan proxies would perform under pressure, especially when they were being asked to take on elite Arab fighters, their own former allies. As U.S. commanders drew up the final battle plan and made last-minute preparations, one of two colonels who would be charged with cutting off al Qaeda in the high mountain passes had an uneasy feeling. It was the kind of "sixth sense" they teach you about at West Point, where Col. Paul La Camera had studied over a decade earlier. The short, stocky, young colonel, a former high school football player and avid weightlifter who liked to think of his men as underpaid "warrior-athletes," had been covering Mulholland's back for four months in Afghanistan.

La Camera's concern for the safety of his forces as well as his gung-ho enthusiasm for the hunt made him wildly popular among his men. His first reaction upon seeing the Twin Towers collapse had been, "Payback is a mother[fucker] and there is someone in a cave somewhere who has just opened up a can of 'Whoop Ass.'" Still, La Camera, a soldier's soldier, refused to take for granted this mission of attacking an al Qaeda enclave. As the attack on Shah-I-Kot loomed, the young commander didn't like what he called the Fifth Group commander's "body language" during eleventh-hour planning briefings.

"I guess I just looked at his body language and thought, hmm, there is something wrong here," he said. "There was something uneasy about Mulholland's movements. I mean, I had been working for him since October and I just—you know—had a sense of something."

"We knew who we were fighting," said La Camera. "They were hard-line Taliban and al Qaeda. We also knew we would probably be fighting Chechens, though other nationalities were unknown. In any case, these were the hard-core guys and so as a commander I was thinking, 'Let's plan for the worst.' We had all read the classic Soviet texts about fighting in this area—including *The Bear Went over the Mountain*—and we were now moving in the same direction. So I went and talked to him, Mulholland, the day before the battle and said 'What is going on here?' And that is when he explained to me about the numbers, and he said that his intelligence could not say precisely if the al Qaeda forces were in the valley going to the hills for resupply or in the hills going to the valley."

Colonel Mulholland could not be specific when it came to telling La Camera what to expect. But Mulholland wasn't going to beat around the bush, either. "I was almost in a second skin by this time and I was getting more and more concerned about what we were flying into," Mulholland told me much later in Kentucky. "I guess La Camera sensed that."

Early on, Tenth Mountain and parallel forces from the 101st Airborne Division had been told to expect from two to three hundred enemy fighters in the valley, but Mulholland was thinking on the eve of the battle that the figure was probably closer to six or seven hundred. The latest guesses at enemy strength got to the ground troops at the last minute. Yet, as with the changing situation at Tora Bora, it was not clear whether the enemy was goading for a major showdown or just hiding out and regrouping for guerrilla attacks across Afghanistan. "I told the Tenth commanders that as soon as you get off the chopper you should be looking up the hill," said Mulholland.

"Then I said right before the insertion that they had probably fled up into the mountains, but that was nothing more than pure gut."

For La Camera to find this out at the last minute was disconcerting, but he did the math to make sure he was prepared. "I wargamed it and thought, OK, well, we have enough. Our three hundred guys will be enough considering the close air support and the mortars that we were taking into the battle." While La Camera still believed that he would be on a blocking mission, with the Afghans approaching the whale in a convoy of light vehicles, he also knew that his role was no less important. "Everyone wants to score a touchdown, but you still need blockers for the quarterback to throw the pass," he told me.

Despite the uncertainty only hours before the most important ground battle for U.S. troops in the war in Afghanistan, the basic game plan remained the same. Much of the heady optimism had to do with the knowledge that American ground troops—and their trained spotters on the ground—would have aerial bombing support. They would have the best assets of the U.S. Air Force, Navy, and Army on constant call.

In a sense, the Anaconda battle plan was a compromise between the use of Afghan proxies—which had worked early in toppling the regime but failed miserably at Tora Bora—and a conventional U.S.-led attack, which had not yet been attempted. For the Tenth Mountain Division's chief of planning and operations, Col. David Gray, the attack would be "as close to a siege" as you could get in Afghanistan. "There were to be three concentric rings in order to isolate the objective area," he said. "We wanted to cover all the rat lines, any of the escape routes they might attempt to use. We decided not to have prolonged air campaign, because we felt that the Soviets, when they had tried similar things, had made the mistakes to begin these kinds of operations with a long bombardment." Heavy bombing, it was believed, might well "spook" the bad guys and get them on the run before the blockers fell into place. This was, of course, a consideration that planners had left off the table at Tora Bora.

For each of the seven helicopter landing zones, or HLZs, some fifty troops, or two platoons, would be inserted, with two choppers touching down initially. Command could accelerate the insertions depending on the resistance at hand. Soldiers would march from each HLZ to a "blocking position" of the same name up in the mountains, sometimes as much as two thousand meters higher than the HLZ, but less than a thousand meters as the crow flies.

Col. Charles "Chip" Preysler of the 101st commanded the forces that would move into the first four blocking positions—Amy, Betty, Cindy, and Diane. The savvy Michigan State Reserve Officer Training Corps graduate and father of two felt uncertain about what he would confront in the mountains, but he too was anxious to prove his mettle. He met with Colonel La Camera, who informed him that his own Tenth Mountain outfit would seize positions Eve, Ginger, and Heather.

For some of the boys, the idea of attacking positions like Heather and Cindy sounded like a raucous Saturday night party with ladies galore. But for Preysler, a thin, sometimes jumpy beer drinker dedicated to his men, it was to be deadly serious work. He and La Camera went carefully over their plans to round up the enemy—to separate the chaff from the wheat. Several psy-ops teams were to be attached to the fighting units in order to show fleeing fighters and civilians signboards in Pashtun and Dari asking them to halt and surrender to save their own lives. In addition to the signs, the psy-ops teams had megaphones and barbed wire to halt the enemy and to set up temporary holding pens as needed.

# 7

## MEETING YOUR MAKER

The vile and horrid mutilations, which the tribesmen inflict on all bodies that fall into their hands, and the insults to which they expose them, add, to unphilosophic minds, another terror to death. Now, it takes at least 4 men, and very often more, to carry away a body. Observe the result. The group of men bearing the injured are excellent targets.

—Winston Churchill,
*The Story of the Malakand Field Force*

### Moon Landing

In the black Afghan skies, twinkling with stars, several shooting across the horizon, the Tenth Mountain Division began loading seventy-pound rucksacks onto Chinooks at the Bagram Air Base. Sgt. Tom Finch's head had been buzzing for hours with anticipation; the inspirational speeches that his commanders had made had gone mostly in one ear and out the other. The stocky, blond Georgian with sparkling blue eyes was twitching like a bird, and, as usual, he wasn't able to keep his mouth shut. His endearing southern drawl, spinning tales of chasing ladies and hunting wild animals in swamps hung with Spanish moss, had calmed the nerves of his colleagues in the weeks of anxious waiting in Uzbekistan and then in Afghanistan for their first shot at a still faceless enemy. As far as Finch was concerned, these so-called terrorists could just as well have been "zombies."

Earlier that night of March 1, when the mission commander, Colonel Frank Wiercinski, had addressed his men, he had reminded them of the courage of the New York City firemen who died trying to save lives in the 9/11 inferno. However, that kind of talk meant nothing to Finch this late in the game. For him, the motivation had always been the same: al Qaeda were "a bunch of bastards" who threatened his own ideas and the 225 years of freedom through which his own nation had struggled. He knew that because it had been repeated like a mantra back home in Georgia in the aftermath of September 11. Now he just wanted to get down to business and maybe—as one of the commanders had joked—have a long drink in a bar somewhere back in the States and share war stories about the "big battle." That was a nice, pleasant thought, and as the big Chinook flew through the starry Afghan night, Finch, normally a ball of cheer, grew dreary and dozed off. It might have been the most important day of his life, but he also needed some shut-eye.

Across from Finch in the flying machine sat two dozen elite fighters of the Tenth Mountain Division from Fort Drum. They included New York native Eddie "Doc" Rivera, who wasn't there so much to take on the bad guys as to save his buddies if and when they went down. For him, this struggle was about a civilian he had trained with in New York, a fire department medic who had died in the World Trade Center collapse. Rivera's memory of this innocent, kindhearted man who had not deserved to die kept him focused on what lay ahead. This was it—the moment to prove something. As he psyched himself up for the fight, the rotor blades of the big Chinook sounded like the thumping beat of a favorite rap music song. "Whap, chook, whap, chook, whap, chook." As he listened, the wiry, young Afro-Latino had only one thought that kept spinning like the blades of the giant bird. He said it felt almost like a gangland rumble in the making: "I was just thinkin', Yo, OK. Bring it on, al Qaeda. Let's see what you got! Play me now, bitch!"

The Tenth and 101st commanders who had planned the surprise attack had hoped to get the choppers down under the cover of the night to avoid taking ground fire. But as the Chinooks swept in from two directions around the "Whale," a two-mile-long hump in the earth at the base of the mountains, the sky took on an inviting pink hue. Apache helicopter gunships had flown in ten minutes earlier to survey the terrain, a move that had given the al Qaeda remaining in the three main villages of the Shah-I-Kot time to lock and load. Scores of al Qaeda fighters, who had arisen early to the sound of the reconnaissance craft, scrambled up through the small wadis, or ravines, to join colleagues higher up in the deep folds of the Shah-I-Kot mountains. They began digging into the very "blocking positions" that the U.S. forces hoped to seize. Despite extensive U.S. air surveillance of the valley in the weeks and days leading up to the offensive, dozens of hidden al Qaeda positions had gone unnoticed. Indeed, these positions, hidden in crevices and behind rocks, amounted to a drawn-out stairway into the heavens above, two miles in the air and overlooking the entire valley. In effect, the Shah-I-Kot provided a nearly perfect guerrilla redoubt, in that it allowed Arab and Chechen fighters, who had no air power of their own, to use the steep, jagged cliffs to fire down on an approaching enemy.

As the morning sun began to streak the landscape, two Chinooks set down a few hundred meters apart, and young American fighters began to leap into the desolate, seemingly abandoned valley at the base of the mountains. As the ramps lowered, Charlie Company fighters skipped out over the parched, frozen landscape of dirt and shale onto landing zone (LZ) thirteen. The first step for Sergeant Finch felt a little like his own, personal moon landing. He jumped out and looked up behind him into the snow-capped mountains, three thousand feet above the seven-thousand-foot plateau where he had touched down. Behind him stood the Whale, which, though flush with al Qaeda, looked mostly uninhabitable from Finch's vantage point. If the enemy had the high ground, they were "in for the shit," he thought to himself.

For the first ten minutes, the deployment went without a hitch. The only sound was the "whap chook, whap chook" of the rotor blades. Charlie Company moved quickly to link up with their fellows. They assembled from their two Chinooks at a point a stone's throw from the intended landing zone but close enough to begin the planned march into the mountains, where they still planned to take up their preassigned blocking position.

Lt. Bradley Maroyka, a twenty-six-year-old Charlie Company

platoon leader, knew as soon as the first shot rang out that a major battle had begun. As bullets began to rain from the mountainous high ground above them, the riflemen dove for cover wherever they could find it. Maroyka ordered his soldiers to set up the two 120 mm mortars. The initial enemy fire was coming not from the Whale but from the crags and boulders farther up in the mountains, and Maroyka knew that the heavy mortars were the only artillery that could wreak havoc that high. The platoon scrambled for several minutes to put in place the three-hundred-pound system, but the heavy incoming fire soon made it impossible to continue.

Cover in the frigid earth near the landing zone proved difficult to find. After the first shots, Sergeant Finch ran for a small gully a short

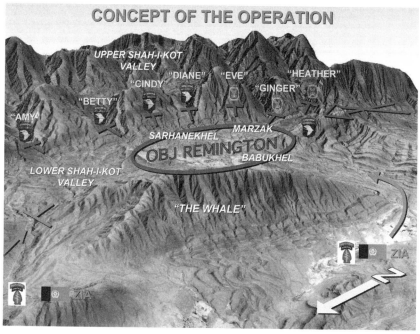

*Operation Anaconda: In the original battle plan, U.S. forces intended to take up "blocking positions" on the high ground, with the 101st Airborne holding Amy through Diane, and the 10th Mountain at Eve, Ginger, and Heather. Afghan allies commanded by Zia Lodin, and accompanied by Green Berets, were supposed to sweep into the valley from both sides of the Whale, forcing al Qaeda to flee the three villages of Sarhanekhel, Marzak, and Babukhel (objective Remington) and into the shooting range of U.S. forces on the ridge.*

distance from where he had just put down. He opened the safety on his machine gun and started returning fire into the hills. For the young Georgian, the firefight unfolded like a war movie. It felt thrilling and also a little terrifying as he caught his first glimpse of the men he thought of as "zombies." The enemy he saw wore black turbans and long capes "like something out of the Arabian Knights." They ran between rocks, switching positions, with their robes billowing in the air. Hitting them was one immense shell game that made the range exercises back at Fort Drum look comparatively easy.

"There were two kinds of guys shooting down at us," Finch would recall. "Some of them, the chickens, would just stick their guns over a rock and spray over the tops at us. Their fire almost never hit anywhere near us. Then there were the hard cores, many of them with high-powered rifles, who were putting down slow, meticulous fire from about two thousand feet up. These guys were potentially deadly and they kept us on the move, rolling right and rolling left." Finch's rifle company was in the hottest LZ in the valley, and for the first full day of the fighting in the Shah-I-Kot it would receive the heaviest fire from al Qaeda positions.

As soon as the battle kicked off, ground control informed Capt. Bill Ryan, piloting one of six Apache helicopters belonging to the 101st Airborne, that their mission had switched from acting as forward gunners for the approaching Afghans and Special Forces to covering the Tenth elements pinned down in the valley. Ground control offered no immediate explanation, and Ryan had no time to ponder. This was the first time that the deadly Apaches would see action in Afghanistan, and if the game in the hills and valley was shoot and dodge, it was so with the air war as well. Al Qaeda fighters knew how to knock a bird out of the sky—some had years of experience taking out Soviet choppers—and so Ryan, sitting in the front of the bubble on top of a bucket of Kevlar plating, started zipping back and forth in circles and dives. He felt a little like a fly getting chased by a swatter. While he dodged fire from an enemy DSHK 12.7 mm, his copilot, Jody Kilburn, in the backseat, took over the guns. Kilburn began to lay down pairs of the Apache's thirty-eight rockets. It would have been nice to be shooting at large tanks, the targets often used in practice back in Kentucky, but the crew had to make do with the instructions they were getting from the ground. Even from the air, the al Qaeda positions were tough to spot.

The Apache pilots knew the general vicinity of the al Qaeda fighters, but since maintaining one single heading for too long was too dangerous, they found it difficult to home in. Further, there was an added risk of "fratricide," since the al Qaeda fighters had popped up in locations where the war plan said U.S. troops would be. Just fifteen minutes into the fight, machine-gun fire hit the first Apache, stitching its belly with bullets. Capt. Jim Hardy steadied his bird and radioed that he would try to remain and draw fire away from the other choppers.

Captain Ryan still felt safe in the bucket of Kevlar armor, which came up around his hips. He knew he had to work quickly, because his distance from the refueling post left him just an hour in the air. "The guys on the ground were driving our fire and target selection. They gave us distance and direction. If it hadn't been for them, we wouldn't have known what or where we were shooting. It was what we call 'running fire.' We were always changing altitude, dipping and bobbing to make ourselves a hard target. After forty-five minutes, al Qaeda hit another of our choppers. A surface-to-air SA-7 hit an Apache, ripping out part of the fuel system and setting a black smoke trail billowing out the back. It was all the bird could do to dip down the backside of the mountain before it cut and run for cover. The other four craft, two in the north and two in the south, kept up an incessant fire that gave the ground warriors more time to arrange their own positions.

"We were putting a lot of rounds in on them when a DSHK bullet popped through the plexiglass of my right window, hit me in the jaw, deflected off the door and went out the top bubble," said Ryan. "I looked around. There was nothing loose and my face was bleeding but it wasn't gushing. I put down some more rounds and noticed that we were almost at bingo fuel [just enough left to return to base], so we turned back and headed out."

Maroyka, Finch, and company watched the retreating Apaches with a sense of despair. They would have liked to have them around longer, but they had been warned in prebattle briefings that the Apaches, never tested in combat at two miles high in close air support for infantry, had only limited staying power. In the end, "they fired their load and they were gone, we never saw them again," said Maroyka. "They were taking so much fire, it just sounded like someone had lit off a whole bunch of firecrackers every time they flew over. It wasn't their fault. They just couldn't hang."

As the Apaches zipped off into the rising sun, the fire raining down on the U.S. fighters from the mountaintops intensified. The "anvil" was struggling to take up its position, but the "hammer" had not appeared on the scene. Col. David Gray, one of the chief architects of the attack plan, was getting itchy back at Bagram Air Base. "The Special Forces column coming in with Zia Lodin's fighters was strung out," he later recalled. "The ground was slippery and several vehicles overturned as they approached the Whale." Zia's men, Colonel Mulholland still insisted, could be counted on. They were what he liked to call "tier one Pashtuns"; "They were just awesome and did anything you asked them to do."

But there was one thing that the Afghans would not do no matter how much Mulholland had paid them up front—and that was to go head to head with an American AC-130 Spectre gunship. With an autoloading 105 mm cannon, a Bofors 40 mm cannon, a 25 mm Gatling gun, and smaller chain guns, the Spectre can decimate anything in its path. A huge, low-flying plane, however, it usually attacks at night and must rely on good on-the-ground intelligence to put its heavy weaponry to proper use.

Several of Mulholland's best commanders, under Lt. Col. Chris Haas with the Fifth Special Forces Group, had begun their approach to the hammer positions the night before, after loading dozens of pickup trucks with heavy guns and 380 of Zia Lodin's Afghan fighters. The Afghan force planned its approach to the Shah-I-Kot so as to move through the three major villages of Sarhanekhel, Babukhel, and Marzak. The idea had been to push the enemy into the waiting arms of the U.S. conventional forces.

Hours before the Chinooks had touched down, Zia's fighters had been approaching the left flank of the Whale, with Mulholland's Special Forces troops in the lead. As the convoy struggled through mud and sporadic al Qaeda fire, a Spectre gunship dropped out of the night and opened up with cannons and heavy machine-gun fire. In the Pentagon's initial reports of the fighting, U.S. officials would incorrectly report that Zia's men made a hasty retreat after coming under fire from al Qaeda. It was the "Afghan way," they insisted, to retreat and fight again another day. A U.S. officer in the Pentagon was highly dismissive of Zia. "This is the way everybody fights over there. Fight and fall back. You don't want to take too many combat losses yourself. You save your resources from attrition, to make sure you stay in power when it's all over." But in a second, more complete version of the incident, which took eight months to work its way through the Pentagon's after-battle reporting system, U.S. military investigators determined that the Spectre had strafed the convoy in repeated runs, having mistaken the U.S. troops and their Afghan protégés for al Qaeda. Fire from the gunship wracked the convoy, cut holes in engines, and blew out tires, killing Chief Warrant Officer Stanley Harriman and several Afghans.

Harriman, second in command of the "Cobra 72" Green Beret unit, one of two special teams moving into the Shah-I-Kot, was wounded in an initial strafing. He managed to jump out of his vehicle and run down the line ordering everyone, including the Afghans, to dive for cover. After issuing his orders, the young warrant officer sprinted back toward his own vehicle, apparently to try to call off the Spectre. He was hit again and killed almost instantly. Combined with unexpectedly heavy fire from al Qaeda and Taliban positions in the hills, the AC-130 drove the Afghan "hammer" into hasty retreat, concluding one of the more unfortunate friendly fire incidents of the war. Zia Lodin's men left their guns and vehicles strung out on the muddy approaches to the Shah-I-Kot Valley. They had failed to make it into the heart of the battle—and would not return to the fight for nearly a week. Zia's day in the sun and his big U.S.-dollar bonus had to be put on hold. Back in Gardez, his men complained bitterly about the American cock-up.

As soon as the U.S.-led Afghan convoy cut and run, the battle plan—at least everything on paper—for Operation Anaconda fell apart in tatters. The fate of both the enemy and the young U.S. infantrymen would have to be decided by creative, often spontaneous, thinking on both sides of the lines. Elements of the Tenth, and the

101st Airborne were hanging tough, but they could already see that they were outmaneuvered and outgunned.

Just over three hours into the battle, al Qaeda attacks on the U.S. units in the valley became sharper. Al Qaeda fighters, through less sophisticated means than their adversary, targeted U.S. positions with mortar fire—they used their height advantage to watch their rounds land and then adjust their barrels. This kept the Americans on their toes, dodging incoming rounds. For some of the fighters it felt like a fatal game, a dance with death that some would surely lose. They suspected that their foe had been setting this trap days and weeks in advance. As Maroyka, Finch, and company rolled away from one mortar round, they moved directly into another burst that hit in the middle of a dozen men. "There was a massive explosion and shrapnel hit me in four places: my thigh, my ankle, my hand and my hip," later recalled Lieutenant Maroyka, who was moving his men out of the line of fire. "It was strange, though, because I felt almost nothing at first. Then I looked down and an artery in my leg was spurting blood all over the dirt. I was pretty rattled, but I didn't realize how bad it was. I looked back and seven of my guys were on the ground, none of them moving. I thought, for sure, that most of them were dead."

The Tenth's fighters still standing threw down their packs and started dragging the wounded down a slight incline into a natural crater with an overhanging rim that provided cover. It took two, sometimes three men to help pull one wounded man into what Tenth soldiers quickly dubbed "the Bowl." A half-dozen fighters screamed in agony. It would be the start of what would be for some of the most religious in the ranks a ten-hour prayer vigil.

Doc Rivera immediately realized that he would be hard pressed to save lives. As Rivera pulled the wounded under the lip of the Bowl and helped cut through shirts to get at the injuries, he also ripped off honeycombed Kevlar "interceptor body armor." On many of the soldiers it had been indented, crushed inward, but had kept out the heaviest shrapnel. Despite some gashes, the armor had done its work impeccably. Rivera's forty-five-pound medical kit hadn't nearly enough bandages to stop all the bleeding that erupted after the first major strike. "I got to work immediately," he said. "I grabbed my bandages, my IVs, and just started wrapping up whatever I could." Rivera also kept an eye on everyone's blood pressure and alertness. He knew that if his patients slipped into unconsciousness at this altitude, and with the long wait ahead, it would mean almost certain death. Kyle McGovern, a twenty-year-old kid from New Hampshire, had suffered the worst injuries, as though he had been through a malfunctioning meat grinder. The mortar attack had mangled his legs beyond recognition. He had dozens of small and large metal fragments still lodged in his lower body.

Rivera already saw the shadow of death hanging over McGovern. "He was in a daze and you could just look at him and know that he wasn't all there. I shot him up about two times. He asked me what was wrong and I was like, don't you worry—just get some rest. Just lay back. We started to realize after a while that we were going to be there for a long time. That is when the frustration and fear started to set in. All you could hear was the whiz of the incoming."

The Arabs, Chechens, and Afghans shooting down from the mountains also had comrades just across the valley, ensconced on the high ground of the Whale. One mortar team consisted of two men and a mule, moving constantly from one camouflaged position to the next. The low-tech fire teams would prove agile enough to survive for a full ten days on the same ridge. Al Qaeda fighters, their robes and lambskins flying behind them as they sprinted back and forth between boulders, had moved in closer to the Bowl even as the Tenth took its worst casualties. They circled their prey like wolves or vultures, coming within one hundred meters, then dropping back to two hundred to wait, looking for the right moment to finish the infidels off.

The only hope the Americans had of fending off the enemy was to seize at least some of the high ground. Both al Qaeda machine gunners and forward artillery spotters would have to be eliminated with—as it were—extreme prejudice.

Behind the LZs, across from the base of the Whale, the Tenth's Colonel La Camera, perched safely on a mountain ledge overlooking most of the battlefield. He was in communication with his fighters in the Bowl, though conversation was limited because some of the heaviest comms equipment had been left on open ground when fighters dove for cover. He knew that Maroyka and his men needed to eliminate the sharpest resistance, and he had a pretty good idea of who would be up to the task. This was the time when a commander's close eye on those who had excelled in training became crucial. La Camera sent down an order through Maroyka to take out the spotters. Sergeant Finch, who had remained above the Bowl with a scout team and could see the scene deteriorating before his eyes, would lead the charge.

"We started firing up as much lead as we could muster," said Finch. "Most of the fire was coming down from the high mountains—about 2,500 feet above us, but the only way they could see us was with their spotters."

It looked to Finch like a single sniper on a ridge about a thousand feet up was doing almost all of the target spotting. "He was right up on the edge of the rocks, in a grouping of boulders and trees. When we started moving up, he went around the other side of the rock to put more fire down the hill. He was peeking around the rocks."

Finch and his team of some half-dozen fighters crept up the mountainside, darting from one large rock and overhang to the next. Gaining a ridge on a level with the sniper, the team fired several rounds but hit nothing. Then the al Qaeda fighter, swathed in black, slipped out from behind a boulder back into the open, and the team fired several 203 mm rounds from the launcher—grenades suspended beneath the barrels of assault rifles. That was it. "We moved over and all I saw was a bent up sniper rifle and a half of a leg stuck in a boot," said Finch, who kept right on shooting, jamming new clips into his gun as he moved.

Then came the surprise. When Finch's team began moving forward toward the dead fighter's position, thinking they had wiped out the sniper's lair, four more al Qaeda shooters popped up from behind a nearby cluster of rocks. For Finch, it was turning into a nightmare video game. "Once we killed him, his security unit opened up on us—like blam, blam, blam. We started taking mad, blistering fire. We quickly took cover and started leapfrogging across the ridge with guys laying down cover for each other and dashing ahead. We were moving across killing everyone who was along that ridgeline. Someone hollered at the top of his lungs, 'I got one!'" Finch, who was always talking, chattering like a bird, felt his own vocal cords freeze up. Suddenly, there was too much fighting to breathe a word. Finch's team of a half-dozen took down eleven enemy fighters in the matter of about ten minutes. Their work done, they beat a retreat back down to the Bowl.

Almost as soon as his fighters had left their choppers, the idea of complete extraction had been on the mind of Colonel La Camera. There was talk of how to get at least the wounded out. Over twenty—nearly a quarter of the total eighty-five—of his fighters were injured, many of them in dire straits. Al Qaeda fighters still had the high ground on two sides, and dozens remained holed up in the adobe rubble of the nearby villages of Marzak, Sarhanekhel, and Babukhel, ready to pounce on any choppers that tried to make a landing. "We still had to set the conditions to bring the choppers back in," he said. "We knew that the enemy knew that choppers without cover would be our greatest vulnerability. That is what they hoped for." Charlie Company's commander wanted the first and second platoons out of the Shah-I-Kot as soon as possible, but he also knew they had the staying power to dig in and fight through the day. "In this kind of a situation, you aren't fighting for mom and apple pie, a piece of paper or a plaque," added La Camera. "You fight for each other, to protect your buddies. My guys were fighting because they didn't want to let their buddies down."

Following the early departure of the Apache attack choppers, heavy U.S. air support—including Air Force and Navy aircraft—moved in to fill the holes. From heights of several thousand feet, however, the fresh bombing runs served mostly to suppress al Qaeda fire, not eliminate the enemy.

Other commanders, such as Colonel Wiercinski of the 101st Airborne Division, were having troubles of their own. While hovering over the fray, Wiercinski's Black Hawk had been hit by a rocket-propelled grenade (RPG) that hadn't exploded, but had severely damaged the underbelly and forced his command unit to set down in the valley. Almost immediately, al Qaeda fighters, keen to turn the battle of Anaconda into Mogadishu II, attacked the chopper and unleashed a fury of small arms and RPG fire. With little notice, the colonel, who was now commanding Operation Anaconda on the ground, found himself in the midst of a major defensive firefight that would continue sporadically for eighteen hours before his extraction. In the meantime, he continued to issue orders from his embattled post.

Several kilometers to the north of Maroyka's team (or to the left, facing some forbidding mountains, which spilled into Pakistan), 140 of Wiercinski's troops of the 101st were slowly slipping into a vexing predicament of their own, albeit one that would take longer to develop. After jumping off their Chinook onto the designated landing zone, Sgt. Earl Beaudry, thirty-one, a Gulf War veteran who had never seen close combat, began struggling up the mountainside toward his assigned blocking position, along with the rest of his platoon. He had been training hard as a soldier for over ten years, but he could have done without the added bulk around his gut. He had the good cooking of his second wife partly to blame for that. In addition to a lighter load, he figured it might also have helped to have a pickax as well, to negotiate the steep incline. Rather than shoot straight up the mountain, the platoon skirted around to the side and made a half-circle approach to their destination. "I was suckin' air at nine thousand feet and we were slippin' in the snow even in our cold weather boots," Beaudry said later. "The planes were hitting the mountains so al Qaeda did not shoot back at us. After about twenty minutes we spotted one person in a bunker about five hundred meters away." Oddly enough, the 101st fighters had not yet received orders to shoot at anything that moved. Orders to turn the valley into a "free-fire zone" would come, but as it was the platoon had to radio to Lt. Col. Chip Preysler for permission to engage the target. As soon as a voice on the other end said, "Go ahead," the Americans fired, and the al Qaeda fighter slouched over from a direct hit, bleeding to death in his bunker.

Beaudry's mate, Adam Skillen, a tall, strapping farm boy from Suzanneville, California, hadn't bargained for an uphill battle of this nature, but he figured he was up to the task. As the climb continued, more and more al Qaeda fighters popped up from behind boulders. About four hours into the march, a group of Arabs and Chechens slipped down on their left flank, knelt down behind rocks, and started shooting. To Skillen, it felt like something out of a western, with the Indians, al Qaeda, harassing American cowboys. "Every fifteen or twenty minutes they would jump up and shoot again and then pop back behind the rocks," he said. Across the valley, from one end to the other, the taunts began, echoing off the high walls of the Whale and back across the valley. The al Qaeda fighters were shouting, sometimes laughing. They bellowed taunts, one even in English— "C'mon, Let's see what you can do for George Bush!"

"A couple of guys grabbed the M-203, the 40 mm grenade launcher, and tried to shoot up at them," continued Skillen. "They shot one short and then one long and then the al Qaeda guys popped back up again. I dropped down with my own rifle and fired from a prone, but he dropped down. So, I took a scope from one of my gunners and put it on my weapon. There was a tree right next to where he was coming up. So, I fired a couple of shots at the tree to gauge my point of aim. I had it set just right, so I waited."

It wasn't a sure thing, but Skillen was hoping the al Qaeda fighter was dumb enough to pop out at the same location. He sat motionless, in position, for a couple of minutes that seemed like an hour. As he waited, Skillen thought about what he was about to do. "I wasn't thinkin' about judgment or revenge," he thought to himself. "That was God's job. My job was simply to arrange the meeting. I put my point of aim right back on the spot where I had seen his head come up, I just waited, and when he popped his head up, I shot him. I hit him in the forehead and there was a little burst of red mist that filled the air."

Beaudry saw Skillen's kill and gave a whoop. He was impressed, but he was also getting furious about the fix he was in. Most of the al Qaeda fighters were not brave enough to come out into the open for long, but they still had a huge height advantage. "We knew they would be up there because we had had a last-minute intelligence drop that said some of them had already made it up into the mountains. But now they had the high ground and as soon as we came under fire, we had to hunker down and start building up our own shooting positions from scratch. We just rolled boulders and stacked big old rocks. But even as we did this, we were getting pissed. They were shooting RPG's right over our heads as we worked."

## Bleedin' Bad

Back at Bagram, Mulholland and Hagenbeck knew by midday of the first day that they had a major battle on their hands. Mulholland, whose estimates of the numbers of anti-American fighters in the valley had risen substantially as the battle unfolded, was concerned, along with General Hagenbeck, about the possibility that several hundred more al Qaeda and local jihadis were trying to join the fray against U.S. forces.

With boots on the ground and eyes in the air, U.S. commanders at Bagram were equipped to keep track of the enemy influx. This was, after all, the age of robotic warfare. One of the most fascinating—and potentially useful—advances was the ability of commanders, even several thousand miles away, to view frontline fighting through real-time video images. The Predator drone, flown by a ground controller stationed in the Gulf, could, in addition to shooting Hellfire missiles, take constant pictures of the enemy as U.S. infantry units advanced through the valley. Mulholland and Hagenbeck had the same video stream crossing their monitors in Bagram.

Mulholland found the footage coming from the al Qaeda positions useful, but he cautioned himself that he was still only seeing "a piece of the action and not necessarily everything." The ability of the drones to monitor the maze of caverns and overhangs was limited, not least because of the clouded skies. The colonel already knew from the sound and pictures, though, that this fight was bogging down.

Afghan commander Zia Lodin was already back in Gardez licking his wounds when Mulholland asked one of his own most trusted lieutenants, Lieutenant Colonel Haas, to try to persuade the Afghan warlord and his 350 men to reenter the fray. It was a tall order. The Afghan mercenary leader said that his men had not been given proper air cover moving into the Shah-I-Kot, on top of which the Spectre gunship had attacked his men. Still trying to recover from the deadly incident, Zia and his men would decline to reenter the battle for days to come.

Across the valley, which ran northward between the high mountains and the Whale, the 101st Airborne's Lieutenant Colonel Preysler heard over his radio that Charlie Company was in dire straits. He still had 135 of his own 101st Airborne troops, and their positions had held up better than expected. He consulted his superiors and suggested that there wasn't any point remaining halfway up the mountain when there wasn't anyone down below—namely Zia's Afghan fighters—to push the enemy up toward the blocking positions. "I told him that we were blocking, but we didn't have a hammer, so why don't we get out of here and re-cock this thing and then sweep the valley. There was no reason just to stay there and circle the wagon. At this point, al Qaeda was not coming out to press the fight and we were not going down there to get them."

General Hagenbeck, too, knew his fighters had lost the upper hand. He already had scrapped the "hammer and anvil" plan. On top of that, several Apache helicopters belonging to the 101st were out of commission. The AC-130s he had were required to do double duty, but daytime fighting was not their forte; they worked best by night under the moonlight, when their hulking frames were less easy to spot.

Hagenbeck's initial thinking back at HQ was to pull all the U.S. infantrymen out of the Shah-I-Kot pocket and devise a new plan of attack. He would be willing to wait until Mulholland could get his Afghans back up to speed and return them to the fray. In other words, Hagenbeck and Mulholland were ready, in Preysler's words, to "re-cock" the attack in anticipation that al Qaeda might stick around and still be ready for a showdown with the American "infidels." With intelligence reports indicating a steady stream of al Qaeda reinforcements streaming in from Pakistan, the latter was certainly true, but devising a new plan to squeeze al Qaeda, whose fighters had already seized the high ground, would be easier said than done.

Under the first new plan, most of the three hundred–plus U.S. soldiers in the valley would move back down out of the foothills and then northward after dark to prepare for extraction. Meanwhile, other units, including Green Beret teams, would continue to provide eyes for the air war. But then another, more daring, idea arose—not to abandon the valley but keep as many U.S. soldiers in the fray as possible and simply clear it out, in hopes of killing as many remaining al Qaeda fighters as possible. It was a risky but arguably braver option. Hagenbeck ordered Preysler to pull down the mountain but hold onto the valley. In addition, Preysler would get another company—135 fighters—to bolster the force he already had. At the same time, small Green Beret teams accompanied by special forces units from Australia, Norway, Canada, Denmark, Germany, and France, were asked to move higher into the mountains to both chase al Qaeda already there and block those who might flee from the three main villages at the base of the Whale.

A total of 187 fresh Tenth Mountain troops were also to be sent to reinforce their own units hunkering down farther to the south. While some of the highest ground had already been conceded to al Qaeda, American commanders were now banking on their dominance in the skies and on their overwhelming firepower to win the Anaconda battle. American and allied spotters, working their way on foot into the mountains, now became as important to the final victory as the infantry left to fight in the valley. Still, without the U.S. fighters still slogging through the valley, al Qaeda might not have bothered to keep fighting. They might well have, as they had done at Tora Bora, pulled up stakes and fled back into Pakistan to regroup.

Back with the Tenth, the situation grew tougher by the hour, even after Finch's heroics. As Charlie Company fighters defended the perimeter of the Bowl, they got better air support, mostly from Air Force jets, but they were still taking hits along the rim that faced up the mountain. Jeff Almy, twenty-four, a feisty, blue-eyed gunner from Rhode Island who was firing cover for the two dozen injured fighters under the lip, had taken hits in the helmet and Kevlar vest, but had held his ground until a large-caliber round wrenched into his thigh. Finch had been watching his back. "He is about twenty feet above me and he gets hit hard. All I can think is—Jesus Christ—this is my buddy. He just falls back and rolls down right into my arms. He had his leg clenched tight and he was calling for a doc. I could see the bullet just sticking out of his leg and all I could think was I gotta get it out and reduce the pain."

Finch told Almy his plans, and he heard back, " 'Do what you gotta do,' so I pulled it and it didn't resist, but his leg was so tight, I guess, that when I got it out and he relaxed it, it just burst out with blood like a fountain. It was spurting in my eyes and in my mouth. I gagged for air. To top it off there was this wretched smell of burning flesh eating at my nostrils. I had him clamp his own leg and grabbed some bandages. The first four bandages I put on his leg soaked through completely. It was like trying to stop a water spigot with tissue paper." Doc Rivera saw what was happening and ran over to help. He had already run out of his own bandages and the Charlie fighters just started ripping up their shirts and pant legs to make more. If there hadn't been so much blood flying, it would have looked like a demented version of one of those college fraternity parties—everyone trying to rip each other down to their underwear. Only the young ladies were missing.

"You had to jump over the casualties and tuck in their heads," said Rivera. "You could hear them asking, 'Why are you covering me, what is going on?' And when another mortar round hit, you would have to gauge where the next one was going to hit and move your ass and everyone else's who couldn't move theirs to a new position. They couldn't just pick up and run, I mean, you had to drag them. After you'd been doin' this for a few hours, you were exhausted."

For Rivera and those still fighting, about two-thirds of the original eighty-five, a mental exhaustion had set in that equaled the physical strain. "I was upset and it was becoming hard for me to reassure myself that we would get out of this thing alive. At the same time, it was my job to reassure the others. Everyone was askin' me, 'Am I going to see my daughter, my wife, my kids?' You live with these guys for months, right next to each other, every day all day. You get to know them so well that you start to love the ones you hate. I mean, you know everything about them, you know who has kids and who doesn't. You know who is a cowboy and who isn't. Some of our men had been bleedin' bad for ten hours and that was a pretty bad thing to be watchin' and not being able to do much. On the other hand, it was like a miracle that we had two dozen down and no one dead. I looked up at the starry night and thought someone up there must be on our side. But there were still guys who could have gone down for good any minute. Sergeant Black had the back of his leg shredded from his knee down to his ankle. I was thinking that he was going to go into shock any minute. That could happen if he lost too much blood and his body would have just shut down." In the mad scramble to take cover, the men had thrown down their rucksacks containing blankets and bandages some two hundred meters away from the Bowl. These items were out in the open. It was simply too risky now to crawl through the al Qaeda fire to retrieve them.

As the sun set, al Qaeda showed no sign of letting up. The Bowl was beginning to look like a possible last stand. Most of the trapped fighters had lost hope of the choppers' getting in to evacuate them, until about six, when an AC-130 Spectre swept down through the valley's barely fading light. The sound of the mammoth fifty-year-old flying freight train turned the wails of pain in the Bowl to cries of joy. Its Gatling guns whirling, the big ship cut up al Qaeda positions, killing only a handful but sending most of the others fleeing deeper into caves and bunkers. When the big guns rained their terror down on al Qaeda, Almy and Maroyka, both suffering from injuries and sharing a blanket, began screaming with joy. They had been pulling each other closer to keep from freezing in temperatures that had already plummeted below zero. Maroyka recalled, "We had to keep each other warm, so we just kept wrapping our arms around each other. It was basic—Survival 101—but our hugs, meant to keep us warm, were now—suddenly—about something else."

Salvation was upon them. Maroyka couldn't help but think that if he survived he would have a pretty good story to tell. "Al Qaeda turned out to be a bunch of pussies!" he said later. "They were a bunch of talk until they got into the fight. When they realized what kind of combat power we had, they didn't want anything to do with us. They cut and ran. We had finally done what we were in country to do and we killed a lot of them. They hightailed it out of there and they were gone."

At about ten o'clock that evening, sixteen hours into the battle, two Chinooks settled into the dust of the Shah-I-Kot Valley. Maroyka's weary rifle platoon moved its injured—a third of its fighting force of four score—into the choppers for extraction. The al Qaeda guns in the hills had fallen eerily silent, but despite Maroyka's sentiments, many other fighters in the Tenth and 101st had a new impression of al Qaeda's staying power. The young Americans credited the enemy, in these initial stages of the battle, with outfoxing them.

The dawn of the second day broke over the Shah-I-Kot, spreading a pink hue over the rocks and bringing with it the renewed taunts of al Qaeda fighters from the mouths of their caves and crevices above. Under a new, redesigned battle plan, orders went to the 101st to continue marching to the north. They were to sweep the valley and hook up with the remaining elements of the Tenth. To get across the valley, though, the infantry troops would have to pass Marzak, a redoubt still held by small bands of al Qaeda fighters.

Skillen and Beaudry set out along a path that ran about two hundred meters from a walled compound in the village of Marzak. They still had their packs from a day earlier, though some food and water had been discarded to lighten the loads. "We were approaching a creek bed with a ten foot drop-off and right before we got there, they opened up on us from three positions," said Skillen. "They shot from the mountains, from the Whale and from within the compound." The attack commenced so suddenly and heavily that the platoon members dropped their rucksacks, including their food and radio equipment, and moved into a dry streambed to take cover. The firing continued relentlessly and, coming from three sides, made it tough to set up and shoot back without giving al Qaeda snipers a prime target.

At 10 A.M., soldiers from the 101st dashed across the creek bed and dove for shelter in an even tighter, almost tunnel-like indentation that ran down from the mountains. "We were taking rounds— 'Teeww, pop, pop'—all around us and we knew we had to make it into that gully. We were ordered to face out—up and down the mountain—and post security, but we were still on a low ridge and this meant exposing yourself. We were like in a half moon and I was the last guy on the end. And all I heard was 'woosh, boom,' and then I caught something coming at me out of the corner of my eye, I ducked and I turned and that was the last I remember."

A mortar round had landed next to Beaudry and exploded into him, hitting him in five places—his helmet, his magazine, his shoulder, and both buttocks. The large fragment that hit his helmet knocked the Georgian out cold.

Skillen looked over at his much shorter colleague, who had keeled over and had evidence of wounds up and down his torso. "I lifted him up and rolled him over on his back. I shook him. I actually thought he was dead and was wondering how I was going to have to tell his wife how he died. I was thinkin', 'Aw, shit.' Then, all of a sudden, he starts to move again. Me and the doc grabbed him by the ankles and drug him down the hill and under better cover."

Beaudry came to three minutes later. "My shoulder was all shot up and I had both butt cheeks peppered with shrapnel. I was just praising the Lord that those shots to the buttocks were not two inches to the left or two inches to the right." Even in his pain and anguish, Beaudry had the strange premonition of making a "Forrest Gump" appearance at the White House and having to explain or demonstrate his injuries for the president. The force of the blast had actually blown out the protective plating around Beaudry's chest, yet another sure sign that the Kevlar plating had saved an American life. Efforts to evacuate him for medical assistance on a four-wheeled motorcycle proved useless. Any position, back or front, to which his colleagues turned him left him in sheer agony. The incoming fire was also too heavy to risk the race to safety. Medics, ducking for cover as they moved, finally gave up and had two men carry Beaudry a few meters down the hill, at which point he managed to lift a middle finger into the air in the direction of his attackers.

For the next twelve hours the young Georgian's thoughts would jump from anger to pride and back again to frustration. "I felt it was a great opportunity lost. We didn't get shit, but I was still happy to be the one out there doing the job. It wasn't like we had asked for this fight. They came onto our land and made the first attack. We wanted to hit back, but in this case, the terrain made it very difficult."

Neither Skillen nor Beaudry, hunkered down for the next twelve hours to avoid al Qaeda's incessant fire, was impressed with the planning at higher levels that had put them "in the shit," as they called it. For Skillen, the annoyance of not being able to shoot back at a tangible target or even talk on a radio, which he had dropped when he fled for cover, started to take a toll. "I was sitting in a ditch for twelve hours on day two, it was raining steel and I was just staring at pictures of my family wondering if I'd get out alive. Al Qaeda was too far away to shoot and for some reason, we couldn't get the Air Force to help us out. We went three days without food or water. We hadn't slept in two days. I had to dig me a little hole at a sixty-degree angle just to lie down and keep from rolling down the hill. When we finally made it down on the third day, they told us that we would have to go right back where we came from. We were told that Tenth Mountain had been pretty beat up and that the U.S. Army wasn't going to let this stand. But for us, this was like returning to the scene of a crime. This is what really got me, our platoon had to go back to the damn blocking position, starting from the same creek bed where we had been pinned down."

The Anaconda battle looked good or bad depending on the position you were fighting from in that first decisive week. Even while some fighters were pinned down and frustrated, they were serving a larger purpose, holding ground, drawing fire from the enemy and allowing others to pick off al Qaeda fighters with guns, mortars, and aerial bombing.

There had been indecision at the highest levels, but then, this was war, and battle plans never survive first contact. With al Qaeda moving in small units in and out of the "concentric rings" set up in the original battle plan, Hagenbeck ordered more fighters into the fray. He wasn't keen to have the Western press ripping into his men for backing out of a major confrontation with the enemy.

After U.S. infantrymen got their bearings, their own small-unit commanders found it easier to confront the enemy by moving in smaller groups, shifting units, one by one, to higher ground and homing in on the enemy. On days three through five of the battle, another Georgian, Lt. Benji Croom, and a reconnaissance/battle-support team snuggled into the side of the mountains above the village of Marzak with a good view of al Qaeda fighters scampering around below them. In his words, the Tenth Mountain was "seeking a little satisfaction, payback and a chance to implement training. We also wanted to know how far we could push ourselves."

Croom, a tall, strapping kid with blue eyes, could frame an enemy in the crosshairs in just a split second. But getting a clean shot down at al Qaeda proved next to impossible. Even the unit's firing-range practice with moving targets hadn't prepared them for hitting the streaks of black and brown they could see zipping back and forth through the rifle sights. The physically fit Arabs and Chechens didn't appear to need to stop and catch their breath. They carried almost nothing on their backs, allowing them to dash behind adobe walls and hide behind rubble. They could even move their equipment without exposing personnel, by kicking a mule and having it run through the line of fire with a big gun on its back. But Croom's Tenth Mountain unit held its position and waited patiently for the right moment to arrive. The first came when two al Qaeda fighters walked below them through Marzak. "It was weird. They didn't bother to dive for cover on the first shot we fired so we had time to adjust the fire on our 81 mm mortar and then send in corrections to move the tubes and fire again. The second chance was similar. We spotted five enemy fighters walking through an eroded gully headed roughly our way. We engaged them with our 60 mm and killed all five personnel. I watched them crumple in the dirt through a pair of binoculars."

## Gloom and Doom at Ten Thousand Feet

U.S. forces fighting in the Shah-I-Kot Valley might well have inflicted heavy casualties on the enemy and escaped with all of their lives had it not been for a controversial decision made back at Bagram to insert a reconnaissance team at a mountain pass above blocking position Ginger on the third day of the battle.

With Mulholland at his side, General Hagenbeck issued the order. He wanted a "Black Ops" Green Beret team inserted at the Ginger pass to monitor al Qaeda movements. "This was done primarily to put eyes on the top of the mountain where we believed enemy fighters were either coming into the fight or trying to leave," explained Mulholland. For this mission Hagenbeck tapped Navy captain Bob Harword, whose elite SEALs were based at Kandahar airport in southern Afghanistan.

The insertion point would be a dominating piece of terrain, a vantage point with a 360-degree view from the Shah-I-Kot and over into an adjacent valley where hundreds of fresh fighters were thought to be massing. It was risky business, but, in the view of Hagenbeck, it had to be done. Little did the U.S. commanders know, but Ginger, where they were about to insert the "Black Ops" team, was probably the most essential entry and escape route for al Qaeda during the entire battle. The planned landing zone was already "hot" with the enemy, especially after two days of indecisive fighting that had encouraged al Qaeda to send more men into the fray.

In the early morning hours of the third day of the battle, die-hard al Qaeda fighters, Chechens, and Arabs got what they had been pining for, a major firefight on the ground with U.S. forces, who landed smack in their gun sights, crawling and climbing uphill toward their dug-in positions above the Ginger landing zone.

A team of Navy SEALs had split up between two choppers at the base of the mountains. Rather than move on foot to the objective at 10,200 feet, commanders decided to fly a pair of Chinooks, guided by an elite team of "Night Stalker" pilots, to insert the SEALs under the cover of night. One of the two fifty-two-foot Chinooks moved ahead to attempt the tricky landing on a ridge and managed to set down successfully. But the Chinook was a cumbersome beast, best used for transport from one safe haven to another. It offered an easy target for shoulder-launched grenades or SA-7s, as had similarly slow and lumbering Soviet choppers in their day. Had Hagenbeck realized what awaited the SEALs, he would surely have chosen another means of insertion.

Mulholland and Hagenbeck, watching events unfold from Bagram, thanks to the Predator videos, heard initial reports of an unmanned heavy machine gun about 150 feet from the landing zone. However, as the hatch lowered and the SEAL team prepared to exit the chopper, fire erupted from at least two sides. As the pilot cocked the rotor blades and swept the craft up and away, one of its crew members, Petty Officer Neil Roberts, teetered over the edge and slipped down an oily ramp onto the ground below. The Predator drone hovering overhead lost its focus, and Roberts disappeared from sight. After several minutes a vague, grainy picture emerged of what looked to Mulholland and Hagenbeck like al Qaeda fighters dragging an injured American off behind a tree line.

The pilot, unaware that he had lost a man, struggled at the controls to see into the starry night. His chopper rattled like an ancient refrigerator as he sped down the mountain with several SEALs screaming in his ears for him to fly faster. Even amid the confusion, however, other crew members became aware that they had lost a man overboard. Indeed, one of them, Alexander (who provided only a first name for the press), had lunged for Roberts and slipped off the ramp as well, snapping against his own safety harness; another alert crew member hauled him in by the collar. Alexander had scrambled back up the oily ramp into the craft even as bullets pinged off the ramp beside him. The pilot, finally learning that he had lost a man, swung around to head back up the mountain. However, as he began his ascent, the Chinook's sensitive hydraulic system, already pulverized by bullets, froze up. He had no choice except to turn back and set the bird down.

The next mission was a given, though no real plan of action had been thought through. From the opening day of Anaconda, superiors had assured every soldier that no U.S. fighter would be left behind. Those were the rules. Most commanders had agreed that even a corpse would not be left to al Qaeda, especially given the Chechens' atrocious reputation for severing heads and mutilating corpses of Russian soldiers in their homeland. Back at the Bagram command base, Hagenbeck approved an extraction plan to be executed by the second Chinook of SEALs, but no one told the next chopper to wait for backup, despite video images that had already displayed fierce resistance atop the objective. Within minutes, the second helicopter headed into a second firefight. As the big Chinook throttled down for a landing with its blades kicking up snow and dust twenty feet below, a shoulder-fired grenade slammed into the right engine. In the same instant, the cockpit came under intense small-arms fire, bullets popping willy-nilly through the glass windows.

The pilot remained undaunted. He knew he had to drop off the SEALs. Back in Bagram, Mulholland and Hagenbeck watched as the SEALs rushed headlong into the fray, ducking for cover. Moving right off the front of the chopper, the team skirted blistering machine-gun fire, scampering toward the wooded position where the grainy picture had shown al Qaeda dragging a prisoner. Exemplifying the solidarity of the rescue mission, a young Air Force technician, Sgt. John Chapman, an air controller, was out front. From a concealed bunker near the trees, two al Qaeda gunners opened up. The SEALs and Chapman returned their fire, but the young technician collapsed, dead in his tracks. Two more SEALs were wounded, and the team decided to disengage and retreat down the mountain.

Even as the situation deteriorated, two more Chinooks packed with twenty-two Army Rangers lifted off the tarmac at Bagram under Hagenbeck's orders to assist in the rescue. Their instructions were simple—find the SEALs and go after Roberts. But they had no way of knowing that the SEALs were already in full retreat, moving back on foot down the mountain.

The third Chinook, with the fourth waiting farther down the mountain, attempted to land but was immediately hit by a rocket-propelled grenade. The crippled helicopter hovered under intense machine-gun fire for a few seconds before plunging down on a ledge, disabled. As soon as the chopper hit the ground, the nine Rangers rolled out to take cover. Another rocket-propelled grenade hammered the wall of the chopper, igniting a small fire. Four Rangers died of gunshot and shrapnel wounds within minutes of their landing.

The fourth chopper, which had remained behind, landed several hundred meters down the mountain. Its crew, led by Staff Sgt. Arin Canon, quickly began the arduous uphill climb toward the burning chopper full of their fellow Rangers. At eight thousand feet against a steep incline, with the enemy firing down on them, they would be hard pressed to reach the precipice alive. The Rangers moved to out-flank the incoming fire as they began the trek. They also struggled to haul up two large M249 machine guns.

As reinforcements trekked into the fray, U.S. Air Force technical sergeant Keary Miller tried to treat wounded Americans at the top of the mountain and fend off encroaching al Qaeda fighters with an M-60. Meanwhile, Sgt. Gabe Brown called in air support, anything available, to fend off the attackers. Two F-15E Air Force Strike Eagle fighters already airborne took the "SOS" and raced to the scene. Brown called in his coordinates and asked the fighter pilots to use their 20 mm Gatling gun, usually used for air-to-air dogfights, to home in on the al Qaeda fighters, who were moving about three hundred feet from the front of the downed chopper. Lt. Jim Fairchild unleashed a volley from the 940-round Gatling gun into the line of approaching enemy fighters. The fire was dead on. It held off bin Laden's men and kept the "rescue" on track.

Two hours later, Canon's Rangers reached their rendezvous point at the downed chopper. An assault team continued farther up the mountain to take up a forward position in defense of the smoldering chopper. The dawn of day three at Anaconda had broken to reveal carnage along the ridge; the Rangers had to step over both al Qaeda and American corpses before taking cover. After the F-15E jets spun off for refueling, a B-52 Stratofortress and two F-16s, also on patrol over the azure skies of Afghanistan, arrived to lay down their loads. The Rangers fought through a blaze of al Qaeda fire, aided by the air support, and soon seized a bunker where they found Roberts's body along with those of two enemy fighters, one dressed in the young American's jacket.

Tribal fighters, inspired by al Qaeda firebrands and word that the infidels had finally come to fight, had now massed in Pakistani valleys adjacent to the scene of the fight. Some al Qaeda fighters had already withdrawn over Ginger in the direction of Pakistan. But reinforcements of double the original numbers had also begun to filter back into the battle. At 11 A.M., fresh machine-gun fire riddled the Ranger positions. The U.S. Army would not send a chopper in by day, so the Rangers knew they had to bear down and get ready for a hard fight. The injured were moaning, sometimes gurgling, but they would have to await the setting of the sun for their evacuation. Their own wait under withering fire would resemble what elements of the Tenth and 101st had lived through on days one and two of Operation Anaconda.

Even as evacuation plans were moving ahead, al Qaeda fighters held the upper ridgelines. They had fanned out in a semicircle and left the cover of the mountain to gain a better firing position. An estimated seventy al Qaeda fighters were bobbing up over the rocks and spraying the ground at the feet of just over a dozen Rangers. But the advantage was not all theirs. The Rangers called in more devastating strikes. Bombs throttled the ridge, slicing through the semicircle of

Chechen and Arab fighters. The ones not cut down by the intense aerial assault picked up their gear and began backing down the mountain and into the passes leading into Pakistan—this despite the fact that Pakistani military officials had assured their U.S. counterparts before the battle that they would thoroughly seal off a sixty-mile-long track of border adjacent to the fighting. Yet again, an avowed ally had failed to cover our rear.

At eight that evening, two hours after a seventh and final U.S. soldier, P. J. Cunningham, expired from his wounds on the mountaintop known as Takur Ghar—dubbed "Roberts's Ridge"—help arrived to evacuate the dead and injured. Three choppers landed on the ridge, taking only minimal ground fire; al Qaeda had all but vanished into the desolate, fogged-over mountains.

## Counting the Dead

The battle of Anaconda continued with sporadic fighting for another week, but never with the intensity of the first three days. The fighting of the first two days had been so severe that thirty-four U.S. infantrymen had been seriously wounded. It was a miracle that none of them had been killed. Including the one Green Beret warrant officer killed entering the valley, eight American soldiers had died in combat in the first three days of the battle.

What had begun in the planning stages as another U.S.-assisted "proxy war" had flipped 180 degrees in the first hours of combat with the AC-130's accidental attack on the Afghans, who had been the "hammer" of the U.S. battle plan. The allied Afghan and Green Beret retreat had left the al Qaeda fighters with full run of the rugged Shah-I-Kot Valley. Bin Laden's men had seized the high ground and sought to fight the U.S. forces toe to toe. Five days into the battle, there were still isolated clashes between small groups of al Qaeda fighters and both U.S. special and conventional forces. Pockets of bin Laden's fighters in the three villages set between the Whale and the highest peaks received reinforcements streaming in from Pakistan. Afghan commanders told Mashal, now on the ground amid the heaviest fighting, that their foe was operating in groups of four and five guerrilla fighters. Each day, though, the number of these units diminished as they fled or were killed in fighting.

After the tragedy at Roberts's Ridge, U.S. forces adjusted to the terrain and gained the upper hand. Despite the disabling of several Apache helicopters on the first day, the 101st Airborne Division managed to ship another dozen birds to the battlefront on C-17 transport planes within a week, a testament to the amazing speed with which the U.S. military can move assets. Rounding out the required air assets were A-10 Warthog "tank busters," low-flying planes capable of pinpointing bunkers and small enemy units.

Six days into the battle, Pentagon officials announced that "over six hundred al Qaeda fighters" had been killed. Green Berets and Afghan fighters on the ground called those estimates into question almost immediately.

General Franks had approved the deployment of 1,100 U.S. fighters and another one hundred foreign allies into the Shah-I-Kot pocket. Rather than abandon the idea of Afghan proxies entirely, however, Mulholland agreed that the Northern Alliance should send several hundred of its fighters from Kabul. Gen Mohammed Fahim hand-picked Commander Gul Haidar for the task. The predominantly Tajik force, which moved cautiously down an icy main highway with Russian tanks and heavy artillery in tow, ran up against serious ethnic friction as it approached the Shah-I-Kot Valley. Zia Lodin's men, mostly ethnic Pashtuns, were finally prepared to reenter the fray and were not keen to be fighting alongside their ethnic rivals. But Haidar's arrival did not add up to much in the end. His fighters were not in place and ready to go until March 12, well after the lion's share of the fighting against al Qaeda was over.

Chechen diehards, who had reluctantly left Tora Bora and regrouped in the Shah-I-Kot to face off again with their American foe, fought on through the second week of the battle. They were getting a taste of what they wanted, a real fight with U.S. ground troops, something they had missed at Tora Bora. Yet they were few in number. During the second week of fighting, Zia Lodin's men, finally back in the fray, flushed out trenches in the three villages of Marzak, Sarhanekhel, and Babukhel. Hagenbeck wanted al Qaeda out in the dusty terrain where they could be corralled in a "killing zone" for

U.S. pilots. Tenth Mountain and Green Beret snipers, supplemented by Canadian and Australian special forces, kept an eye on the valley sweep from high positions along the mountain walls overlooking the three villages. Forced out into the "free-fire zones," a few dozen Chechen and Arab fighters were slaughtered, their corpses left to rot in the sun.

The battle, projected to take seventy-two hours, wound down after ten days. Maj. Bryan Hilferty, a spokesman for the Tenth Mountain Division, suggested that the fighting at Anaconda had spared the world mass killing. "We killed hundreds of terrorists," he said back at the Bagram air base. "It took twenty terrorists to kill three thousand of the world's citizens in the World Trade Towers. Twenty. We killed hundreds. That means we've saved hundreds of thousands of lives."

Major Hilferty and other military spokespersons insisted that the U.S. strategy had been flawless. "I don't know what we could have done differently," he insisted. Indeed, by the tenth day of the fighting, al Qaeda and its allies had had enough. They were in full retreat over the dozens of goat paths leading away from the Shah-I-Kot Valley in the direction of Pakistan. American troops could not prevent a major exodus of enemy fighters as U.S. "blocking positions" halfway up the mountains were still beneath retreating al Qaeda. Special Forces troops tried desperately to get their allies to do the work they were paying them to perform, but the task was hampered by altitude and terrain.

## Spin Doctors, Winners, and Losers

The Pentagon's official view of the battle of Anaconda exaggerated success and minimized failure. Secretary of Defense Donald Rumsfeld was, after all, still the last man on the ladder when it came to military briefings and carefully distributed press releases. He had, from the start of the war in Afghanistan, as one Army public information officer explained to me, "demanded that we not air our dirty laundry—and that had us all running for cover."

Even after the battle, reports, weighted heavily with wildly rounded estimates of enemy dead, reflected this fear of serious self-criticism. General Hagenbeck, who, on the one hand, admitted that his men were not keeping close track of the enemy dead, still managed to provide the Western press with convenient estimates, in round and rough numbers. On March 6, five days into the battle, after the bulk of the fighting had been completed, Hagenbeck said, "In the last twenty-four hours, we have killed lots, lots of al Qaeda and Taliban. I won't give you precise numbers, but we've got confirmed kills in the hundreds." Other commanders and spokesmen said that U.S. ground and air assaults had already killed "as many as four hundred hostile fighters or perhaps eight hundred." Lt. Col. David Gray told reporters that "about five hundred enemy fighters" had been killed in the first week of fighting at Operation Anaconda. Subsequent investigations of the battlefield by Afghan and U.S. forces, however, would provide little evidence to back these vague estimates.

Operation "Polar Harpoon," involving both U.S. forces and Afghan allies, began after the completion of the battle. Tenth Mountain's Capt. Chris Johnson sent Lt. Benji Croom to the top of Roberts's Ridge, to comb the ground for weapons and corpses. "We found thirteen bodies, all of them intact," said Croom. "I saw one with red hair and I assume he was a Chechen, but the others looked to be Arabs. We didn't turn over all the corpses, fearing that some of them might have been booby-trapped. One fighter had clenched teeth and a grenade in his right hand. You couldn't help but be impressed by their endurance. The air was so thin up there and they carried with them just what they needed to survive—in some cases, American-made rifles and Goretex pants." The al Qaeda fighters had left behind an array of killing devices, including large guns that had been difficult to transport into the two-mile-high redoubt. Chinese-made 30 mm grenade launchers, a DSK machine gun, and 75 mm recoilless rifles littered the frozen earth. In the caves, smoked mutton hung from the ceiling, and Lay's potato chip packets littered the damp floor.

Command Sgt. Maj. Denis Carey's Tenth Mountain fighters, who spent several days going over enemy positions on the Whale, uncovered complex redoubts, some of which contained camouflaged stables for pack mules. "They made amazing improvements to natural holes," he said. "As much ordnance as we dropped, there were many men who escaped. The several corpses we did find were intact, not real shredded or beyond recognition. At the same time, their custom is to remove their dead from the battlefield and I believe, given their affinity with the area, that it would have been possible for them to pull some bodies away."

Empty tents set in the open as decoys succeeded in the same way that they had at Tora Bora. A rough-hewn Afghan commander, Hamid Khan, whose men helped comb the valley with U.S. forces, said his fighters working with U.S. Green Berets discovered a total of forty-two bodies. He claimed that a majority of them were young Chechens, all of whom had arrived from Tora Bora vowing to avenge the deaths of their comrades in that battle. Many had lived in the area with their families for a full three months prior to the fight, according to local residents. Colonel Mulholland told me in an interview in his offices at Fort Campbell, Kentucky, that "there were no shortage of ways for those guys, especially for people who knew that area like the back of their hands, to continue to infiltrate or exfiltrate." At Fort Drum, New York, a British major, John Lockwood, attached to Tenth Mountain Division, spoke to me over lunch in the mess hall. He used the analogy of a large anthill to describe the difficulty of winning a final victory in Afghanistan. "You can try as you like to hammer down on the top of the mountain, kill the Queen and destroy the hill, but you'll still have them running all around you."

The ease with which the al Qaeda fighters had managed to come and go during the fighting was also illustrated by the limited number of prisoners. Twenty captives fell into U.S. and Afghan hands, but most of them were Afghans. Others were Arabs on the verge of death. Fighters from the Tenth and 101st described one such unfortunate character, a rag on his head and holes in the toes of his shoes, who had stumbled down the mountain into their positions halfway through the battle, with the back of his head blown off. Handcuffed and treated by a U.S. medic for severe frostbite, the prisoner became something of a one-man freak show. American fighters lined up to have their picture taken with the elusive "enemy," who soon expired from his injuries.

Most of the brave U.S. ground combatants would remember the battle of Anaconda as a victory—if only because they survived an ordeal that taught al Qaeda a lesson about U.S. military capabilities. Finch, the brazen Georgian who may have saved dozens in his own unit by leading the charge to take out al Qaeda's forward positions, said a year later in the frigid confines of Fort Drum, "We went up there with a bloodied nose and knocked the hell out of them and we had taken the entire mountain from them ten days later," he said. "When they realized we were coming to get them, they just ran."

Other young warriors were not as happy with the battle plan. Many were astounded that the basic strategy had not changed at the last minute when fresh intelligence reports had suggested a far larger number of al Qaeda fighters than had first been expected. "I would have liked to have known how many enemy we were going up against," said Staff Sgt. Steve Achey of the Air Force, who had helped call in the air strikes on al Qaeda from his position in the Shahi-Kot Valley. "There was a certain degree of complacency that went into the planning process. Other branches of the military had better, more realistic estimates of the enemy than the Army, but instead of planning for the worst-case scenario, they planned for the best case. This was because almost every time we would go on a mission in Afghanistan, there was nobody to fight, and with what they, the Army infantry, were originally told [for Anaconda] there were only about 250 people and they probably wouldn't put up much of a fight. When we landed at dawn [not under the cover of night], we blew the whole element of surprise. The whole thing, as far as I could see, was set up so that the Afghan [proxies] could claim a victory there, but all that collapsed like a house of cards." Despite his sharp criticism, however, Sergeant Achey insisted that U.S. air strikes became increasingly deadly over the course of the battle and turned what could have been a defeat into victory.

Col. Paul La Camera, Tenth Mountain's savvy ground commander, suggested that the tide of the battle turned in time for his forces to claim a clear victory. Early on, stricken teams, like that of Lt. Maroyka, had retreated to safety, but at the same time an undaunted General Hagenbeck had ordered new platoons deployed to replace them. "Initially, at Anaconda we were going to provide the outer ring and then shrink the perimeter," said La Camera. "Al Qaeda was moving in and out of the battle zone and the question then was, should we have moved back? But we didn't need to. They came to us and we stopped some of their guys who tried to escape. This was maneuver, not attrition warfare. We went in there and took control of the valley. There was a terrorist training center and we ended up denying the enemy sanctuary. It sent a message to the world that we had the stomach to fight even when we were taking casualties."

La Camera, drawing the battle lines with a blue felt pen on a whiteboard at Tenth Mountain Division headquarters at Fort Drum (set in the flatlands beside Lake Ontario, a long distance from the mountains), became pensive as he spoke about the bravery of his men at Anaconda. He recalled a recent seminar in which he had participated along with a veteran commander of the Vietnam War, who had complained bitterly that his troops had never been motivated in that war. "So many of them were draftees and so many of them didn't really see the point of that earlier war," La Camera explained. "The difference was that in Afghanistan, I had volunteers on my side and every one of them understood what they were fighting for. You can't beat that for motivation and they showed clearly that they could think outside the box when called upon to do so. This was about guys using their heads and adjusting. The single most valuable resource and weapon system in our army is the individual soldier. As T. R. Fehrenbach explained in *This Kind of War* [a classic history of the Korean War], you can bomb it, you can pulverize it, but in the end, you have to do what the Roman legions did, that is to put boots on the ground in the mud. We could bomb things from various distances in Afghanistan, but, in the end, it was that infantry soldier from the Tenth Mountain Division who stood in the Shah-I-Kot Valley and said, 'Make me move.' There is no substitute for that."

# Conclusion

## CHASING THE MAD MULLAHS

If a strong man, when the wine sparkles at the feast and the lights are bright, boasts of his prowess, it is well he should have an opportunity of showing in the cold and gray of the morning that he is no idle braggart.

—Winston Churchill,
*The Story of the Malakand Field Force*

On the surface, there were great similarities between Tora Bora and Anaconda. Both were set in the forbidding Afghan highlands, where guerrillas have traditionally fared far better than conventional armies. Both battles pitted some of the best technology of the U.S. military, by far the world's most potent, against the seasoned fighters of al Qaeda, the world's most lethal terror network. Tora Bora and Anaconda, the former at the end of December 2001 and the latter in March 2002, also fed into each other. Hard-core al Qaeda fighters who had finally left Tora Bora under the heaviest of U.S. bombing and after missing a chance to meet American fighters head to head had fled south and regrouped in order to continue their guerrilla struggle.

The intensity of both battles gave evidence that many of bin Laden's foot soldiers were spoiling for a fight—a chance to prove themselves on the ground against an American military about which many of them harbored strong doubts. The decision to pull U.S. forces out of Somalia after the "Black Hawk Down" battle had left some network members, who had fought there, with a sense that the Americans would not tolerate casualties. Simply stated, they did not respect the U.S. military. As bin Laden had boasted in his speech to tribal leaders in Jalalabad before the start of the battle for Tora Bora, the al Qaeda was ready to "teach the Americans a lesson."

It was the difference in tactics, however, that led to different outcomes in what were arguably the two most crucial battles of the entire Afghan campaign. At Tora Bora, where the al Qaeda leadership remained for a time, the U.S. tactics mimicked earlier successful efforts to overthrow the Taliban regime. Colonel Mulholland, while struggling to capture Kandahar in the south and deal with a harrowing friendly fire incident in that same area, sought to make quick use of a fresh lot of "Afghan allies" in eastern Afghanistan. The result was an inefficient offensive and ultimate betrayal of the American cause. Even the intense bombing of Tora Bora, which had begun in October, proved counterproductive, serving to alert the enemy and alienate the very tribesmen that the Pentagon had been hoping to win over. On the ground, the strategy played out as an effort to liberate the surrounding valleys and force the enemy to flee. No real "manhunt" ever got off the ground.

As Colonel Mulholland explained to me, the "lessons from Tora Bora" were many, and they were applied directly to Anaconda. Still, in retrospect, it appears that a decision to try again to meld an Afghan warlord's small army into the "sharp end" of a crucial U.S. military operation failed for a second time at Anaconda, in part because the Americans accidentally bombed a group of Afghans before they even made it into the battle. Colonel Mulholland, whose intention it had been to rely once again on the Afghans, was clearly disappointed. But in an interview in Kentucky a year later he also defended the Afghans. "Zia took a lot of hard hits and unjustifiably so," he said. "The issue of the AC-130 strike didn't help things but the fact of the matter was that Zia's guys were under direct and indirect fire from the Whale. Truthfully, I think that we asked Zia's guys to do something that we shouldn't really have asked them to do. What we asked him to do with two or three hundred of his own men, we would have probably asked one or two thousand Americans to do. But we were banking on the Afghan knowledge of the terrain and up to this point these guys, al Qaeda, had not really stood and fought. There were also some serious issues of air support—American air support for the Afghans. Rightly, so, when this thing started, the preponderance of air support went to American soldiers in contact with the enemy. I understand that, but our Afghan buddies didn't really understand that, of course. What happened is that Zia was unable to make the progress that we had hoped he could make because of the fire he was taking. What is important to keep in mind is that despite the fact that he was a major part of the op, if you are an Afghan warlord, you leave the battle so that you can fight another day."

Nevertheless, Anaconda did not end as a draw. The network's hard-core fighters learned not to doubt the killing capacity of the U.S. war machine. The brave young infantrymen of the U.S. conventional army made sure of that.

In contrast, at Tora Bora, the top brass—and by implication the secretary of defense and commander in chief—had flinched at the idea of inserting U.S. ground troops into a battle that had promised far greater rewards, in terms of destroying al Qaeda leadership, than Anaconda. Indeed, the U.S. tactics at Anaconda begged the question of why only a handful of Green Beret spotters fought at Tora Bora. The arguments that both Green Beret and conventional military commanders had given for not infusing more U.S. troops into the fray had been their fear of alienating the local population as well as the inherent difficulty of transporting conventional forces into the Afghan mountains. Yet the terrain of Anaconda was several thousand feet higher than that at Tora Bora and even more forbidding than that of the White Mountains to the north. There had been no parallel concern, in this case, for the potentially negative views of the local tribesmen. So why had the U.S. military not employed the same "hands-on" fighting tactics in that all-important battle? The Tenth Mountain colonel who had stood in the wings, waiting to enter the battle for Tora Bora at the request of Colonel Mulholland, had a quick answer to my befuddlement. "That was someone else's sandbox," Col. Paul La Camera told me.

At the battle of Anaconda, as U.S. commanders, Mulholland included, later admitted, they had initially underestimated the amount of resistance they would confront. They insisted that the number of fighters they faced off against when the fighting began more than tripled over the next several days with the arrival of an additional five hundred from Pakistan. The enemy had shown up in droves for a battle many viewed as another showdown.

It is crucial that both at the battle for Tora Bora and at the battle of Anaconda, al Qaeda forces reacted with the same gusto to the arrival of U.S. forces, even to mere rumors of their arrival. The financier Abu Jaffar and another of bin Laden's Saudi foot soldiers said that al Qaeda fighters had hoped and literally prayed for a chance to go up against American infantry at Tora Bora. When Tora Bora turned out to be a battle against bombs dropped from ten thousand feet, and against Afghan proxies, however, al Qaeda fled the scene. Apparently, they still wanted to die a more glorious death than beneath a two-thousand-pound bomb. In Anaconda, hopes of a direct fight with American infantry had lingered on, finally coming to fruition.

In his book *The Hunt for bin Laden,* Robin Moore argues after describing the battle of Anaconda, "There was little doubt that it had freed a large part of southern Afghanistan, and destroyed one of the AQ's last refuges. But [General] Franks's decision to use conventional ground forces would probably be something he would sorely regret, resulting in more than a hundred casualties, and more Americans killed than Special Forces had lost in the past eight years." But these major U.S. losses only came when a Special Forces team was injected into a "hot" landing zone with the help of cumbersome Chinook helicopters. Seven of the eight deaths at Anaconda were due to this decision alone. General Hagenbeck and his colleagues in the Special Forces both took that fateful decision to send Black Ops reconnaissance elements to Roberts's Ridge. In contrast, it was at the urging of the Green Berets that Afghan proxies were again handed a leading role at Anaconda. That arguably flawed choice of tactics appears far more significant to the final outcome—the eventual escape of so many enemy fighters—than the move to take Roberts's Ridge. Had planners chosen a more conventional, all-American "siege" instead of the "hammer and anvil" attack that relied on

Afghans, far more of the enemy might well have been caught in the vice grip of the world's most agile military.

Throughout his book, Moore burnishes the legend of the U.S. Special Forces at the expense of all other elements of the American military. He blames the Pentagon's top brass for not relying more on the Green Berets. History will show, however, that the decision to use conventional American forces was not the cause of the myriad failures of the war in Afghanistan. Rather, it was impatience at the top to rush into a war aimed primarily at "regime change" that left the U.S. military largely empty handed when it came to capturing its al Qaeda prey.

There had been no urgent need to press Mulholland's Task Force Dagger into early action in October 2001 to topple the Taliban, though his units could still have played a leading role in a more developed and focused war plan that integrated conventional forces into the fight. Indeed, a calmer and more collected military strategy that melded the strengths of the Green Berets with the overwhelming might of the U.S. conventional army and air force would have served the American cause better. Al Qaeda, anxious to meet its foe, would undoubtedly have remained in-theater, waiting for the arrival of the infidel.

Though we will never know what the result would have been of an invasion of Afghanistan that fine-tuned a combination of conventional and Green Beret capabilities, it is very likely—even with heavier loss of American life that could well have ensued—that we would have captured more of the al Qaeda leadership and dealt far more of a knockout blow to a terror network that now continues to flourish and expand across the globe. Therefore, blame should not be cast upon either Gen. Tommy Franks or Col. John Mulholland. The American taxpayers did not get what they bargained for. But that was due to decisions made by senior civilian leaders anxious to produce a quick result when more military planning and better timing could have produced a better one.

When I interviewed the U.S. commander on the ground in Afghanistan in the summer of 2002, the mood at Bagram Air Base was decidedly upbeat. From the outside, the immense tented headquarters of the U.S. Central Command could have been a wealthy Arab sheikh's desert haunt. Inside, though, it looked like one giant Internet café, except for the standard blackboards set up on easels. Officers sipped from cups of orange juice and hot coffee as they kept track of the prisoners held in metal containers in a barbed-wire section of the camp. A few of the officers fiddled with the U.S. military's latest "war games" videos, planning for live exercises and sometimes shooting down enemies that popped up from behind crumbling walls. The scenes on the screen were set in what I judged to be a vaguely Middle Eastern city; the enemy fought with automatic weapons from the beds of pickup trucks, no doubt modeled on al Qaeda and Taliban tactics in Afghanistan. It reminded me that the U.S. military's greatest recruiting tool was now a video game in which teenage boys could kill and capture the "bad guys." That was what the American public wanted, and so that was also what its sons wanted. They were once again signing up in droves and making the U.S. military, which had done a painful penance in the desert ever since the Vietnam War, a proud and elite government institution.

On the ground in Afghanistan, the war against terrorists was as real as ever. Lt. Gen. Dan McNeill, a clever Texan and a polished tactician, told me that the hunt was continuing in earnest. "Typically the enemy depends on several things; one is support of the populace. They also depend on the land. We're seeking to deny them both of these things and doing a pretty good job of it." The general spoke with the soft, controlled delivery of a man mindful of his superiors.

"And what about bin Laden?" I asked. "Are you still hunting for Osama bin Laden in Afghanistan?"

"I'm not solely fixated on UBL [Usama bin Laden]," he said. "If [his capture] is incidental in our operations and we get to him, that's fine. I don't have a particular name I affix to what I'm going up against, but the leadership is indeed a target." The general's answer startled me somewhat, because neither the Pentagon nor the CIA had conceded that bin Laden had left Afghanistan. Indeed, many "Osama watchers" believed he was straddling the Pakistani-Afghan border.

But the general's unusual couching of the "hunt for bin Laden" also sounded oddly similar to what NATO commanders had told me for a full two years, between 1995 and 1997, in reference to the Bosnian war crimes suspect Dr. Radovan Karadzic, responsible in part for the mass slaughter of Muslims in Sarajevo and other Balkan cities. They had insisted that if NATO forces came across Karadzic "in the line of duty" they would take him into custody. Until they changed their tune under international pressure, NATO commanders had sounded rather uninterested in the hunt. Now, here was America's top soldier in Afghanistan saying that he hoped to round up the kingpin of terror "incidentally" to his other efforts to tackle the al Qaeda network. The U.S. government's reward of twenty-five million dollars for bin Laden's capture still stood, but on the home front President Bush appeared torn between standing behind his earlier unequivocal-sounding vows and his subsequent statements that one man did not a terror network make. Senior advisers in the White House were all too aware that a leader seen to be fixated on one villain might well be perceived as the "loser" should that villain continue to wreak havoc across the globe.

Still, for some bin Laden watchers, including me, it looked late in the game to change the initial strategy. Bush had already made the lone-wolf Saudi millionaire target number one, and despite a new ambivalence expressed by subordinates, it would be very difficult to change that. The president, also the commander in chief of the U.S. military, had made his vow in a fit of Wild West bravado just a few days after the September 2001 al Qaeda attacks, demanding that bin Laden be brought in "dead or alive." Bush, who by his own admission often acted on "gut instinct," believed he knew what, at that time, the public wanted. "Start with bin Laden, which Americans expect and then if we succeed, we've struck a huge blow and can move forward," he told the National Security Council principals just a day after the World Trade Center and Pentagon attacks.

But General McNeill, until he had new marching orders, was riding the fence. The U.S. government had achieved a semblance of a "victory" in Afghanistan. Within a year of entering Afghanistan, the U.S. military could safely boast that it had captured, chased out, or—in rare cases—killed several thousand of bin Laden's fighters and a handful of his top lieutenants. The desired "regime change" had fallen into place, and Washington had installed its man Hamid Karzai as a new head of state, even though his title of "president" remained more titular than factual outside the capital city. The new government's writ ran up against the strength of individual warlords, many of them still living large off their shares of the tens of millions that Washington had dumped on them during the war. As early as May 2002 CIA director George Tenet had been crediting the U.S. military and his own personnel with a job well done. He told graduating students at Rochester Institute of Technology that al Qaeda was now "dispersed" thanks to U.S. and allied actions in Afghanistan. His exact words reflected the attitude of many of the optimists in Washington: "There in Afghanistan a brutal regime, which had denied the rights of so many and turned an ancient cradle of civilization into a ward of modern terror, has been deposed. There, the authors of September 11th, denied their refuge, have been dispersed."

Still, the successes did not diminish the importance of more senior al Qaeda operatives who still ran free. It is, unfortunately, too late to try to downplay bin Laden's own importance. Even if someone turns up his corpse one day soon, his image as a defiant and charismatic leader will continue to resonate, as have his tape recordings, which continue to urge holy war against the Zionist and Christian infidels. Charles Heyman, the editor of the respected London-based *Jane's World Armies* and one of my principal "analysts" in the war on terror, contends that it was a mistake from the get-go for President Bush to vow to capture bin Laden "dead or alive." "Every day bin Laden survives—or even appears to survive—is a victory for al Qaeda," he told me. "In this guerrilla war against the West, if you live to fight another day, it is a conquest of sorts. Just making it through the initial stages of the conflict shows that bin Laden has survived the world's most powerful military."

"There were as many as five thousand highly trained al Qaeda terror cells who escaped Afghanistan in 2001 and 2002, and now the chickens are coming home to roost," Heyman told me by telephone from his London offices after the May 12, 2003, attacks on a foreign compound in Riyadh, which killed two dozen. "These terror cells have spread out worldwide and are now melding themselves into Islamic organizations and newly formed terror groups. They are secretive and operate in some Islamic countries with relative impunity. Instead of one al Qaeda network, you now have a hundred mini–al Qaeda networks operating with a global scope. They are preparing themselves for the years ahead and we can expect to see a large number of low-level attacks. There is a boasting among the fundamentalist types in the region that they have now won round one against the Americans," said Heyman, a man with twenty-five years of experience as a terror analyst. "This is not, in fact, true, but there may be a tiny bit of truth to it—and this is what it looks like if you are on al Qaeda's side of the fence. Al Qaeda has shown in the last couple of years that it attacks on its own terms in places and at times of its own choosing."

# Epilogue

## A DIASPORA OF SPITE

In the spring of 2002, Mashal and I set out for the lush green valleys of Kashmir in hopes of picking up the scent of al Qaeda along the way. Back at our favorite residence, the Continental Guest House in Peshawar, we finally met up again with Jamal, our jovial Pakistani driver who had taken us into Jalalabad for the two-thousand-gun salute back in November. He was happy to see us but not terribly inspired by the idea of heading off to Kashmir, where the violence between Muslims and Hindus had reached new heights. A sad-faced "Auntie," dressed as always in a flowery sari, again packed sandwiches for our trip and told us to take care of her driver if we met up with some of "those shady characters" up in the north of Pakistan.

On we drove to the base of the mighty Karakoram Highway, which snaked along above the raging torrents of the Indus River. We were not far into our journey, some 2,000 feet above the raging Indus River, before we passed the long, whitewashed balcony of a madrassa, or religious school. Across the balcony was painted: "We are fundamentalist Islam and proud of it!" It was written in English for the entire world to read. It struck me as similar in tone to a sign or bumper sticker you might find in a white trash neighborhood in the deep south reading: "Confederate Redneck and Proud of It!" We turned east toward Kashmir, the alluring Shangri-La that had gone from paradise to hell in recent years. The dark-brown shale mountains parted in an unending climb that—if the road permitted—would take the traveler to the "roof of the world" in Tibet. Driving into Kashmir, we picked up a local guide named Nasir, a twenty-three-year-old, clean-shaven, excessively polite kid in a blue wind-breaker. Our initial impression of him was that he'd had a few years of experience with backpackers in the wilderness and that if this hadn't been the new age of jihad in Pakistan, he would still be plying the slippery tracks with sexy Swedish girls.

Nasir was, we soon learned, a rather typical young Kashmiri—steeped in the myths and legends of holy war. The revelation that I was on something of a "mission to assist my Muslim brothers in Bosnia" resonated with Nasir, who excitedly told me that his own brother had fought in Bosnia through the auspices of an Arab holy war outfit that sent them through Croatia to the town of Zenica. (I recalled visiting a video store in that small Bosnian town back in 1995 and finding the shelves stacked with highlights from jihads from around the world.)

We headed off in the direction of the Nanga Parbat, a spectacular snow-capped behemoth that is sacred to Hindus and Muslims alike. The face of the eighth-highest peak in the world is nearly 15,000 feet on its own, the basis of its name in translation, the "Naked Mountain." The road that we now traversed was not far from the Burzil Pass, British India's only direct link with northern Pakistan. We wound our way around ledges and through shady pine groves. As we approached Astore, the gateway to northern Kashmir, sledgehammer blows echoed across steep valley walls as village men broke boulders and spread gravel for a new strategic road. Pakistani army engineers and villagers were drenched in perspiration and the light patter of the early monsoon rains.

But much of the real work for the control of Kashmir was in the hands of the same militant groups that the government had itself funded and trained for the past decade. As we drove along, heading deeper into Kashmir, a new Pajero, carrying a bearded mullah in a white gown, overtook us. Across the hood was a white sheet painted with the words, "Harakut ul Mujahideen." In 1999, that group's members had slit the throat of a male honeymooner aboard a hijacked Indian airliner and managed to swing a deal that secured the release from prison of British national Ahmed Omar Saeed Sheikh, who subsequently masterminded the kidnapping and murder of *Wall Street Journal* reporter Danny Pearl.

Throughout the 1990s, the Pakistani military's Inter-Services Intelligence (ISI) had worked with groups like the Harakut ul Mujahideen (HuM) to help it set up jihadi training camps inside Afghanistan and Pakistan. The ISI originally intended to provide a steady influx of well-trained guerrilla fighters to infiltrate the Line of Control in Kashmir and to carry out attacks against Indian interests. Eventually, the HuM acted as a link between ISI and al Qaeda because Pakistani HuM militants often trained in al Qaeda camps in eastern Afghanistan, many did frontline tours of duty for the Taliban and signed up for the holy war that bin Laden had announced against America at Khost's Zhawar Kili terror base. Several of Harakut's members had been killed when President Clinton ordered that base attacked by cruise missiles in 1998. Now, these same jihadis, steeped in holy war rhetoric and fast recovering from their bloody beating by U.S. air power in Afghanistan, were flocking back to the rugged Kashmiri terrain to continue the fight for which they had been trained.

Our guide, Nasir, told us that many of the young men from his village had trained—starting in the early '90s—at bin Laden's jihad training centers inside Afghanistan, including Tora Bora and Zhawar Kili.

"Tora Bora?" Mashal asked with raised eyebrows. He was riding shotgun, and I had suggested to him that he take over the conversation and find out what Nasir knew. "So, did anyone fight there last November and December?"

"Oh, yeah," Nasir shot back. "Al Qaeda fighters from Afghanistan have been coming to Kashmir in the hundreds since the battle of Tora Bora. They all escaped."

"How can you be so sure of that?"

"Because I drove them into Kashmir. Kashmir welcomes fighters from anywhere in the world, and there were hundreds of them last March. I, myself, drove three Arab *mujahid*s [holy warriors] into Kashmir. I brought them up to a point and then someone else met them and drove them farther. Hundreds have entered Kashmir in the last several months. In some cases they left their four-wheel-drive vehicles with us and rode into Kashmir in local vehicles. . . . There are basically three kinds of fighters," he said. "There are those, like me, who assist the jihad by helping holy warriors to the front. Then there are fighters who are willing to go anywhere to meet the enemy but who want to fight man to man with a gun and die that way—and then there are the suicide bombers. They are the bravest of all. Many of them are Arabs. They are the elite warriors. If you talk with the most devoted fighters, most of them will tell you that the only way to deal with the *kafir*s [infidels] is to use suicide as a tactic. This, they say, is the way of the true jihad fighter. There were Arabs who stayed in our villages for a time before leaving. During the time that they were here, we usually talked with them." Nasir described one fighter in particular, who went by the name Mohammad Abdullah, as always waving the sacred text in the air and preaching the virtues of holy war. "He always holds up the Koran and shouts, 'This is the way, this is our leader. You have to live for it and die for it.'"

Washington had envisioned its Afghan campaign as one that would help liberate the region from fundamentalist groups. CIA director George Tenet had told the Bush war cabinet on September 27, 2001, "People in the region are on the fence. Action next week would help. Some favor UBL [Usama (Osama) bin Laden], some oppose UBL." But two years later, al Qaeda was launching attacks into Afghanistan from Pakistani soil. Radical religious groups in the North West Frontier Province had swept to the region's parliamentary seat and seized control of the local governments through elections. By spring of 2003, these same zealots had imposed *sharia,* or Islamic law. Those political victories gave the official imprimatur to what Gen. Pervez Musharraf had sworn to fight but was powerless to stop.

Mashal and I continued our own personal hunt for al Qaeda throughout 2002 and into 2003. We always had our Persian carpet and whiskey bottle handy—just in case. Mashal, who finally took a job as the translator for the U.S. ambassador in Kabul in late 2003, was always a pleasure to have at my side. On one of our more adventurous journeys, we rode in the company of heroin traders out to the Iranian border, where we found fresh evidence that al Qaeda leaders were plotting anew, with one foot in Afghanistan and the other in Iran. We cut a course through the blistering southwest desert in the atmosphere of a real-time Mad Max movie. Smugglers whisked past us in jeeps with four and six fighters in the back, an occasional anti-aircraft gun welded into the bed, crushing camel carcasses as they drove. The presence of a new Green Beret base along the Iranian border had sparked a set of tit-for-tat expulsions on both sides of the border. Iran's Revolutionary Guard, which wielded control over the country's police and military, was, we soon learned, treating the Green Beret base on its border as a major threat to its national integrity. Not intimidated, the Special Forces, straddling the beds of new pickups, engaged in a swaggering show of force that upstaged even their drug-smuggling counterparts. Of course, they weren't in Zaranj to round up the drug dealers anyway, but rather to nab stray al Qaeda operatives. The Afghans, in turn, siding with the Americans, were trying to round up any would-be Iranian-sponsored "spies."

When U.S. soldiers headed out on missions into the southwest corner of Afghanistan's Nimruz province, the region's "devil's triangle," a corner that juts out into Pakistan in the south and Iran in the west, they invariably found that important al Qaeda figures had slipped away to one of the two neighboring states. Nimruz's security chief, Mohammed Naim, who treated us to tea, told us that Abu Hafs, "the Mauritanian," a key al Qaeda military and religious leader (claimed by the Pentagon to have been killed in Khost), had been operating alongside al Qaeda's second in command, Dr. Ayman al-Zawahiri. The presence of Abu Hafs in Iran had been reported first by the *Washington Post*'s Peter Finn and had been attributed to unnamed "Arab intelligence sources." Dr. al-Zawahiri, previously reported to be in Pakistan, would pop into the limelight in a few months with important messages to his followers. But as with the messages of bin Laden, no one in Western intelligence circles yet knew exactly where they were coming from.

Indeed, despite declarations from the Bush war cabinet that al Qaeda could run but not hide, many of bin Laden's leading operatives had managed to duck out of sight in the first year after the U.S. invasion of Afghanistan. Yet there were notable successes. In mid-2002, George Tenet contended that the net was closing fast on al Qaeda's top leadership. Key captures and kills in 2002 and 2003 included Muhammad al Darbi, Abu Zubaidah, Ramzi Binalshibh, and Khalid Sheikh Mohammed in Pakistan, and Omar al-Faruq in Indonesia. America's successful raids on al Qaeda hideouts were conducted hand in glove with security services in countries where they were hiding. Some of these countries, particularly in the Arab world, were keen to disguise their close cooperation with Washington, fearing a backlash from radical religious groups, even—in some cases—members of al Qaeda. The FBI and the CIA took the leading roles, as the Pentagon's top brass was still trying to work through the legal and logistical parameters of "snatch and kill" teams that could move quickly across borders and take out terror operatives at blinding speed.

In Yemen, I covered one of the most dramatic U.S. raids, in which a Hellfire missile from a CIA drone killed Qaed Salim Sinan al-Harethi. Al-Harethi was known as his country's "godfather of terror" for his role in the attack on the USS *Cole* in the harbor of Aden in October 2000.

The assassination plot that finished off Al-Harethi had the ring of a Graham Greene spy thriller. The American ambassador to Yemen, fluent in Arabic, made long, arduous journeys into the heart of the ancient kingdom of Sheba to help gather the goods. Along with his small army of security guards and CIA officials, Ambassador Edmund Hull, a short, stone-faced chief executive, braved desert wastelands and jagged highlands where Osama bin Laden's foot soldiers were being openly abetted by fierce tribesmen. Yemeni tribesmen are notorious for not being able to keep a secret, and when Hull crossed their palms with silver, they just could not resist telling the truth. Along with the green mucus of narcotic *qat* leaves that filled their silver spittoons, out came the details on Al-Harethi's new haunts.

Senior Yemeni officials, who had done almost nothing to interdict key al Qaeda figures in their country, nevertheless told me that they were infuriated by the way the ambassador handled the intelligence-gathering phase of the operation. They did not like what they called the "freelancing" of the ambassador in the countryside. "We are not happy with his dealings with the tribesmen," said Brigadier General Mutawakel, who displayed little obvious emotion as he vented his views to me in his own posh sitting room in the capital. "There were 'diplomatic journeys' out to the region, there were discussions and money changed hands. We knew that if we agree or disagreed, they would do it anyway, but we are not happy at all with how it has been dealt with."

Still, the attack had not come as a surprise to the government of President Ali Abdullah Saleh. The U.S. military had been passing the Yemenis its own intelligence on al Qaeda activities for months. Ambassador Hull and his fellow operatives had carefully explained to the Yemeni government officials that they themselves had the option of going after the al Qaeda figures suspected of planning the USS *Cole* attack. If they chose not to, they indicated, the U.S. government was prepared to take matters into its own hands.

Time for the Yemenis to act eventually ran out. American Predator drones, based in nearby Djibouti on the Horn of Africa, were already transmitting real-time video images from the Yemeni hinterlands. Then came Ambassador Hull's intelligence coup. Counterintelligence officials believe that Global Positioning System coordinates transmitted by Al-Harethi Thuraya's satellite phone may also have helped seal his fate. But such intelligence can be fleeting; U.S. officials knew they had to act swiftly. They waited until their foe was in a car and clear of his neighbors, who might have been accidentally killed. In the end, the timing was impeccable. "They [the Americans] didn't hit a wedding party, hit their own people, or kill a large number of civilians," a British diplomat based on the Arabian Peninsula told me. "In that respect the U.S. Hellfire strike was good, clean, and clinical." The Hellfire killed all six passengers in the car, including one Saudi operative, a U.S. citizen from Buffalo, New York.

Another crucial victory in the U.S. "war on terror" came later in the year when Khalid Sheikh Mohammed, believed to have micromanaged logistics in 2001's attacks on the World Trade Center and the Pentagon, was snatched from his bed in Rawalpindi, Pakistan, by local police officers. The catch came after an extensive manhunt by FBI and Pakistani officials, who gathered a key lead from a son of blind Egyptian cleric Sheikh Omar Abdel-Rahman, who is imprisoned in the United States. Mohammed had earlier been linked by a phone intercept to an al Qaeda attack (the aftermath of which I covered) on a historic synagogue on the island of Djerba in Tunisia in

April 2002 that killed fourteen German tourists, six Tunisians, and a French citizen. Though Khalid Sheikh Mohammed told his interrogators that he had recently met with his mentor, bin Laden, near the Iranian border, the information had to be taken with a grain of salt, considering his own history of deceptions as well as his obvious interest in providing false leads to investigators. Regardless, the U.S. government rushed to blanket Pakistan's Baluch tribal areas with fresh leaflets reiterating the old promise of a $25 million reward for information leading to the capture of the terror chief.

Despite measured U.S. successes in the war on terror, the al Qaeda network kept its hand in the mix from Baghdad to Riyadh to Casablanca. Not surprisingly, one name kept popping up in the network's attacks after the war in Afghanistan—Tora Bora. In early May 2003, Saudi police identified Khaled Jehani, who they said had fought alongside bin Laden in the caves of Tora Bora, as the leader of a terrorist cell believed to have planned attacks on Western compounds in Riyadh that killed thirty-four people. Jehani, who had previously fought in Bosnia and Chechnya, had recorded a last will and testament, a "martyrdom" videotape, before leaving Afghanistan. While Saudi intelligence officials said he was the leader of a "sleeper cell" with fifty to sixty members in Saudi Arabia, uncovered arms caches and fresh shoot-outs between government authorities and Saudi militants later in the year suggested that those figures were on the low side.

In the same month, May 2003, I traveled to Morocco to examine the aftermath of a heinous attack in which five suicide bombers had set off charges across the country's commercial center with deadly simultaneity. Morocco, a country of thirty million citizens—long considered by Western travelers a francophone paradise of sandy beaches, orange groves, and exotic birds—had been plunged into uncertainty as citizens shook their heads in disbelief. Local officials had quickly identified members of a fundamentalist group, "The Righteous Path," as the instigators of the attacks on Jewish and Spanish establishments and a major tourist hotel. They discovered that a majority of the fourteen suicide bombers, two of whom survived, had been locals.

While officials had not suspected prior to the attacks that the group had links to bin Laden, al Qaeda's interest in Morocco had already been discovered. Indeed, there was another established Tora Bora connection. Moroccan officials, working with the CIA, had arrested three Saudi nationals in June 2002 for plotting to attack NATO vessels in the straits of Gibraltar. Those arrests—which included another senior Saudi operative, Mohammed Tabiti—exposed bin Laden's broader plans to disperse his cells after the fighting in Afghanistan. The three Saudis, later imprisoned for life in Morocco, told interrogators that after the battle of Tora Bora they had met in the Afghan city of Gardez, not far from the Shahi-Kot Valley, before escaping from Afghanistan and finally arriving in North Africa on a mission to use bomb-laden speedboats for suicide attacks on U.S. and British warships in the Strait of Gibraltar. The Saudis, at least one married to a Moroccan, explained that they had been with bin Laden in Tora Bora as U.S. bombers began their assault there; they insisted that the terror chief had dropped out of sight in late November 2001 but used his closest envoys to direct them to launch new terrorist attacks once they had become established in "familiar areas." Bin Laden's orders, they said, had been for cells to operate in the regions of the world that they "knew best."

In impoverished but moderate Islamic countries like Morocco, the grounds for al Qaeda's brand of extremism had grown more—not less—fertile since September 2001. After several days in the capital, Rabat, speaking with U.S. and French diplomats, I found a driver willing to take me into the slums, or *bidonvilles,* where the attackers had lived. Morocco is nothing like Saudi Arabia, where stern government minders keep journalists from conducting "vox pop" interviews in the streets. The residents in the Thomasville slum were quite talkative. Friends of the attackers had noticed changes in the behavior of one young bomber, Mohammed Larrosi, after September 11, 2001. "He grew a beard and stopped saying hello," Radaa Abdullah told me while sitting with a gaggle of friends at the Café Noir, which sits at the base of Thomasville, a community that appeared from a distance to be a rickety tin staircase running down beneath a row of spacious middle-class apartments. "When he did [greet you], it was only to talk about Afghanistan and those he called great holy warriors." Other residents of the tiny slum, formerly the estate of a

French colonialist, Mlle. Thomas, claimed they had not understood what the bold talk had meant.

Morocco had flirted with various forms of Islam, some moderate and some extreme, for centuries. Many of the Casablanca bombers had continued to wear jeans and drink mint tea with friends, who remained oblivious to their intentions. Certainly, the young men of Thomasville were not acting strangely enough for their neighbors to envision that eight of them, from this and another nearby shanty-town, would go on a suicidal rampage. Yet the Casablanca attacks had also been a tragedy waiting to happen. I took a walk with the young men of Café Noir into the heart of Thomasville and sat down for a haircut in a barbershop. Ahmed, a truck driver, spoke softly while glancing around for police informants. "We have an expression," he said, that "if you apply enough pressure, you will get an explosion."

Mohammed Naji, another Thomasville resident, said he believed the local men were pushed from the outside "by bigger operatives who had more experience with international terror." Indeed, Spain's defense minister, Federico Trillo, speaking from Ceuta, the Spanish enclave in North Africa, had revealed that the Casablanca operatives activated detonators on the attackers' vests using mobile phones. The more senior operatives, dialing in from Europe or elsewhere in Morocco, thus managed to set off five nearly simultaneous blasts.

Between my trips throughout the Middle East and Central Asia, I reside, along with my wife, Ivana, in Cairo, Egypt. It is a city of six-teen million souls divided between religious devotion and sympathy for their repressed Palestinian brethren, on the one hand, and an insatiable hunger for the fruits of Western material culture, on the other. Cairo is a city of low crime and tolerant citizens who suffer inconsiderate Western tourists and their own corrupt politicians with the same laissez-faire cheerfulness. For every scene of irate taxi driv-ers screaming at one another, there is another of wooden boats sail-ing gracefully down the Nile at sunset. While there are plenty of radicals and extremists in hiding, Egyptians are generally open-minded—a quality partially attributable, I suspect, to their long history of integration in great empires, from their own pharaonic dynasties through Ottoman rule, the Napoleonic era, and the British Empire.

Egyptians view their leader, President Hosni Mubarak, as a sometimes benevolent, sometimes cruel modern-day pharaoh. Few other countries can boast the levels of close cooperation with the FBI and Interpol as can Mubarak's security services. On the other hand, President Mubarak does his best not to be seen as too close to Washington. His tightly controlled press is his most useful means of "biting back" at the hand that feeds him, the U.S. government, for its failure to take what he considers the middle road to peace in the Middle East. Ironically, Mubarak's rabidly anti-Washington newspapers permit him to distance himself from his own best friends. Egyptian government officials like to state in private that the two billion dollars that they receive in military and economic assistance each year from Washington is really far less than they deserve for their diligent peacemaking efforts. They never fail to remind an American that "you need us more than we need you."

Arab official views toward the United States are not, however, a good barometer of the mood on the streets. Most Arab regimes, like Egypt, have highly repressive security forces that control public displays of discontent toward both Washington and their own national government. Mubarak even keeps a tight lid on pro-Palestinian rallies. Far more important than street demonstrations, however, is what goes on beneath the surface, where terror cells can grow and reproduce much faster than the world's most powerful army or intelligence network can hunt them down. No country has contributed more to al Qaeda's core leadership than Egypt, which provides nearly half of the network's top three dozen leaders.

Growing anti-American sentiments simmer beneath the surface at every bend in the Nile. On the verdant, upscale island of Zamalek, where I reside, Egyptians, learning of the suicide attacks on the World Trade Center, were initially horrified and expressed immediate solidarity with the victims. But that sympathy was also tempered with an attitude of "I told you so." An air-conditioning mechanic outside my apartment on the Nile River told me ambivalently on September 12, 2001, "It is not fair that these Americans have been slaughtered, but, at the same time, I am not so upset by the attacks because the United States has failed to take the right stand against Israel." A neighbor in an upstairs flat, a retired foreign service officer now working in the tourism business, was more blunt: "This was not an attack on civilization, as you seem to believe; this was an attack from the enemies of Washington who disagree with your policy." I was infuriated, but I also knew what he meant.

Anti-Washington opinions can be just as negative—or more so—in the teeming slums of big Egyptian cities, where the nightmarish mix of disastrous planning and rampant corruption have left residents struggling to survive. Between September 2001 and the end of 2003, I made several trips by taxi and boat into the neighboring slums of Imbaba to take the pulse in Egypt's poorest neighborhood. As with the poor in a Pashtun village, I was treated like an honored guest one afternoon right after the 9/11 attacks. At a small table, dozens of Egyptians crowded around to talk, offering me free tea and a smoke from a *shisha,* the long, tall water pipe popular everywhere in the country. A tired-looking but smiling shopkeeper asked me rhetorically, "What would you do if your wife was raped? If you answer that you might try to find the man and punish him and even kill him, then you must see why we admire Osama bin Laden." The wife was, of course, Palestine, and the rapist was Ariel Sharon. A bitter older man was more direct. "America is the real source of terrorism and racism. It is you who support Sharon, the butcher," he insisted. "The United States finally got a taste of its own medicine Tuesday!"

Every time I returned to the same Cairo slum, the mood was worse. While there was initial confusion in Egypt about bin Laden's role in the 9/11 bombing, as it became clearer over the course of 2002, more residents of Imbaba were willing to express a favorable opinion of the Saudi mastermind. Across from a group of women selling pigeons and down an alley where horses drew apple carts, I met several men discussing their views of Palestine and bin Laden. A young butcher, Ahmed, aged twenty, said, "Osama is a good man because he is fighting to defend Muslims. If Bush wants to end the terror, he better solve the problems in Palestine first." As he spoke, a waiter walked in, dressed for work in my own neighborhood across the Nile. "Many of the young want to go and fight with Osama and al Qaeda, but the government is holding them back. Osama is a soldier of Allah on earth and when he dies, he will be replaced." Bin Laden's own words were now in the ears of far more potential recruits. Though few young Egyptians imagined that he was winning his war against the West, many of them had grown to appreciate his efforts. They praised his ability to remain at large even as the world's most powerful nation hunted him night and day.

From the mountain villages of northern Pakistan to the slums of Cairo, every Islamic country I traveled to after the winding-down of the conflict in Afghanistan—Yemen, Jordan, Qatar, the United Arab Emirates, Pakistan, Morocco, and Egypt—was producing new recruits to fight in the al Qaeda network. My travels made it all too clear to me that eliminating the threat of terror in the United States and across the globe would require far more than military offensives. The actual "hunt" on the battlefield could succeed only as an integral part of a broader campaign; young Muslims cannot be allowed to languish in poverty where disenfranchisement can so easily turn them into walking time bombs. But beyond this vexing problem—one that my own wife works on every day as a nonprofit development planner in Egypt and which is likely to remain with us for decades to come—my own government needs to redouble its efforts to end the bloodshed in Palestine and Israel. Most of bin Laden's foot soldiers were joining him not because they were psychopathic killers looking for a role, but rather because they see al Qaeda as a vehicle to achieve their political and religious aims.

As a reporter covering the war on terror, I had a creeping sense that I had also become a part of the problem. Just as politicians in Washington needed to reinvent their approach to fighting terror, I sensed that those in my profession needed to step back and seize a more constructive role in the ongoing struggle.

After several years on my personal terror trail—winding back to Bosnia a decade earlier—I am also convinced that daily Western journalism has to adjust to the realities of a new world. As mentioned at the outset of this book, many citizens in my own country initially viewed the "war on terror" as a vehicle, emotional and practical, to set things right, to wreak vengeance on an enemy that had shocked them from out of the blue on 9/11. The predictable, knee-jerk reaction from the Western press, some of my own outlets included, was to fuel America's new patriotic fervor by painting the warriors on one side as do-no-wrong wonder boys and the killers on the other side as unthinking fanatics. It was an epic struggle that was taking on perverse, sometimes comic, proportions. Two and a half years after the World Trade Center and Pentagon tragedies, the Western press is still largely treating the war on terror as a simplistic struggle of good against evil. Politicians, appealing to the middling common denominator, stress this same dichotomy over and over again in bland, ridiculous clichés repeated ad infinitum in the mass media.

The results of this unfortunate mindset have become clearer to me. The worlds of "Islam" in the East and "Christianity" in the West are growing further apart as real, peaceful dialogue takes a backseat to the war on terror being fought against a diabolical unseen enemy. A clash of civilizations, by no means inevitable at the start of our millennium just a few years ago, has become a self-fulfilling prophesy with the help of a Western media that thrives on confrontational language and score-keeping.

Indeed, there is a kind of new cold war developing across the six continents. As in the previous Cold War, this one is a shell game—not of ballistic missiles hidden in underground cavities, but of trying to figure out when and where the bad guys will pop up to commit their next obscene atrocity. Retired Adm. John Poindexter of Iran-Contra fame, whose Defense Advanced Research Projects Agency in the Pentagon helped dream up the idea of futures trading on terror strikes in the Middle East (a scheme quickly shot down by his superiors for being in bad taste) was only an unfortunate harbinger of this bizarre new era.

This isn't a game of winners and losers; it concerns of our own survival. Yet the constant message from politicians, emphasized by the press, is "prepare yourself for the worst and be ready to pay in the trillions of dollars for a safer security cordon to protect your precious freedom." Real self-criticism, the cherished and traditional role of the Fourth Estate in our democracy, remains relegated to the back burner. Neither the commanders of our war on terror nor the policy our nation pursues abroad are held up for the American public on a daily basis and truly scrutinized under the magnifying glass of our daily newspapers and television stations. How then are we to devise creative and new strategies to fight terror?

Americans, who still live largely in a self-contained paradise and who rarely examine the outside world, cannot be blamed in full for their own misunderstanding of the legitimate views and aspirations of over one billion Muslims. The U.S. diet of information from leading news organizations provides few clues about the real thinking on the other side of the fence. Moderate academics and religious scholars in the Arab world express their concern that U.S. foreign policy is in some cases "creating conflict" and not fostering peace. Shouldn't we at least be listening with open ears? Their overwhelming concern is the peace process in Israel and Palestine. But there are other burning conflicts like Chechnya, Kashmir, and Iraq that they worry are causing negative reverberations in the world of radical Islam and, in turn, producing more terror cells.

You don't have to be a "liberal" to suggest that double standards have prevented the United States and its closest allies from promoting democracy in the Islamic world in the past century. Many on the American right are now gathering around this same realization. Whereas Asia and South America have seen a relative blossoming of democracy in recent years, largely underwritten by Western support, the Arab world has been left to stew in its own authoritarian juices, with rulers in countries like Egypt and Saudi Arabia stamping out civil freedoms but still receiving the firm political and financial backing of the West. It should be no wonder that the youth in these countries, also at the receiving end of their own anti-Western state propaganda, are turning against us. This is an untold story waiting for more messengers.

I plead guilty, as a member of the Fourth Estate, to having promoted an "us vs. them" view of the current conflict. Even the phrase "war on terror" seems increasingly obsolete and inappropriate in the new environment. Self-examination on both sides of the conflict can help us to recognize what values we have in common and what values can be used to invent a new and peaceful world. My own country, whose image abroad I have never seen sink so low as it had by mid-2003, must reinvent itself as an eager peacemaker, not just a determined warrior. Yet, just as fighting the war on terror is a perilous, often thankless exercise, it is crucial that our leaders understand that peacemaking requires similar hardship and risk-taking. I sense, however, that American can-do optimism, our oldest and most proven trait, can still win us back the respect we have lost in the world. Only then will bin Laden and his ilk run out of fuel to fire their inferno.

# Select Bibliography

Alexander, Yonah, and Michael Swetnam. *Usama bin Laden's al-Qaida: Profile of a Terrorist Network*. New York: Transnational Publishers, 2001.

Anonymous. *Through Our Enemies' Eyes: Osama bin Laden, Radical Islam and the Future of America*. Dulles, Va.: Brassey's, 2002.

Bergen, Peter L. *Holy War: Inside the Secret World of Osama bin Laden*. New York: Simon & Schuster, 2002.

Bodansky, Yossef. *Bin Laden: The Man Who Declared War on America*. Rocklin, Calif.: Forum, 1999.

Churchill, Winston. *The Story of the Malakand Field Force*. London: Longmans, Green, 1898.

Cooley, John K. *Unholy Wars: Afghanistan, America, and International Terrorism*. London: Pluto Press, 1999.

Feldman, Noah. *After Jihad: America and the Struggle for Islamic Democracy*. New York: Farrar, Straus and Giroux, 2003

Fouda, Yousri, and Nick Fielding. *Masterminds of Terror: The Truth Behind the Most Devastating Terrorist Attack the World Has Ever Seen*. New York: Arcade Publishing, 2003.

Gunaratna, Rohan. *Inside al Qaeda: Global Network of Terror*. New York: Columbia University Press, 2002.

Husayn, Kamil Yusuf. *Osama bin Laden: Legend of the Century*. Dubai: Al-Bayan, 1999.

Karsh, Efraim, and Inari Karsh. *Empires of the Sand: The Struggle for Mastery in the Middle East*. Cambridge, Mass.: Harvard University Press, 2001.

Rashid, Ahmed. *Taliban: Militant Islam, Oil, and Fundamentalism in Central Asia*. New Haven, Conn.: Yale University Press, 2000.

———. *Jihad: The Rise of Militant Islam in Central Asia.* Lahore, Pakistan: Vanguard, 2002.

Weaver, Mary Anne. *Portrait of Egypt: A Journey through the World of Militant Islam.* New York: Farrar, Straus and Giroux, 1999.

———. *Pakistan: In the Shadow of Jihad and Afghanistan.* New York: Farrar, Straus and Giroux, 2002.

Woodward, Bob. *Bush at War.* New York: Simon & Schuster, 2002.

# Index

# The Author

**Philip Smucker** has spent the last seventeen years as an overseas reporter, covering conflicts around the world as a war correspondent in Burma, Cambodia, Haiti, Bosnia, Serbia, Afghanistan, and Iraq. Smucker covered the U.S.-led war on terror in Egypt, Sudan, Morocco, Tunisia, Yemen, Afghanistan, Iraq, Syria, and the United States. He has written extensively for the *Christian Science Monitor, U.S. News & World Report, Time* magazine, the *Daily Telegraph, International Herald Tribune,* the *Washington Times,* the *Pittsburgh Post-Gazette,* the *Toronto Globe and Mail,* the *San Francisco Examiner,* and *Newsday.* He has reported on the airwaves for the Voice of America and Deutsche Welle Radio.

Smucker broke the story of bin Laden's escape from Afghanistan in December 2001. In connection with his reporting in Afghanistan, he appeared on *Good Morning America, The Today Show,* Chris Matthews's *Hardball,* ABC's *Nightline,* CNN's *Wolf Blitzer Reports,* and other television programs. He is a frequent guest on NPR and other radio newsmagazines. Philip and his wife, Ivana, reside in Cairo, Egypt.